Camping with the SPIRIT *of* ADVENTURE

Camping with the SPIRIT *of* ADVENTURE

Development of Boy Scout Camps for Youth in Northeastern Massachusetts

THE KEY FOUNDATION INC.

America Through Time®
ADDING COLOR TO AMERICAN HISTORY

To all who camp with the spirit of adventure

America Through Time is an imprint of Fonthill Media LLC
www.through-time.com
office@through-time.com

Published by Arcadia Publishing by arrangement with Fonthill Media LLC
For all general information, please contact Arcadia Publishing:
Telephone: 843-853-2070
Fax: 843-853-0044
E-mail: sales@arcadiapublishing.com
For customer service and orders:
Toll-Free 1-888-313-2665

www.arcadiapublishing.com

First published 2019

ISBN 978-1-63499-110-0

Typeset in Mrs Eaves XL Serif Narrow
Printed and bound in England

ACKNOWLEDGEMENTS

The creation of this book was a three-year effort with contributions from over sixty individuals and organizations. The Key Foundation Inc. wants to thank the primary authors of this work. They are: Brian J. Lobao, Chuck Mahaleris, Robert Sean McLaughlin, Brian P. Eckelkamp, Michael J. Bryant, Keith E. Miller, Charles E. Blanchette Jr., Mark E. Svendsen, and Justin D. St. Louis.

We are also grateful to The Key Foundation photographers, editors, and researchers for their continued efforts: Erin M. Crowley, Linda M. Lobao, Marc Desgroseilliers, Keith Lord, Stephen J. Marchacos, Andrew Pinard, and Raymond Morrison.

We would also like to thank the following individuals and families who provided photographs, documents, and insight in the creation of this book: Michael Henderson, John Halsey, Emily Wilson, Joe Curran, Dennis M. Conway, Jamisean Patterson, Brendan McNeill, John Hovey, Ron Quattrochi, Chris Boran, Matt Bailey, David Crowley. Zack Shepherd, Bruce Colvin, Nick Cortese, Rob Teich, Gaelin Kurtzman, Cole Ogonowski, Ray Theberge, Alexander A. Vervaert, Charles F. Emerson, Neal Grotenhuis, John Goodwin, The Donald Gray Family, The Takesian Family, The Fascione Family, James Batchelder, Mark Lamarre, Ron Fuller, Donald Doliber, Thomas Kehoe, Robert V. Guptill, Richard Becker, Arnie Sheltra, Don Laing, and Al Lefebvre.

The foundation also expresses gratitude to the following organizations: The Lone Tree Spirit Foundation, The Trustees of the Haverhill Public Library, Beam Camp and the Beam Center, Vintage Aerial Photography, Lee Scouting Museums, The Lawrence History Center, Camp Aranu'tiq-Harbor Camps Inc., Center for Lowell History—George H. Russell Collection, Zion's Camp, Mass Audubon Society-Wildwood Camp, Troop 42 (Quincy, MA), Troop 53 (Swampscott, MA), The Hale Reservation, TKF/FStar Productions, and the Town of Lyman, ME.

Special thanks to The Spirit of Adventure Council, Boy Scouts of America: Chuck Eaton, CEO, and Darrin Johnson, General Manager.

Introduction

On a perfect summer day, Tommy goes into the Wah-Tut-Ca dining hall for dinner. It's his first season and he's already been in camp for a few days. As the group starts to eat, the older Scouts of his Troop give him a warning: "Tommy, don't eat too much." The warning from these seasoned camp veterans is justified. The Troop has plans for after dinner. They are going to the waterfront to board the Craig Ryder Whaleboat on a trip that will take them halfway across Northwood Lake. The planned destination is Johnson's, a local restaurant and ice cream stand. The portions at Johnson's are extreme: a small cone is considered mountainous.

The trip had been planned for the night before, but the threat of thunderstorms kept all the boats in. Tonight, the lake is like a sheet of glass and the air is mostly clear, with only a few fluffy clouds to contrast with the vivid blue sky. It is a perfect night. On evenings like this, boating on the lake is akin to slipping into an oil painting.

Tommy had a moment of great anxiety on the first day of camp. Every Scout is required to go to the waterfront for a swim test. He was not a great swimmer and he knew it. He was going to be graded in front of everybody. He didn't pass. He was ranked as a beginner. As he walked from the dock a lifeguard escorted him and said, "Tommy, if you come by tomorrow, I'll help you get your swimmers certification." The next day, Tommy took him up on the offer and, after a few hours, was ready for another swim test. This time Tommy passed.

On this day anxiety was replaced with anticipation. After dinner and a quick stop to their campsite, Tommy and his friends head to the waterfront. As he and his companions put on their life preservers, he stared across the expanse of Northwood Lake. Unable to see the other side, he wonders, "what is over there?" Tommy climbs into the oversized boat and, with oar in hand, he and his fellow Scouts set off on yet another scouting adventure.

The Spirit of Adventure Council, Boy Scouts of America began in 2015. This council serves Boston and seventy-five other Massachusetts communities. Its current membership is made up of over 13,000 Scouts and 5,000 volunteers. The Spirit of Adventure Council spans the eastern coast of Massachusetts from Boston to the North Shore, along the New Hampshire border, and west to Greater Lowell. Its existence is the result of over 100 years of mergers and consolidations of smaller councils. More than fifteen councils have been identified.

We have found historical evidence of over sixty camps. Most of these were "trolley camps," summer programs held on borrowed or rented land lasting a year or two. More than a dozen camps have been catalogued that were owned by councils. We could not capture the rich history of all these places in a single book, nor could we adequately describe the hundreds of dedicated individuals that built them. The focus of this book is to chronicle the evolution of these Boy Scout camps through a then and now theme. Our approach is to follow a trail with many divergent branches that led us to where we are today.

For the first fifty years a major focus of community-based Scout Councils was the acquisition and development of properties to support Boy Scout camping programs—particularly in the summer months. That emphasis lasted until the 1960s when BSA membership peaked.

As Scouting's membership declined in the next decades, councils became stressed as philanthropic funding for council operations diminished. Competition from other youth organizations accelerated that trend. In an effort to improve efficiency, councils were forced to merge. Councils with multiple properties consolidated into one of the camps and sold the others to fund endowments. Despite these efforts, membership and funding continued to decline. Sales of the camps created bitterness among its supporters and volunteers and council politics became ugly. Councils began to borrow against the endowments to fund operations and after a few years would forgive the debt in a pledge to start over. The cycle continued downward. The fact that camps were sold to ultimately fund short-term budget goals only added to the discontentment and disillusionment with Scouting.

As the twenty-first century dawned, Boy Scout camping was still declining while other youth summer camps, many of which were former Boy Scout camps, were growing at amazing rates. Today, most kids live in households with both parents working or are living in a single parent family. The need for summer day care in the form of resident camping has never been greater.

In recent years, Boy Scouting has been doing some soul searching. The Spirit of Adventure Council was formed and is helping plot a new direction. Since its founding, Scouting has become more inclusive by removing barriers of gender and sexual preference. It recognizes the needs of families as they are as opposed to how they were.

The hope is that this book will spark a discussion on the value of our remaining properties and how to best use them. There is a sense of magic in camping in the way that it transforms and impacts young people. Scouting was created in the progressive era of the early twentieth century with the aim to improve the lives of youth impacted by the Industrial Revolution. Now, in the twenty-first century, there is an urgent social need for youth that have been impacted by the Digital Revolution. Kids need more time outdoors and less time online.

When Tommy walks through camp he is unaware of its history. For him, the names inscribed on buildings are locations, not individuals. He is too busy living the daily adventures. Adventure in camp is not an undertaking of danger. The adventures of Tommy's time in camp are exciting, remarkable experiences that collectively create a positive, life-changing experience. He is following an old trail, but one that leads to timeless values.

CHAPTER 1

THE TROLLEY CAMPS

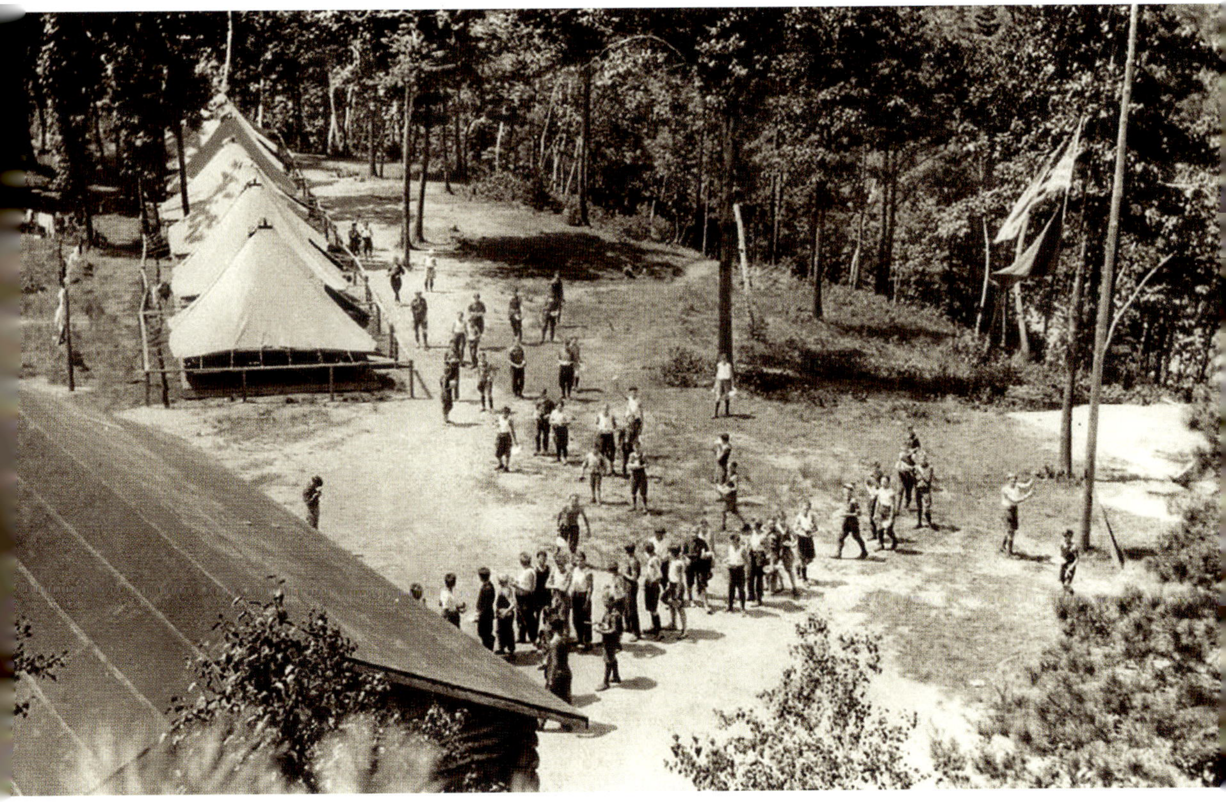

CAMP MANNING, ANDOVER, MA CIRCA 1910: Scouts lining up at Keniston Hall at Camp Manning to eat. Getting to Scout camps was a challenge in the early days of Scouting and remained a hurdle to overcome for Scouts who lived in the city and for families who didn't own cars. The first Boy Scout Summer camps were small and took place on borrowed or leased land that was sometimes owned by a leader in the troop. Many of these camps served just one or two troops from the same town but some served an entire district. There were very few serving whole councils.

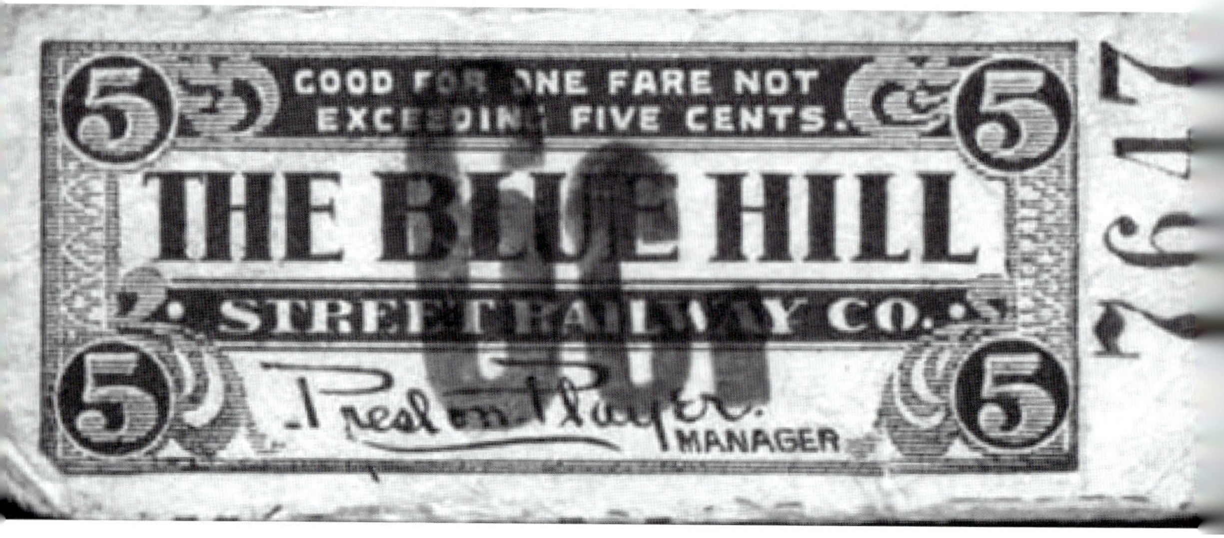

GETTING TO CAMP: In the early 1900s, most Scout families lived in cities close to the industrial mills and relied on public transportation. The suburbs were sparsely populated and were mostly farmland and woodlots. Scouts would often take city trolleys to the end of the line then hike three-five miles to their campsite. Today, at New England Base Camp in Milton, MA, there is a Scout camp in the Blue Hills, and the Council's shuttle vans take them into Boston to explore the Freedom Trail and other city adventures.

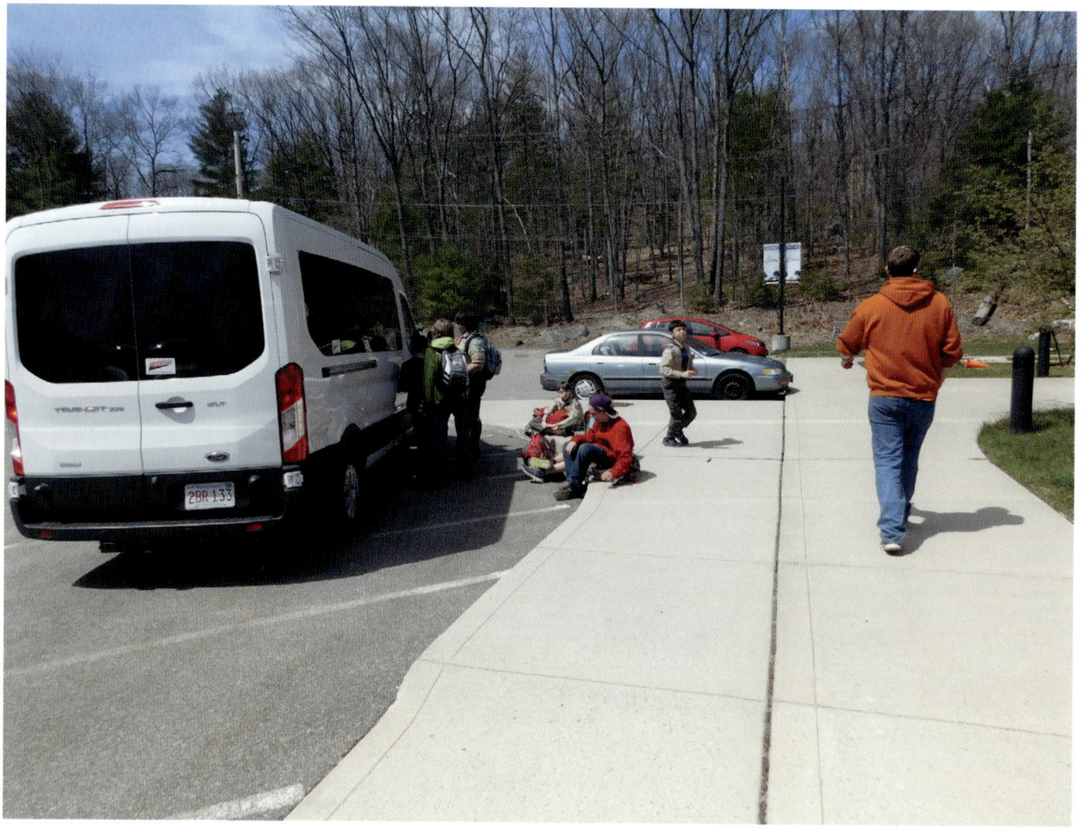

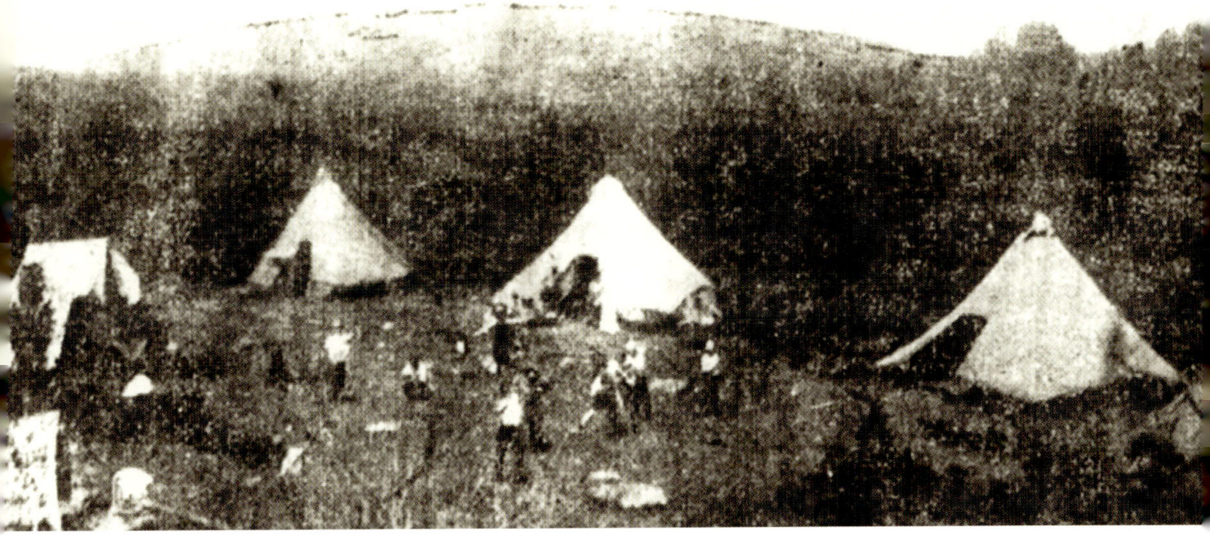

CAMP JACKSON, FRAMINGHAM, MA: Framingham's Lilac Farm is today a privately-owned rural estate. Its timeless pastoral setting makes it easy to visualize the hundreds of Scouts from all over the Greater Boston Council—the BSA who attended Camp Jackson in the Summer of 1920. They stayed in tents and teepees learning scoutcraft and playing sports and games, along with hikes through the woods, trail following, tree reading and other Scout activities. Scouts loved the short hike from camp to the 602-foot summit of Nobscot Hill where, from that height, they took part in bonfires, gazed up at the night sky and listened in on wireless radio dispatches from across the Atlantic Ocean. Scouts from the camp could swim at the nearby Agricultural Fairgrounds.

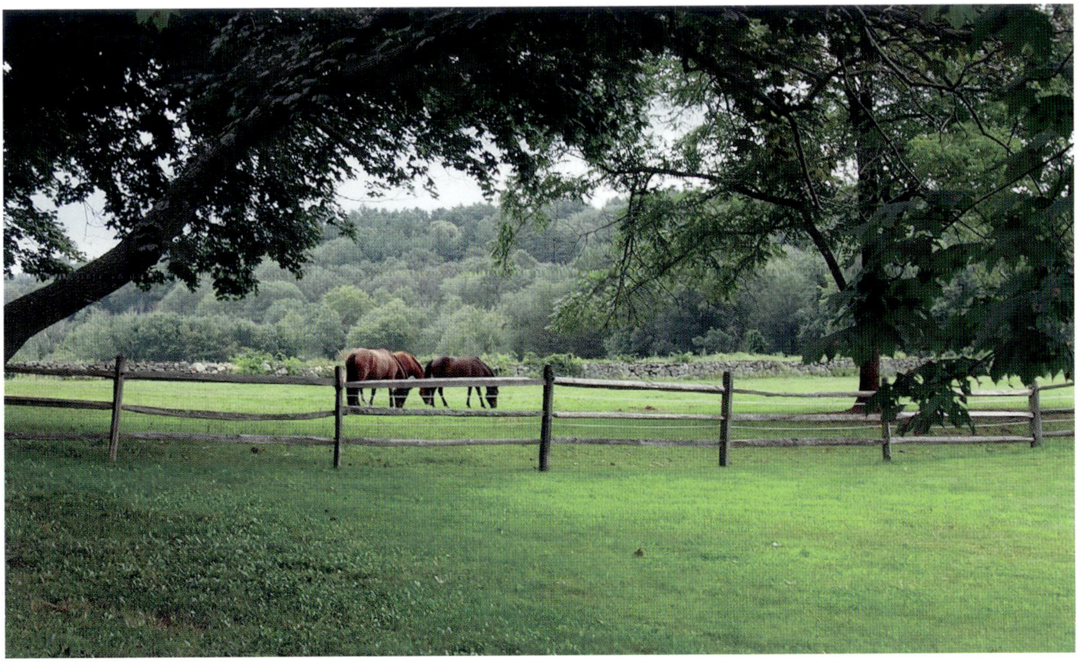

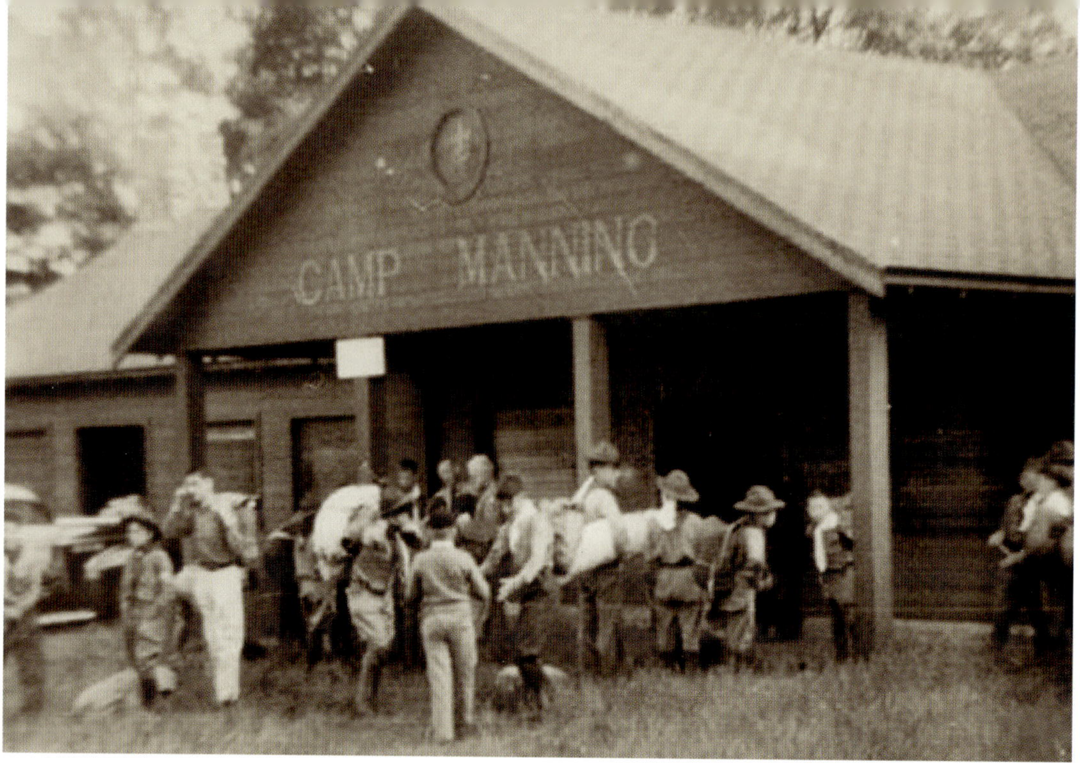

KENISTON HALL CAMP MANNING: In January 1921, Malden Council Scout Executive Herbert L. Patrick signed a lease for twenty acres of land at Pomp's Pond in the Ballardvale section of Andover for the council's summer camp. Camp Manning was twenty miles north of Boston and eighteen miles from Malden. Scouting volunteers built Keniston Hall, named for benefactor Charles E. Keniston, with logs cut on-site, which could accommodate seventy-five at meal time. Volunteers and Scouts cleared the brush for camp sites, built tent floors, and constructed a raft for the waterfront. Scouts even helped dig the trenches to pipe water in from Andover and built the amphitheater as part of their pioneering class. Today, the land is managed by the Andover Recreation Commission who run a summer day-camp on the site.

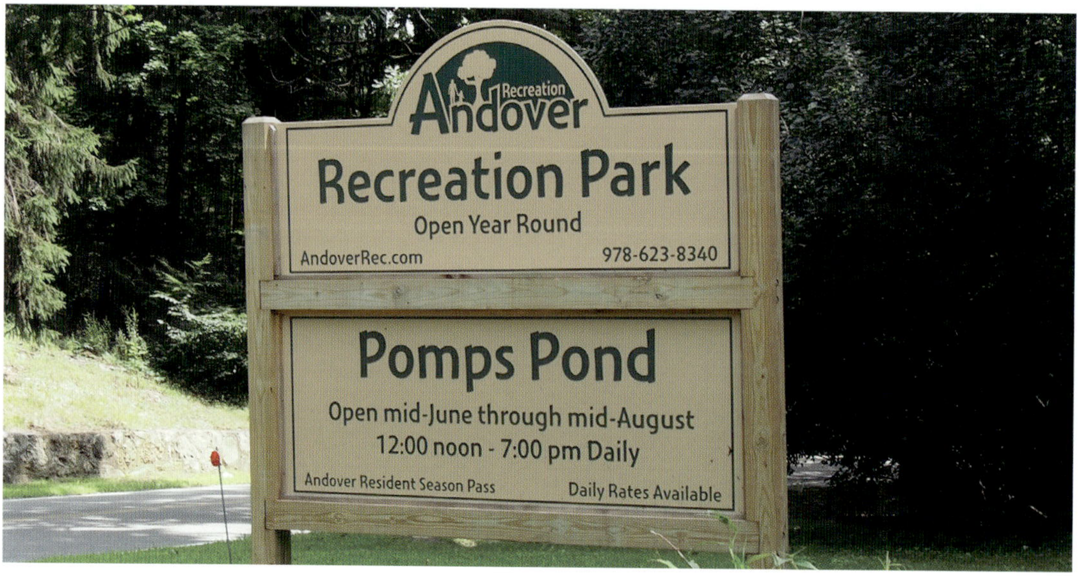

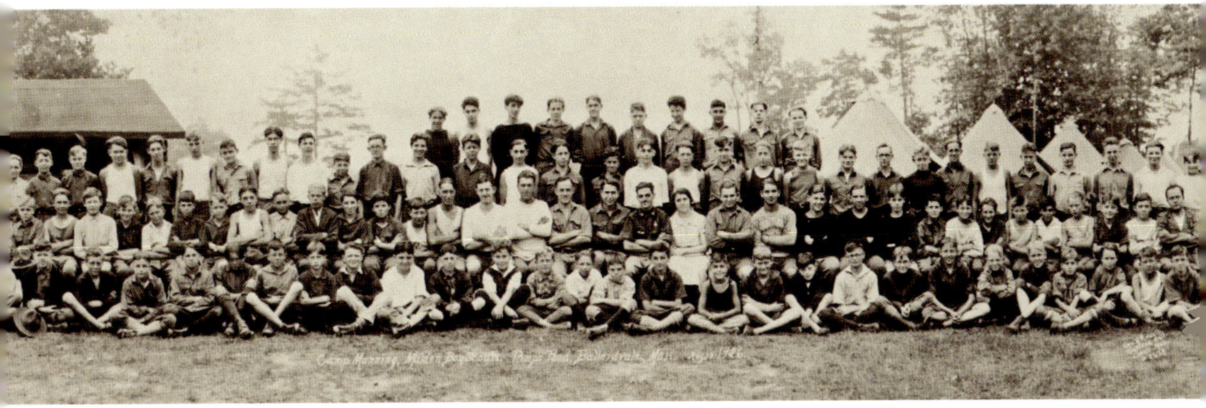

Growing Camp Manning: The 1920s were the booming years for the automotive industry, seeing Americans buy nearly twenty-six million cars and three million trucks in that decade. It was still the norm, however, for Scouts to travel by rail to camp. By 1931, the camp had grown to cover seventy-two acres with the Council owning part of the land in addition to the section that was leased from the Manning family. Facility improvements allowed it to accommodate 200 boys per week.

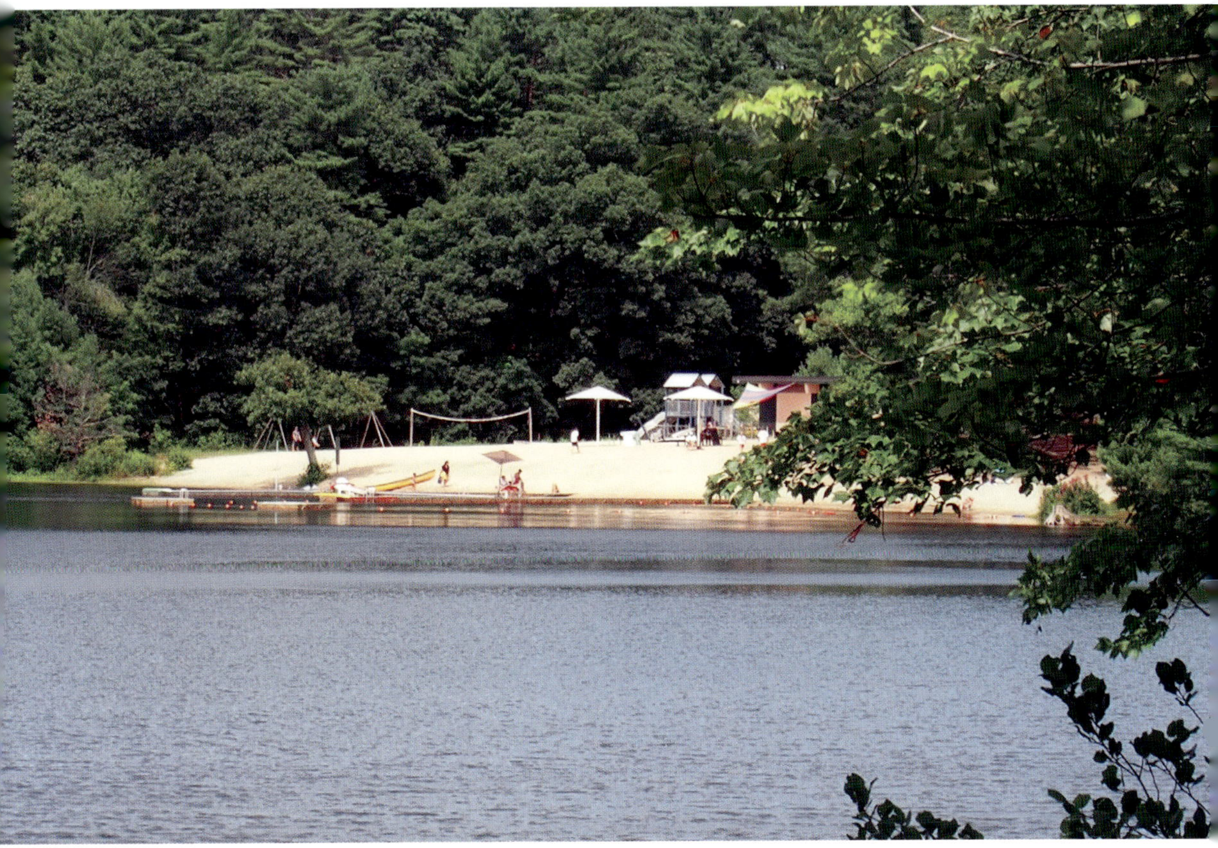

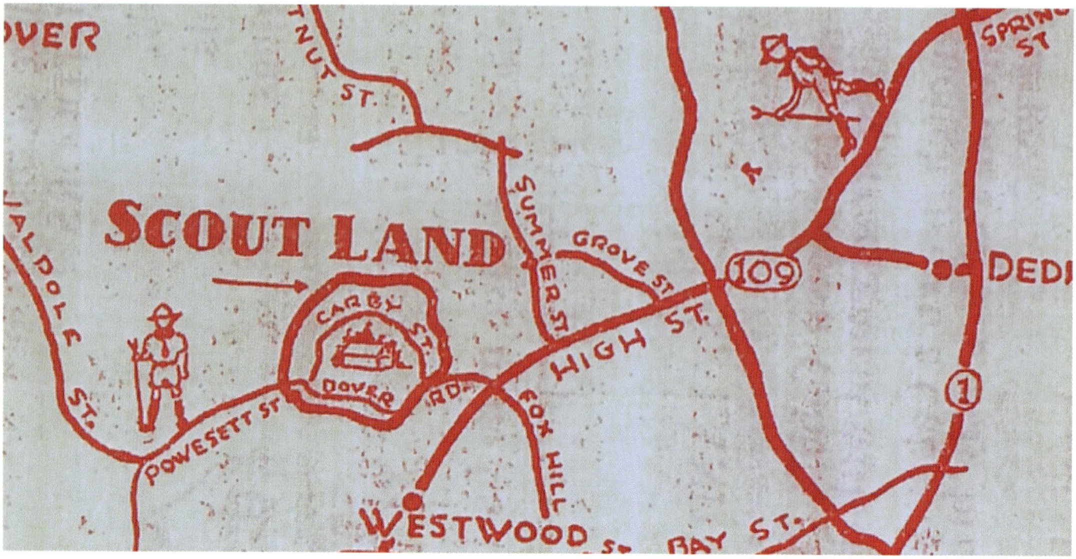

SCOUTLAND-DOVER AND WESTWOOD, MA: Robert S. Hale was a graduate of Harvard, a trustee of Roxbury Latin School, and was a senior official at Boston Edison Company. He was known as Uncle Robert to thousands of New England Boy Scouts thanks to his personal association with Scouting and the camp he created called Scoutland. Beginning in the Spring of 1918 and continuing beyond his death in December of 1941, Hale welcomed all Scouts, church groups, and hikers. Scoutland was for all to enjoy. The Hale Reservation continues to run successful youth camps and environmental programs today just as in the days when Uncle Robert walked among the trails.

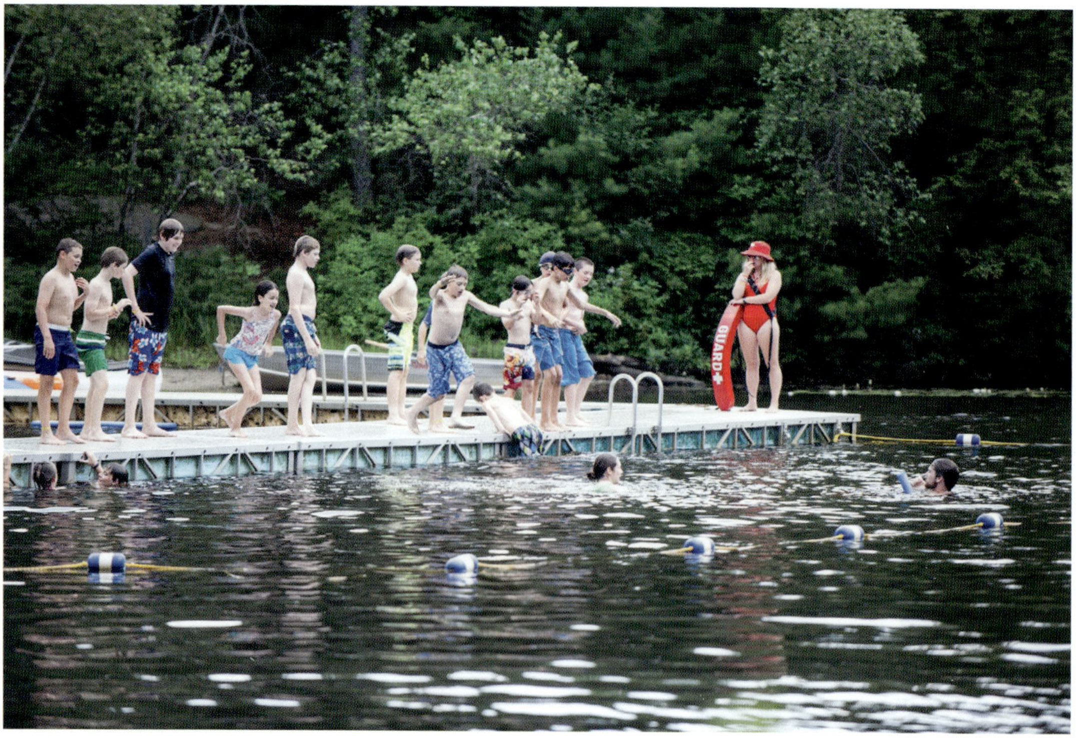

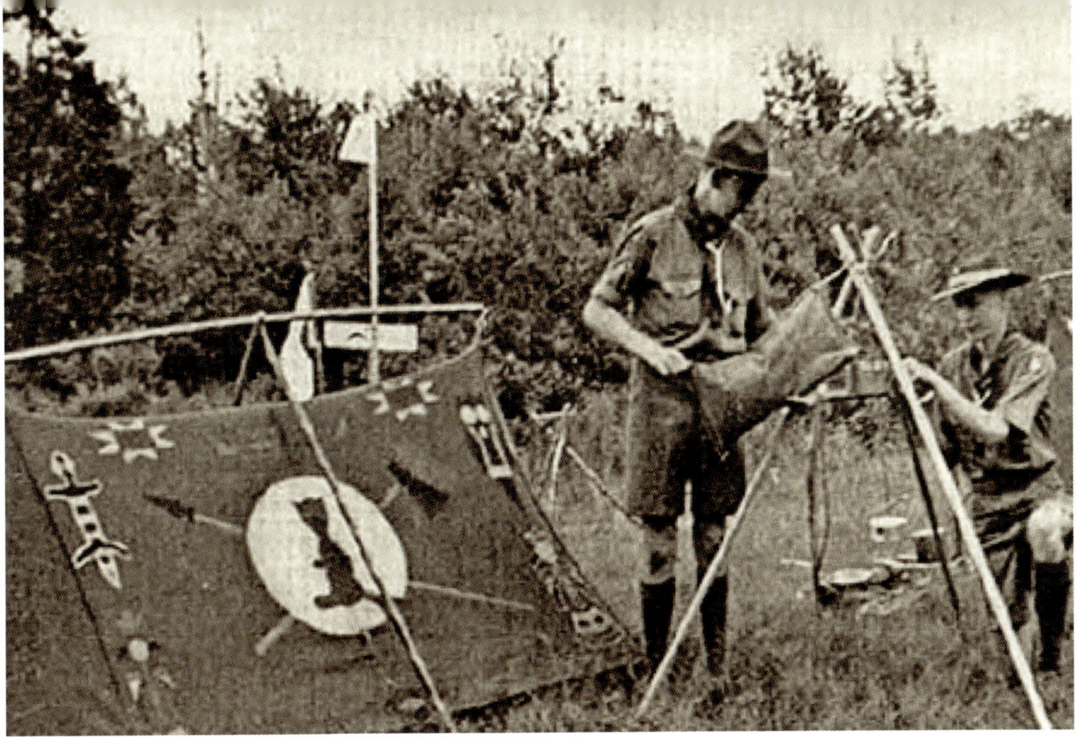

CAMPS AND CAMPING: There are two schools of thought in Scouting. One is that the Scout should make his own camp, do his own camping, and devote their thoughts with this end in view. The other school realizes that when a Scout is just beginning, they cannot be expected at once to take care of themselves, and therefore devotes their thoughts to the camp rather than the -ing. In August 1926, Hale personally turned the valve on a dam that was constructed to block a stream. This created Storrow Pond. It was named in honor of recently passed BSA President James J. Storrow. Storrow had helped create Boy Scout programs in Greater Boston.

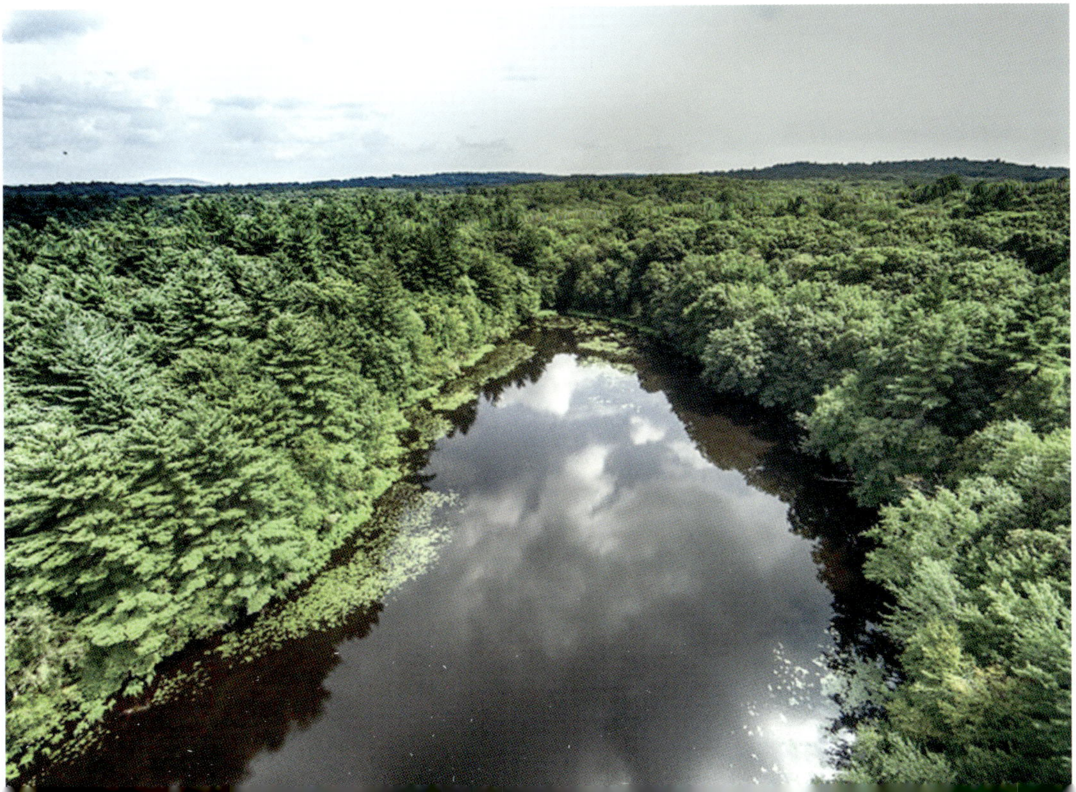

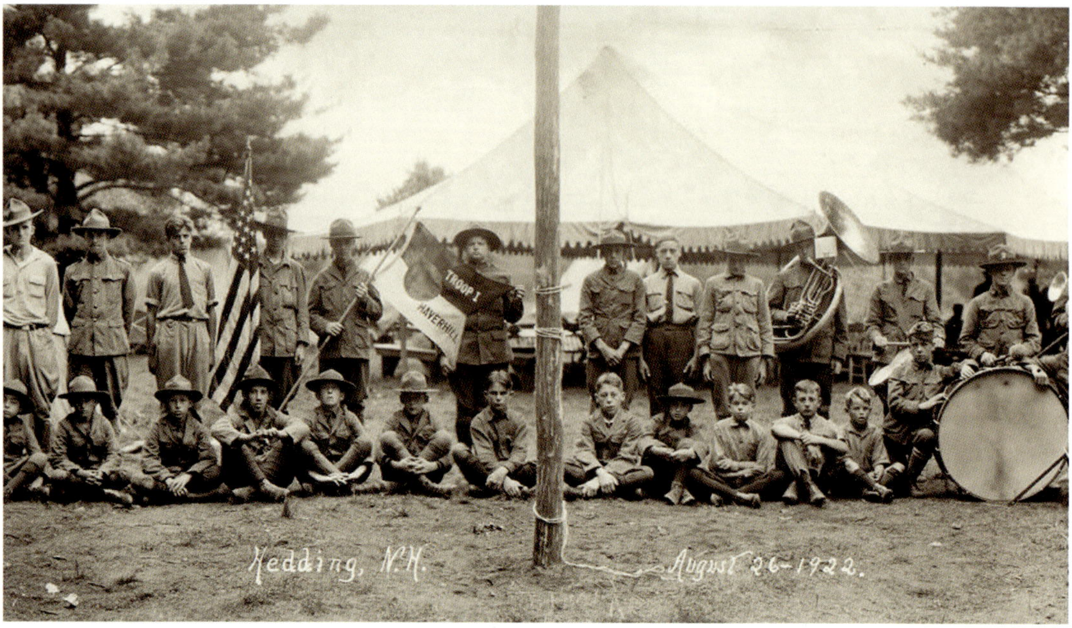

CAMP TRAILS—HEDDING TO KINGSTON: The roots of our current camps can be found in the early trolley camps. Camp Hedding was organized for Scouts in Haverhill, MA and surrounding communities. Camp Hedding, in 1922, was a proving ground that would lead to the establishment of Lone Tree Scout Reservation in 1946. That journey continues today.

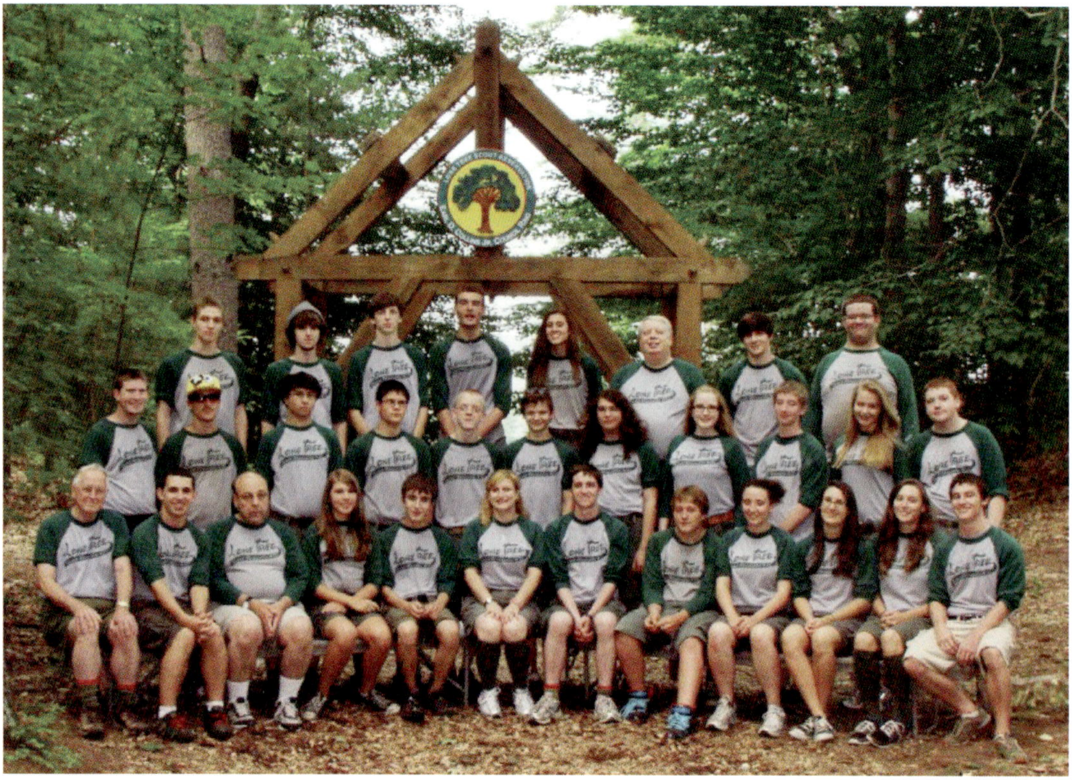

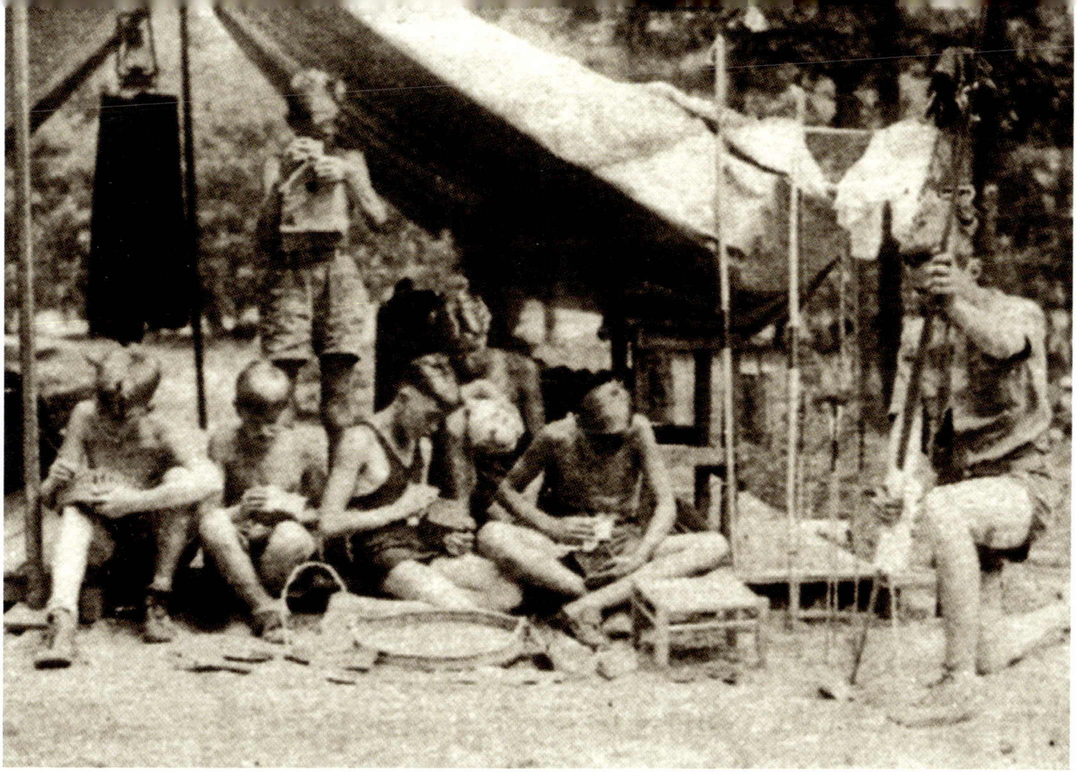

CAMP MAGUNCUG—KEYES POND WESTFORD, MA: In 1918 and again in 1919 the Lowell Council ran this camp for $5.50 per week. A fifty-cent discount was offered if the boys brought their Scoutmaster. For twenty-five cents boys would take the Ayer Trolley out of downtown Lowell to the end of the line. There, they hiked the last mile to camp. Maguncug was largely run by volunteers. Its program and spirit were like the West Wind Cub Scout Day Camp, which runs today on borrowed land with programs provided by volunteer leaders. Discounts are available for parents who volunteer to be part of the staff.

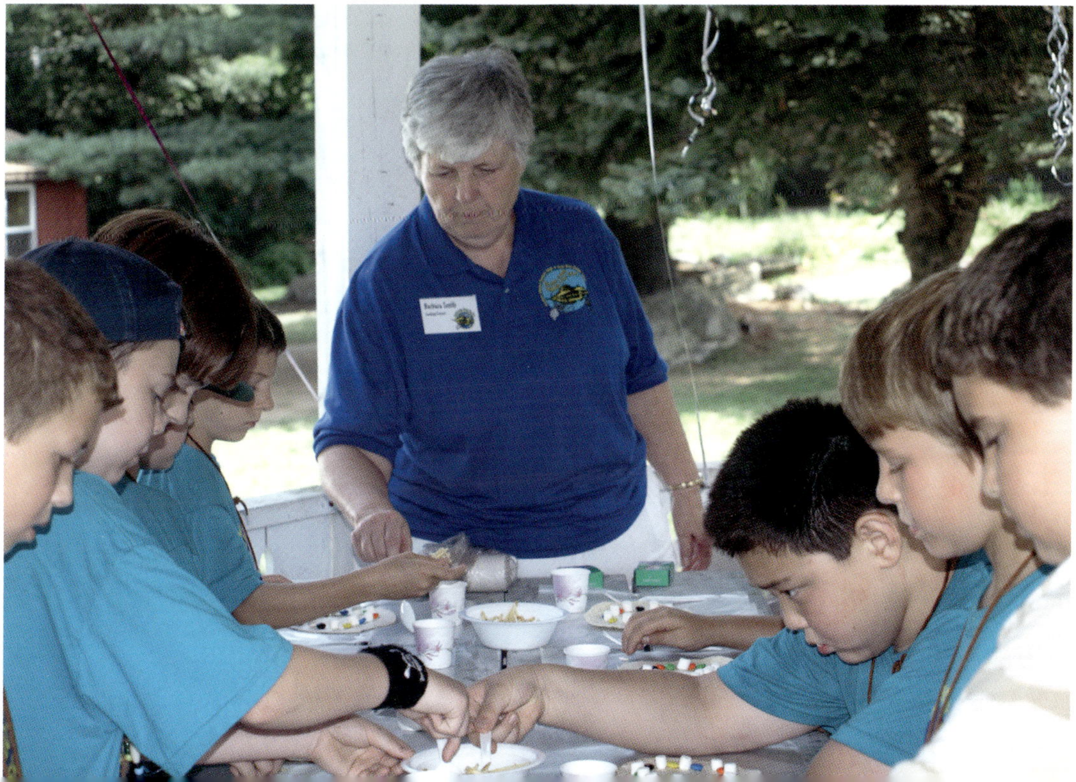

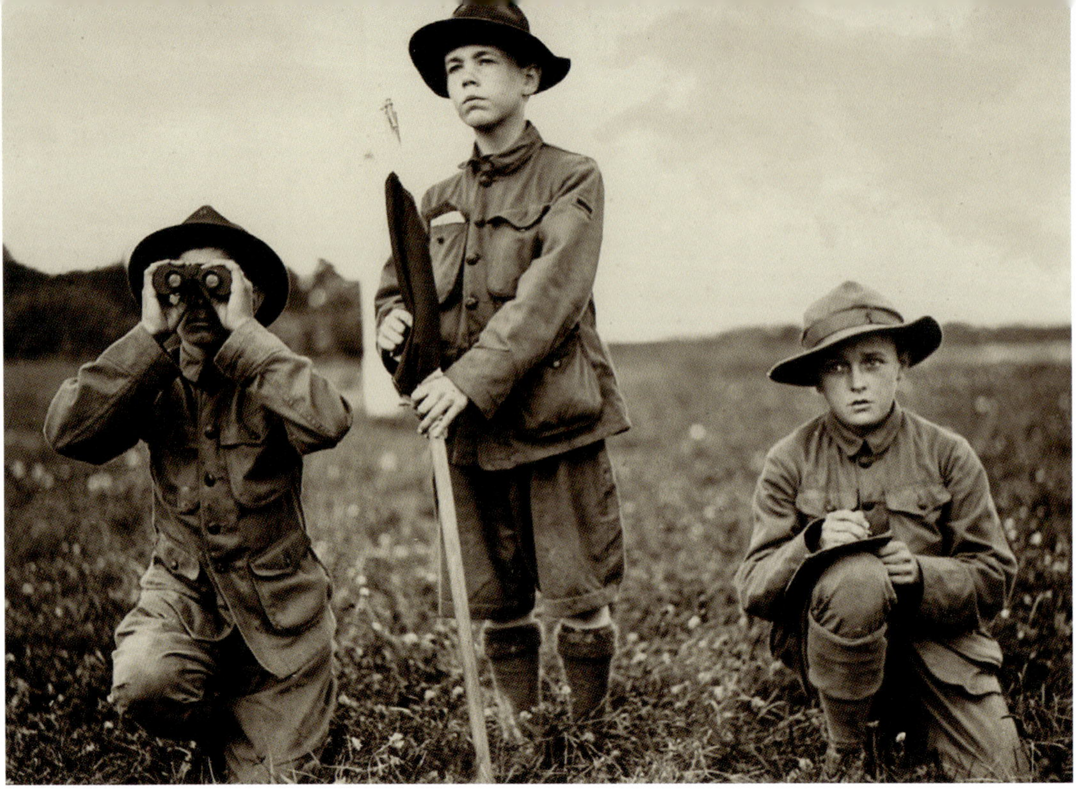

SEARCHING THE BLUE HILL RESERVATION, MILTON, MA: South of the Great Blue Hills, in what is known as the Pierce Devise, was the location of the first Boy Scout camp organized by the Greater Boston Council, BSA in the Summer of 1912. This camp provided outdoor programs for about 45 boys per week. The camp was ethnically and racially diverse. Each day began with a morning dip in Hoosickwhisick Pond. Malden's Charles W. Bradlee Jr. was camp director and activities included training in lifesaving, forestry, animal and plant studies, and knot tying. There were so few summer camps serving the nascent Scouting program that Boston Scouts were joined by those from East Bridgewater, MA and even Portland, ME.

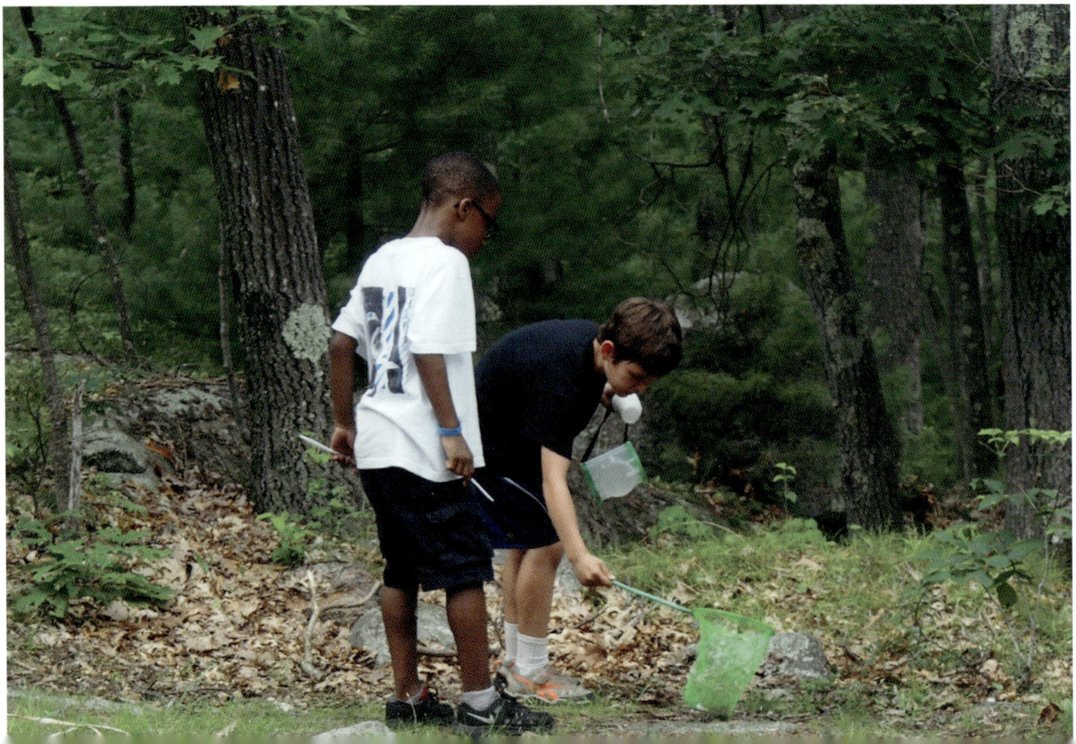

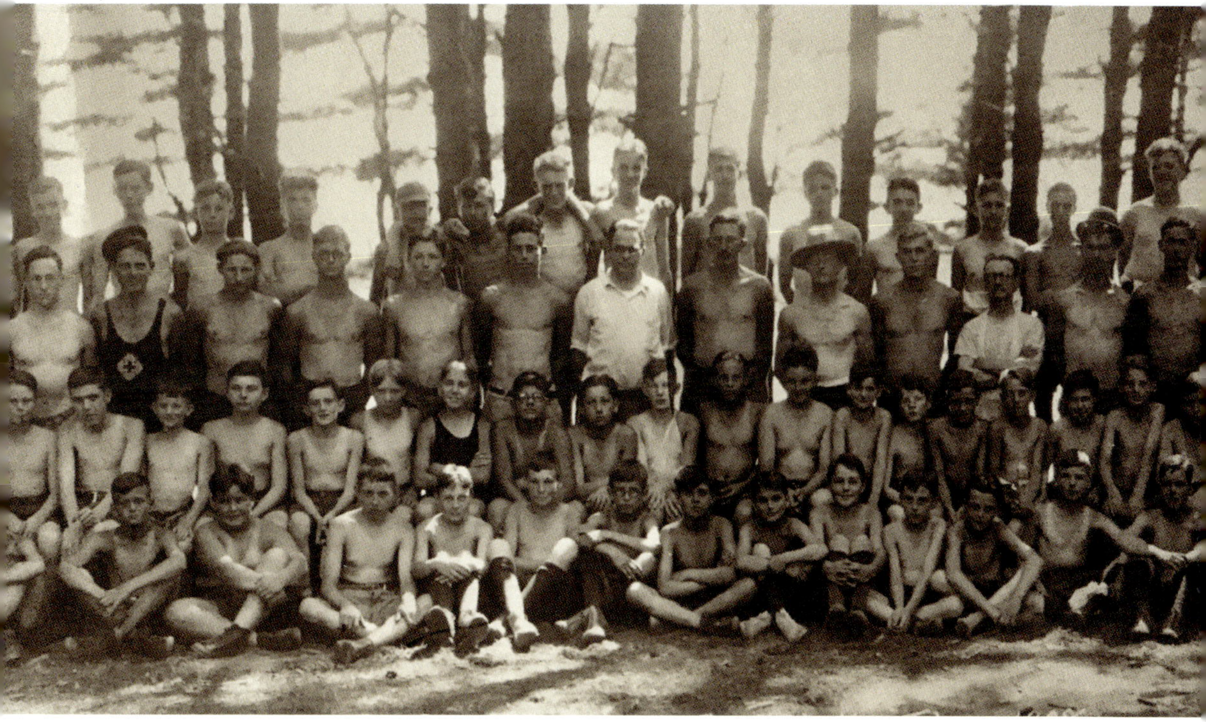

CAMP CHADWICK—DUNSTABLE, MA: Camp Chadwick was one of the most successful and influential of the trolley camps. It was organized by the Greater Lowell Council, BSA in 1926 on a small 11-acre site on Massapoag Pond in Dunstable, MA. At one time it served Scouts not only from the Lowell area but also from North Essex Council, BSA (Lawrence), and the Lone Tree Council, BSA (Haverhill). Three camps emerged from this experience: Camp Onway, Lone Tree Camp, and Wah-Tut-Ca Scout Reservation. In August of 1936, at the final campfire of Chadwick, a steel box was circulated, and each Scout placed a coin within the box. At the end of the fire the box was filled with those ashes from that last fire. The box and its contents were then placed into the foundation of the new dining hall at Wah-Tut-Ca, where it sits to this day beneath the hearth.

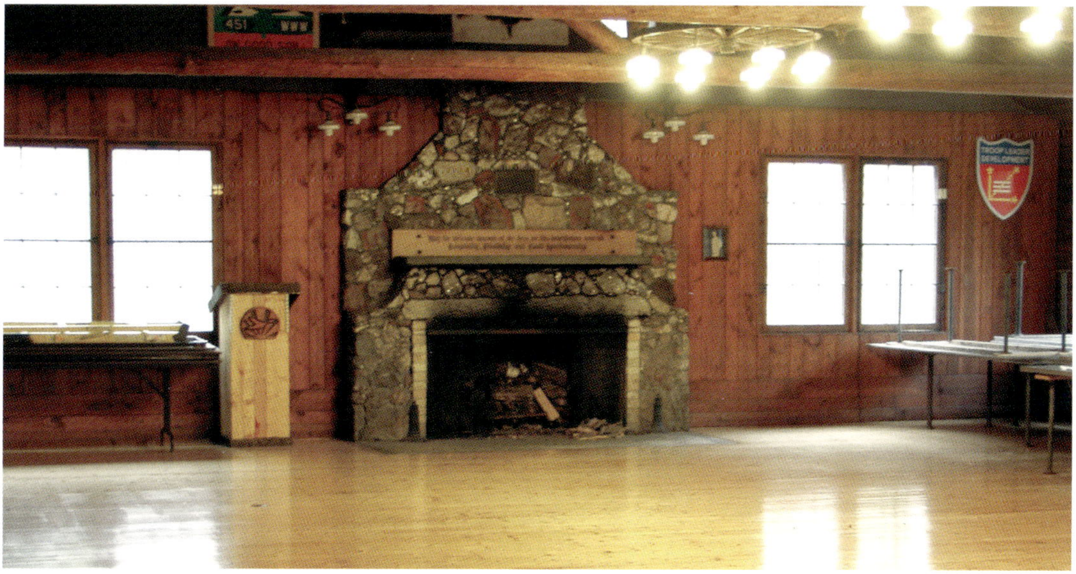

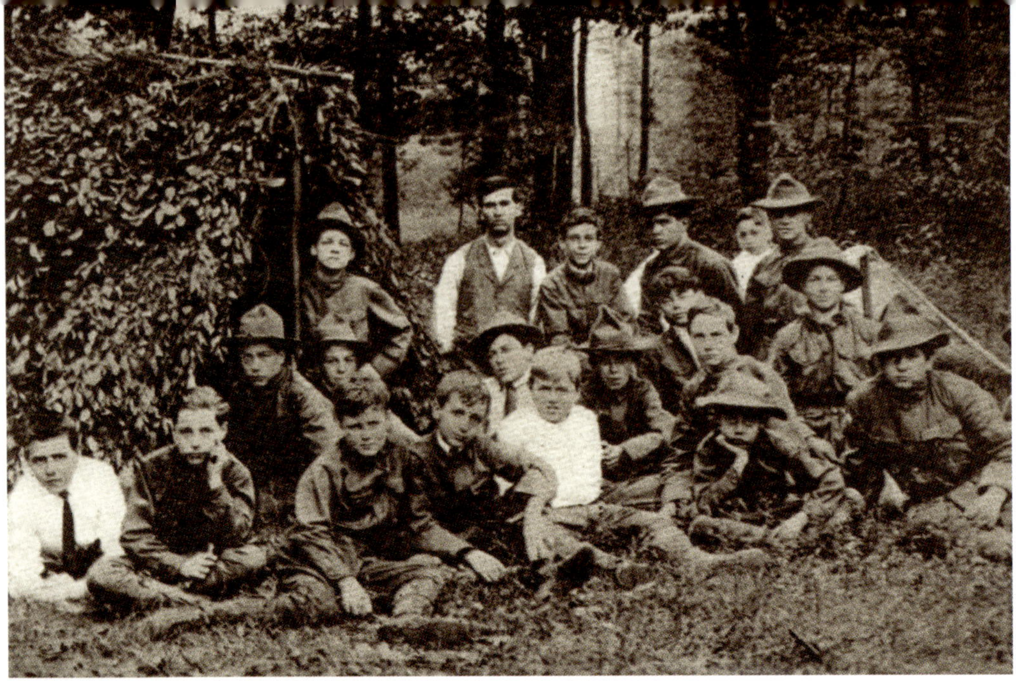

OTHER TROLLEY CAMPS: We have highlighted the most prominent of the trolley camps but there were many others. For example: Cambridge Scouts have a rich Scout camping legacy and in 1911, those Scouts camped on private land in Billerica, MA calling it Camp Hackquinanimen. At Beaver Pond in Lincoln, MA, in 1916 and 1925, the council celebrated their new camp located on Lake Quinapoxet in Jefferson, MA with weekly hikes to Mt. Wachusett. Scouts from District 1 of the Boston Boy Scout Council attended Camp Essex in Essex, MA in 1916. Andover Scouts would hop on the Salem Trolley to Middleton, MA and camp near the Ipswich River in the summer of 1916. Arlington Scouts could camp at Camp Oak in Bedford, MA. There was a lot of media attention for the Three Pond Camp the Boston Council opened outside Plymouth in 1915; however, the attention was short-lived. Scouts from Winchester, Woburn, and Stoneham, MA spent the summer of 1919 at Camp Mystic at Humarock Beach. For several years, Boston area Scouts enjoyed regular outings at Camp Karlstein located on the old Dedham polo grounds. The tradition of one-week camps, on rented or borrowed land, continues today in the numerous Cub Day and satellite camps of the Spirit of Adventure Council such as the Lexington Cub Day Camp pictured below.

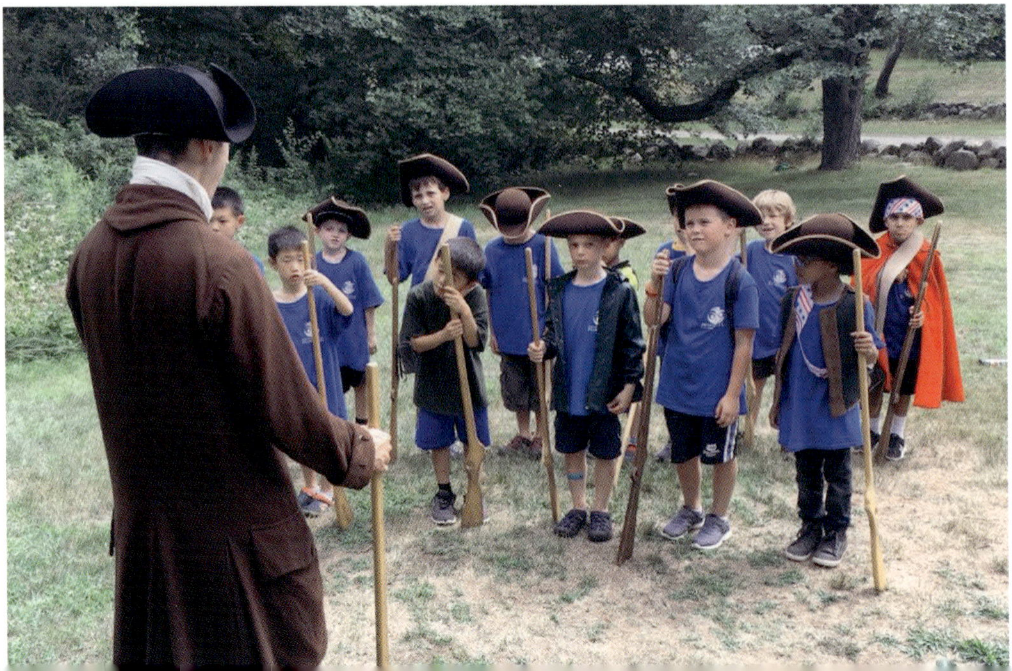

Chapter 2

Long Road from Home
Camps of the North Bay

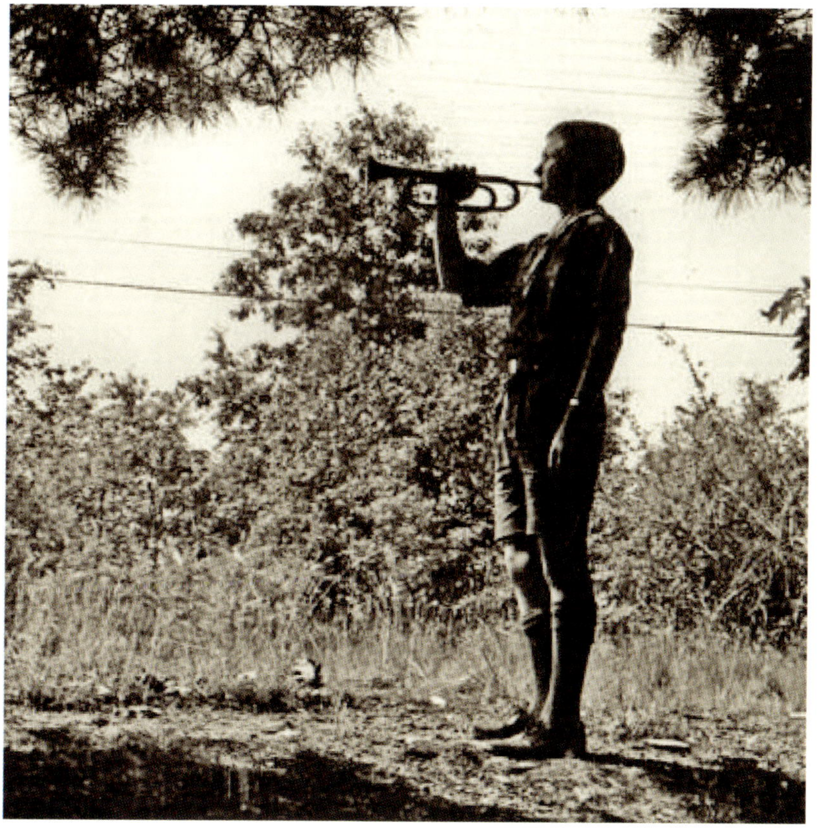

Camp Powow—Amesbury, MA Circa 1960: The North Bay Council, BSA, which stretched from Winthrop to Gloucester along the Massachusetts North Shore, was originally two councils, one of which was the Bay Shore Council, BSA. Headquartered in Lynn, MA, they owned Camp Powow. Powow was a small camp on Gardner Pond that was opened in 1925. It was the successor of a trolley camp named Camp Weston.

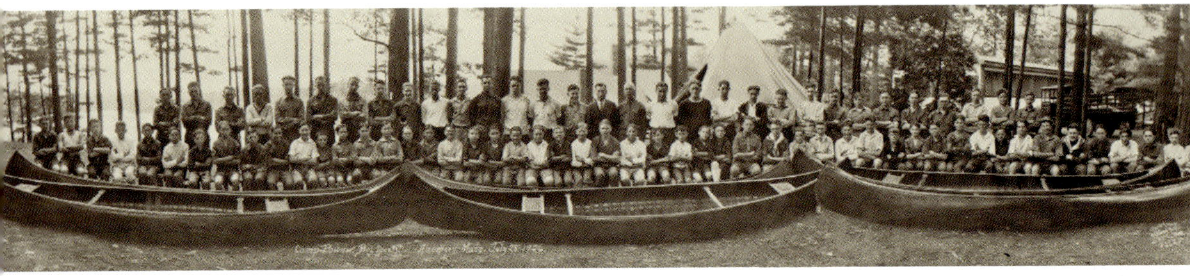

THE CAMP ON A HILL: Powow is named after the hill on the property. It was hardly larger than a football field. By the 1960s only thirteen percent of the Bay Shore Scouts attended it because it was surrounded by other councils with larger camps. Today the site of Camp Powow is partially underwater due to the expansion of Gardner Pond into Lake Gardner in the 1980s.

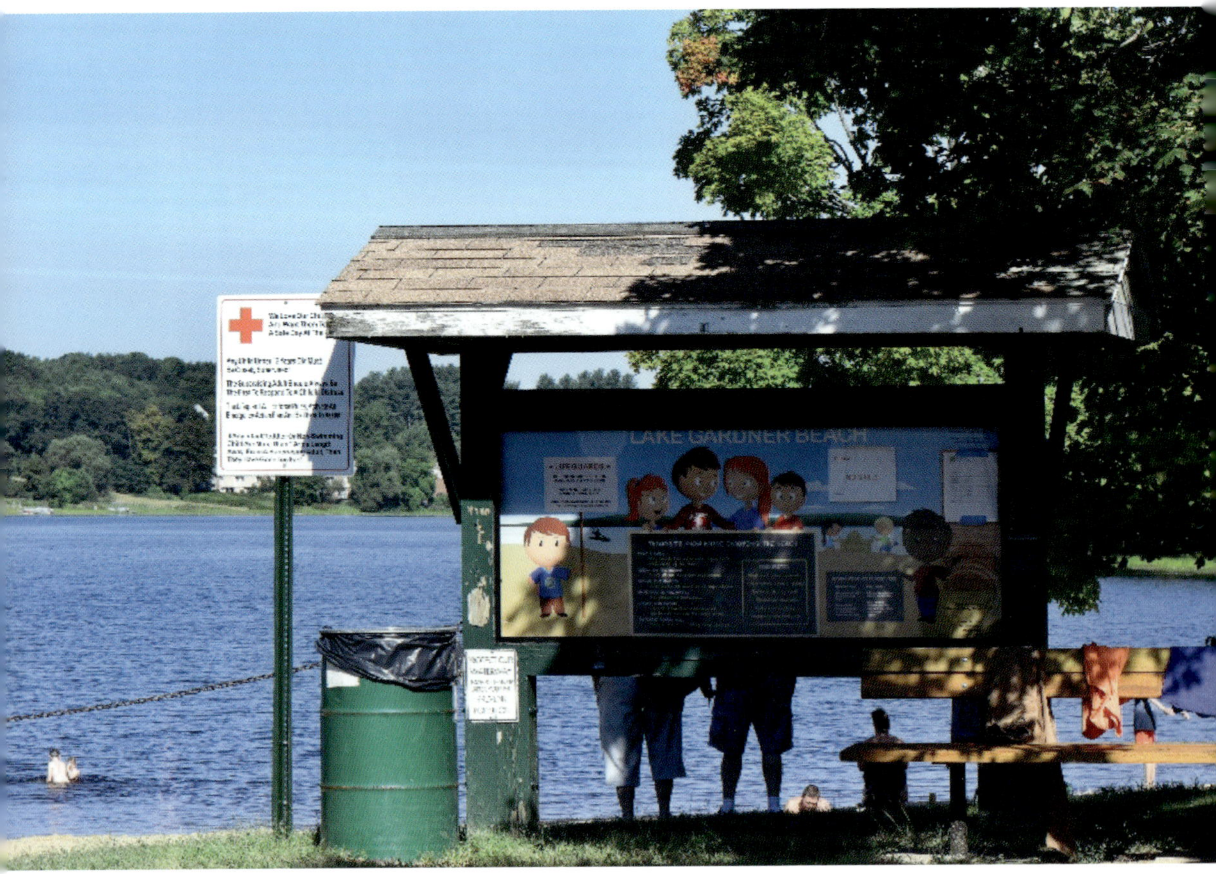

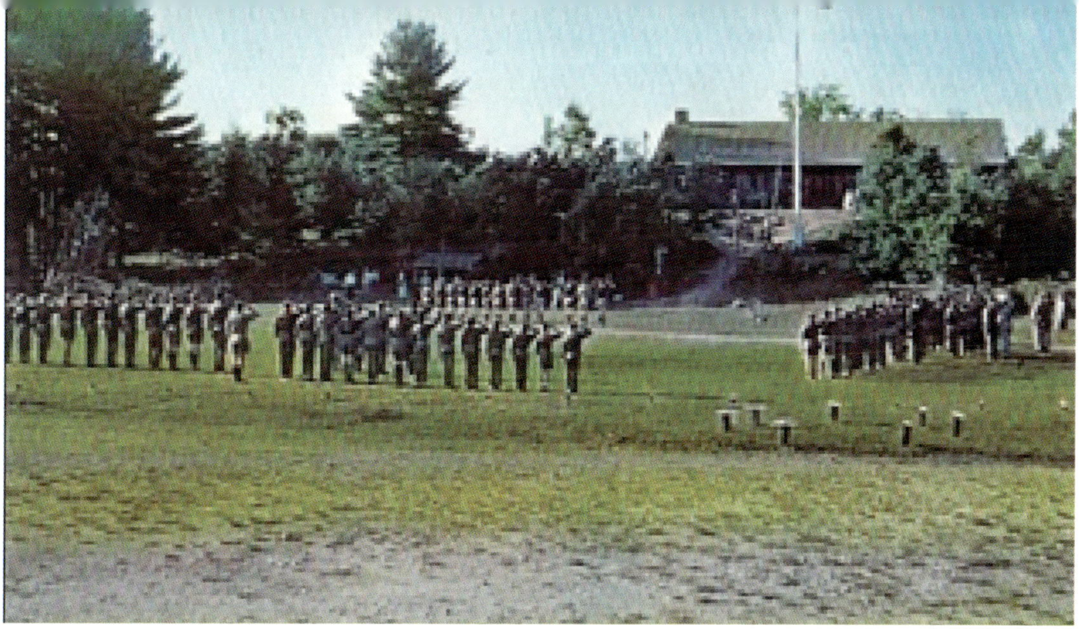

NORSHOCO SCOUT RESERVATION—LYMAN, ME: The North Shore Council, BSA moved out of trolley camps in October of 1944. A group of Council leaders, led by James E. Reynolds, purchased 400 acres on Bunganut Lake in Lyman, Maine. Norshoco, (North-Shore-Council) opened in the 1945 season with accommodations for 100 Scouts to participate in four two-week programs. The cost of camp was $11 per week and Scouts were required to bring their Second World War ration cards to camp. Great pride was taken by North Shore Scouts, leaders, and volunteers in the camp. Their connection to the camp was so strong that the demonym "Bunganut," was used often to refer to those passionate about the property. To this day a good number of former campers and staff react emotionally to being called a Bunganut. The camp today is a town park for residents of Lyman, Maine.

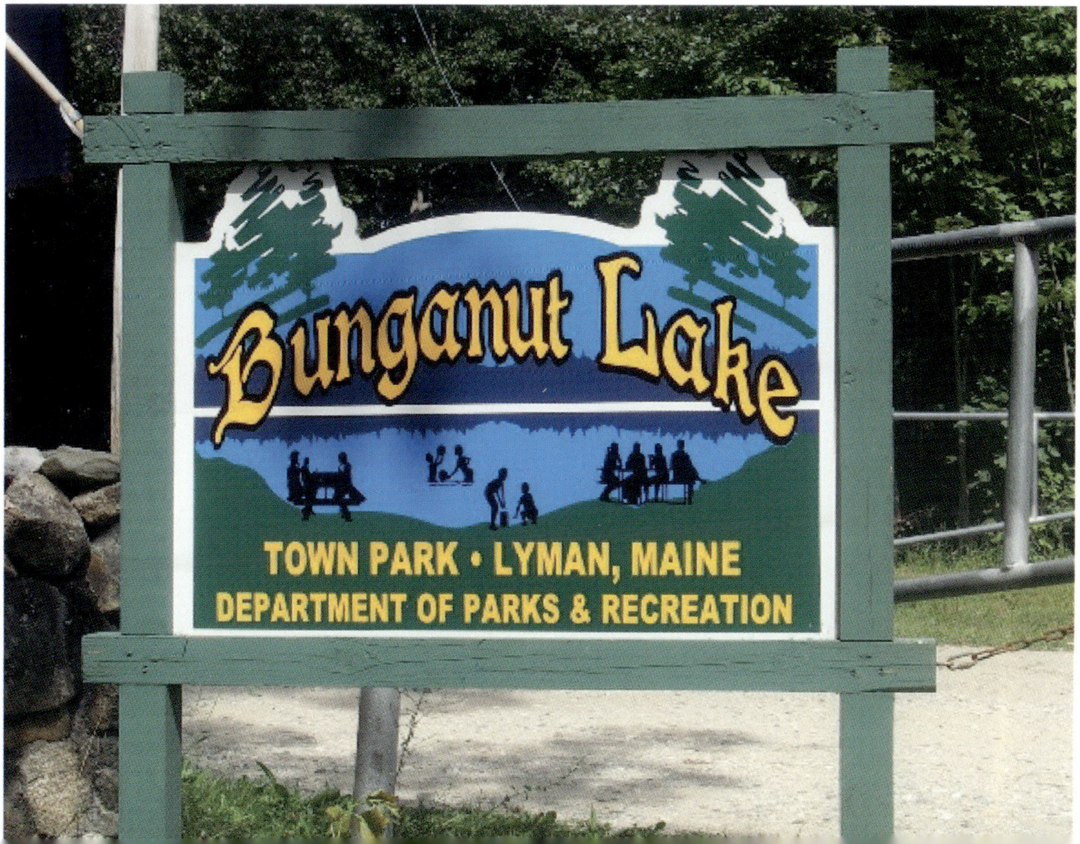

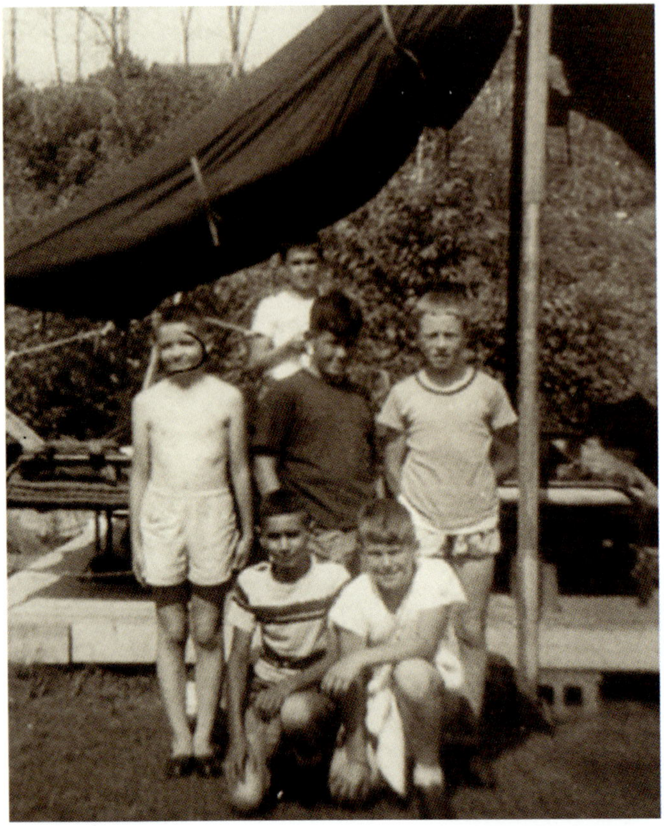

THE NORSHOCO COMMUNITY: Camp at Norshoco was very much focused on community. Staff, campers and unit leaders knew each other well and shared the ownership of the property. Every staff member at camp knew every unit leader and every unit leader knew each other through camp. In the off-season this was further promoted by the incorporation of Amiskwi Lodge No. 505, the local Order of the Arrow Honor Camping Society. Weekly family barbeques that were held on the parade field drew hundreds of extra visitors to camp. Mothers, fathers, and children would all join their Scout at Camp. Many camps continue this tradition, like Wah-Tut-Ca, with their weekly family barbeque.

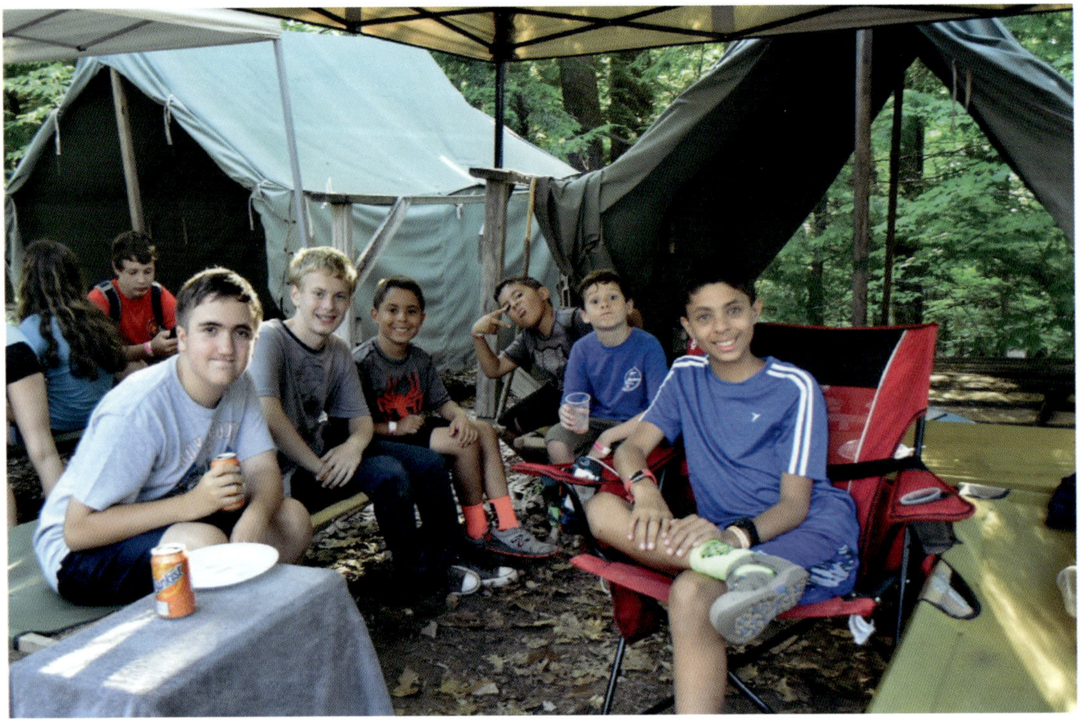

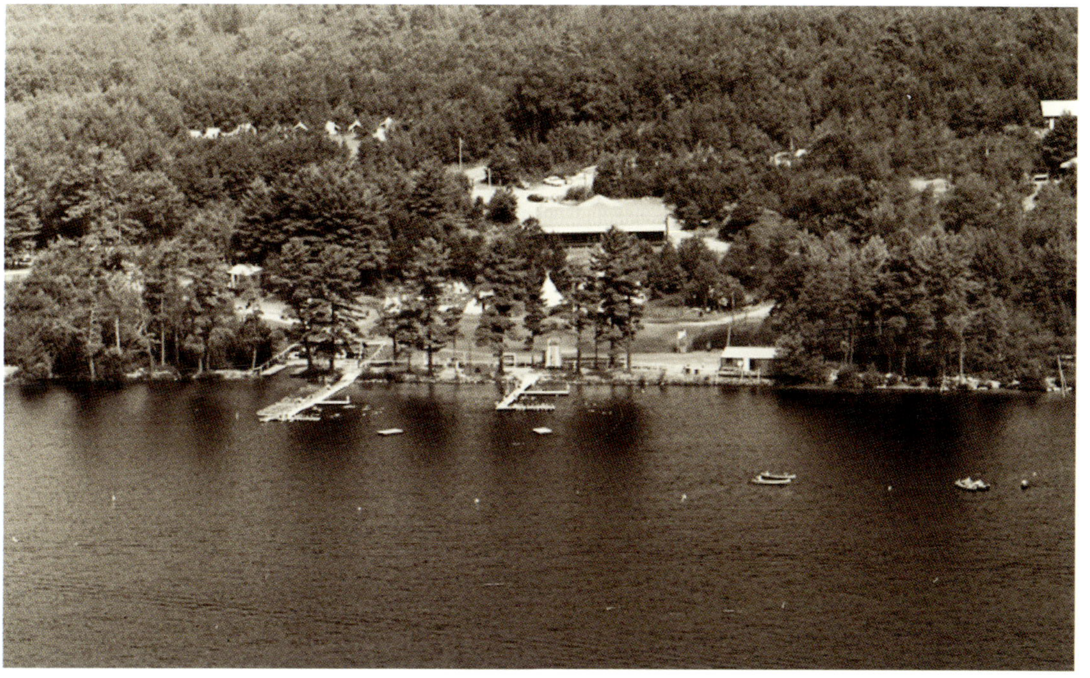

Norshoco From Above: By the early 1960s Norshoco had greatly expanded and was conducting programs for nearly 300 Scouts a week for eight weeks. Thriving camp programs were established, including a weekly water carnival and a camp-wide relay race called the Bunganut Cup. The expansion was most noticeable at the waterfront which had grown from a small collection of seven canoes and rowboats in 1945 to a fleet of various watercraft, an expansive swimming area, and floating rafts. In its peak years the dining hall was filled. Today, the shadow of the camp can still be seen from the air above Bunganut Lake.

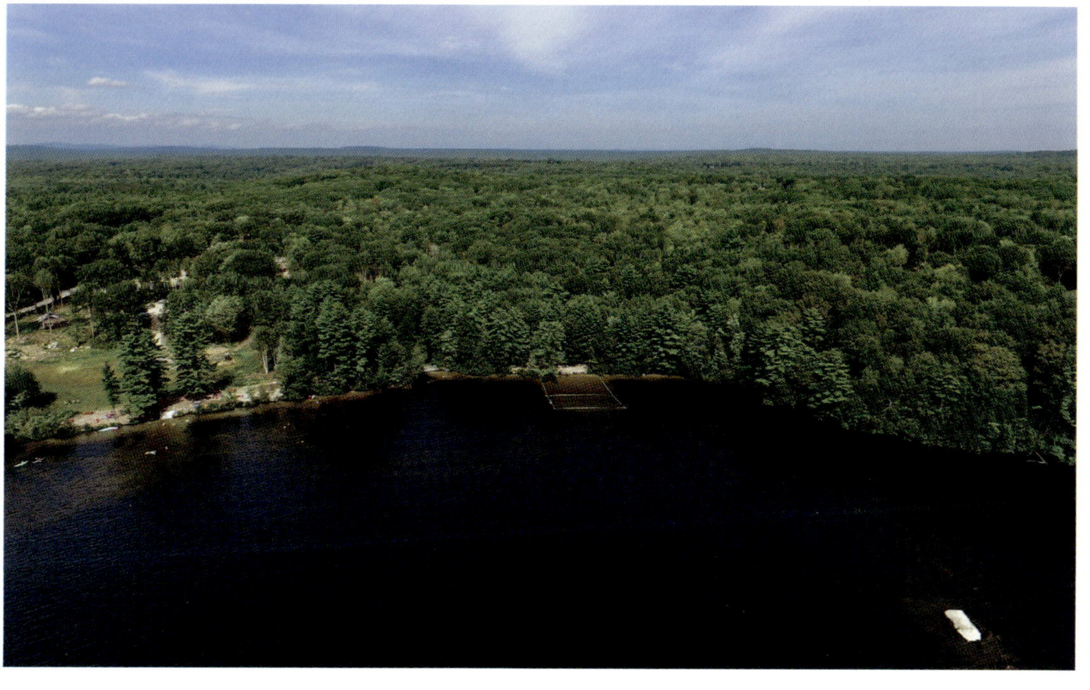

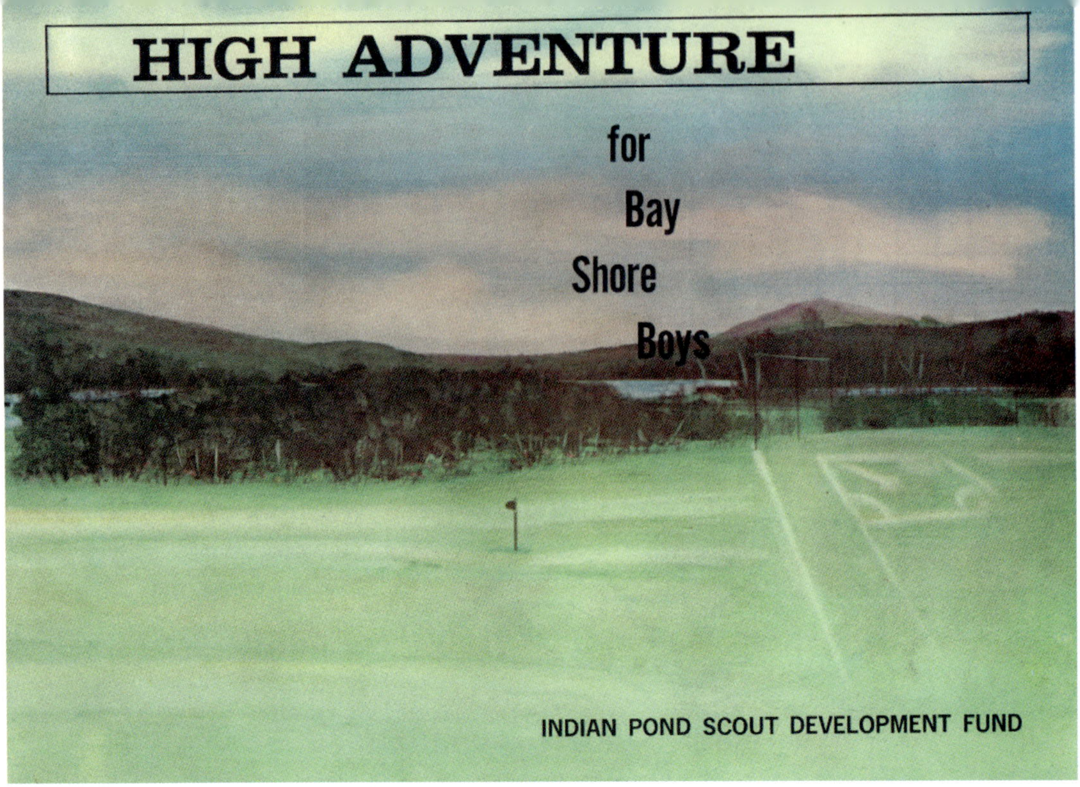

INDIAN POND BOY SCOUT RESERVATION - ORFORD, NH: By 1962 it had become clear that Powow needed to be replaced and the Bay Shore Council, BSA would need to expand camping operations. A very optimistic proposal was put forth by the Council to purchase a recently closed camp in Orford, NH for $125,000. The camp was 150 miles from Lynn, ME and was 1,200 acres. It was near the Appalachian Trail, Cube Mountain, and Indian Pond Mountain. It was designed to hold double the current number of campers at Powow. Everything about the new camp was about predicted growth.

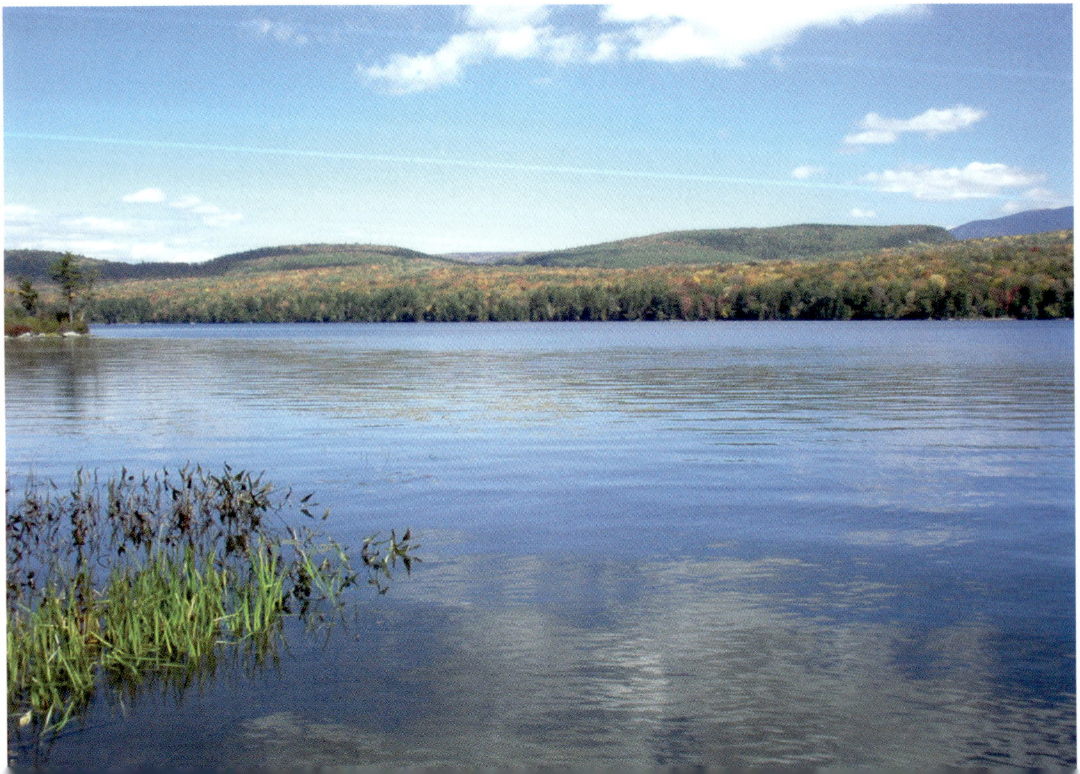

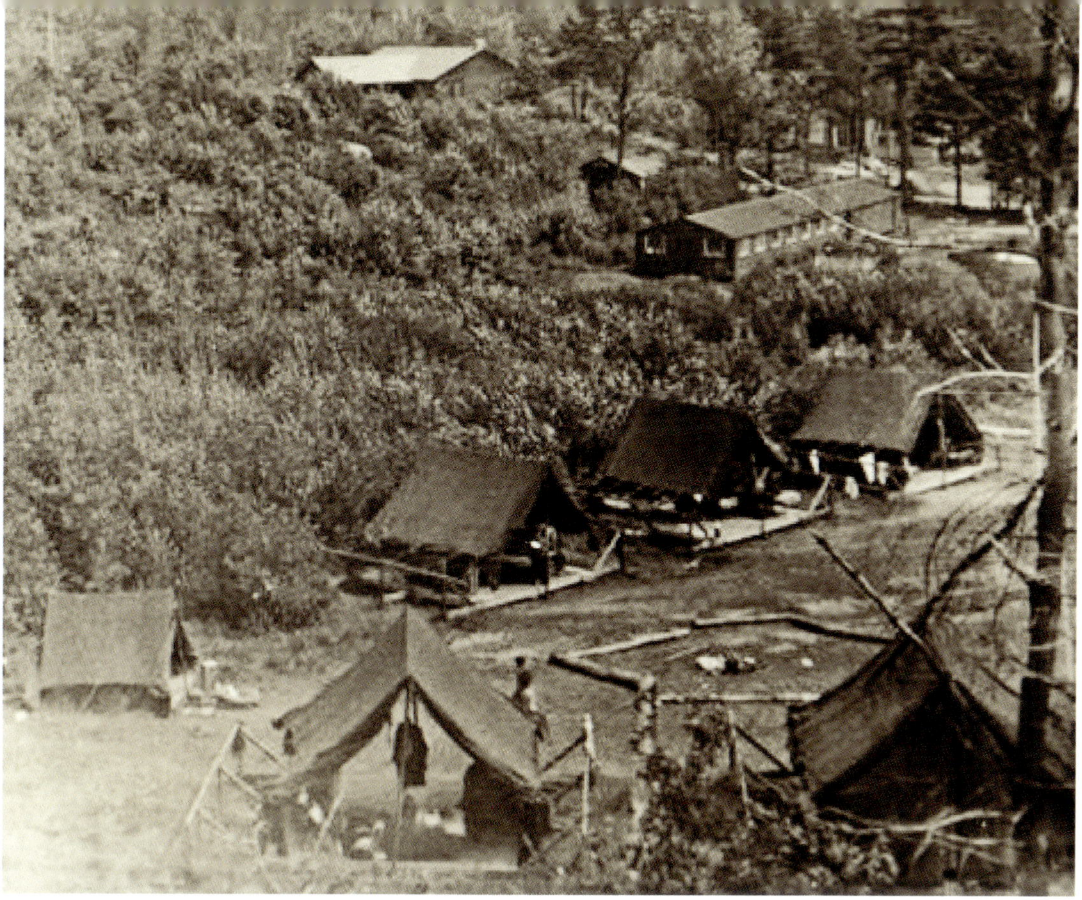

CLOSING OF NORSHOCO: Campsites like Skunk Hollow at Norshoco were jam-packed week after week during the summer. The camp remained incredibly popular among Scouts and Scoutmasters. In 1966 one of the first of many mergers of Councils (mergers that continued into the next century) was a merger of the North Shore Council and the Bay Shore Council. In 1971 the newly formed North Bay Council, BSA made the decision to shutter and sell Norshoco. All camping operations were moved to Indian Pond because it was a larger property. Today the remains of Skunk Hollow are disappearing from history and being reclaimed by the woods.

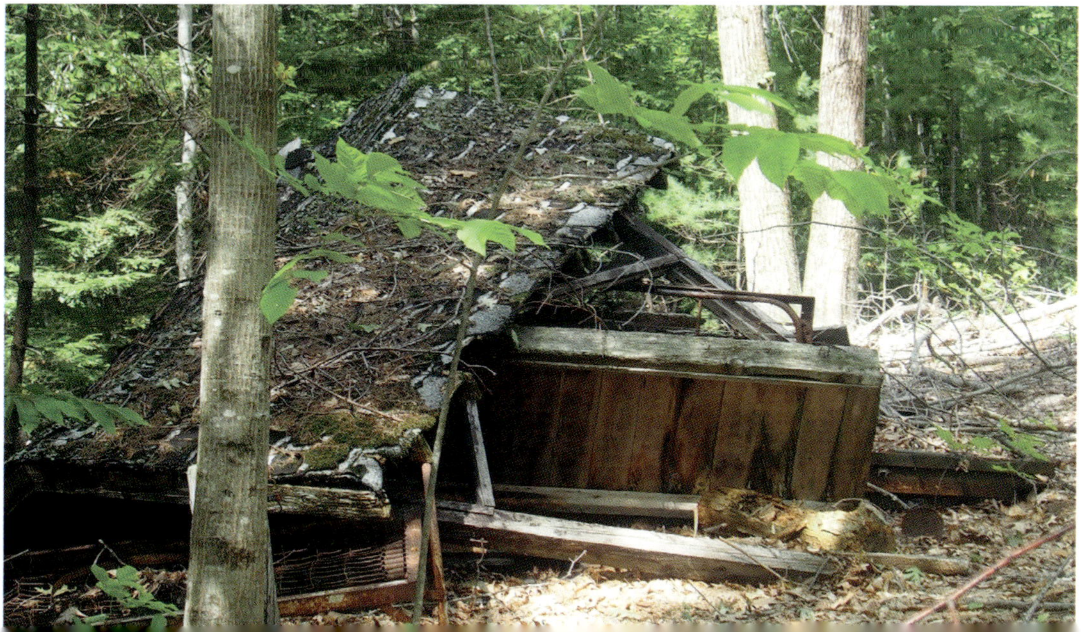

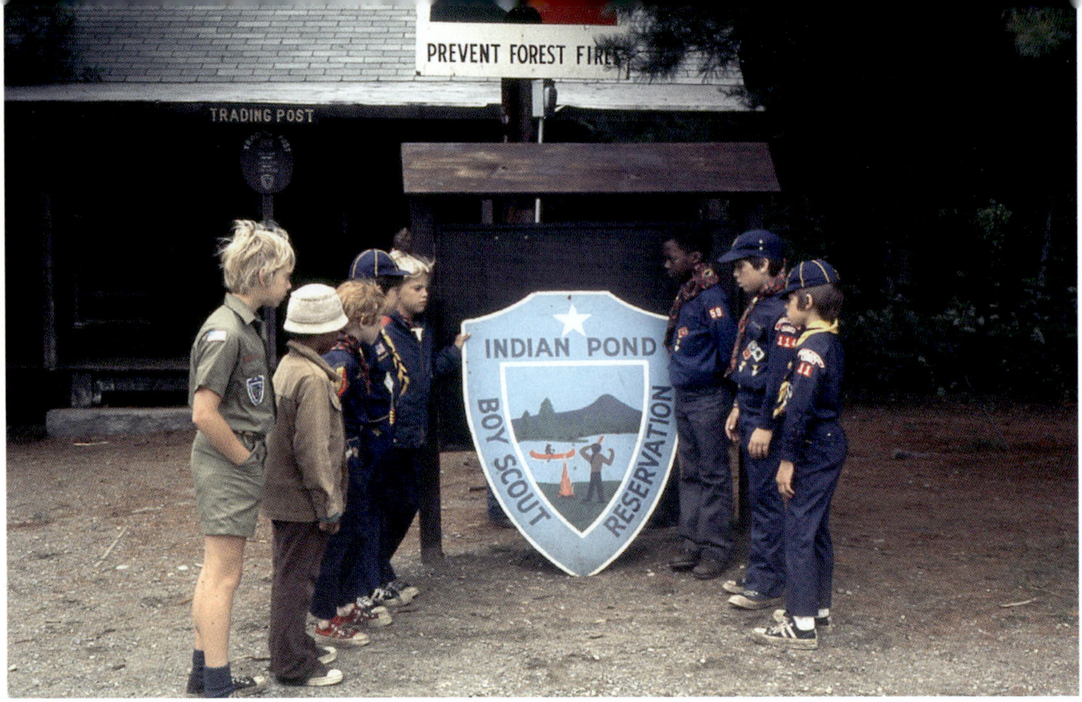

ARROW OF LIGHT WEEKEND: With the closing of Norshoco, Indian Pond became the go-to camping location for the North Shore. As the camp grew older, a new culture of camping began to emerge which included the birth of the Arrow of Light (AOL) Weekend. The weekend was hosted at Indian Pond by Amiskwi Lodge. This event was designed to introduce Cub Scouts to the new world of Boy Scout camping. Every year hundreds of Webelo Scouts would go to Orford, NH to get a taste of what they would experience the next summer. AOL Weekends continue to this day and are hosted by Amiskwi's successor, Pennacook Lodge.

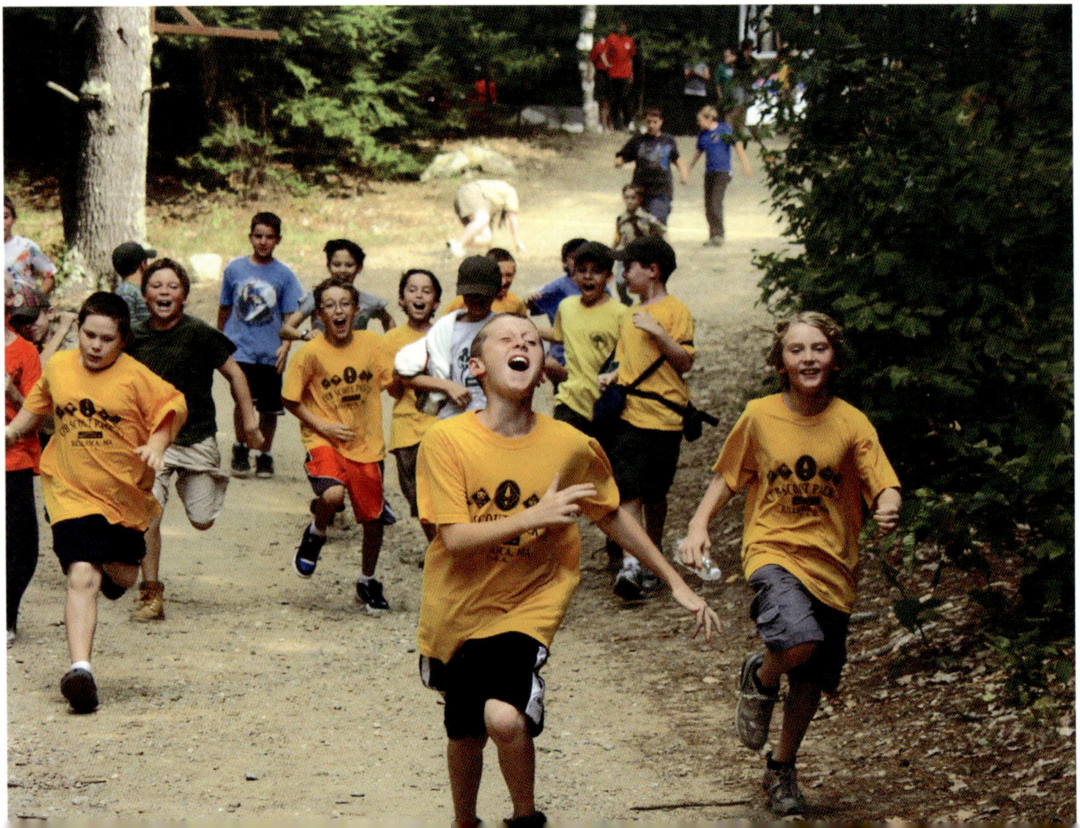

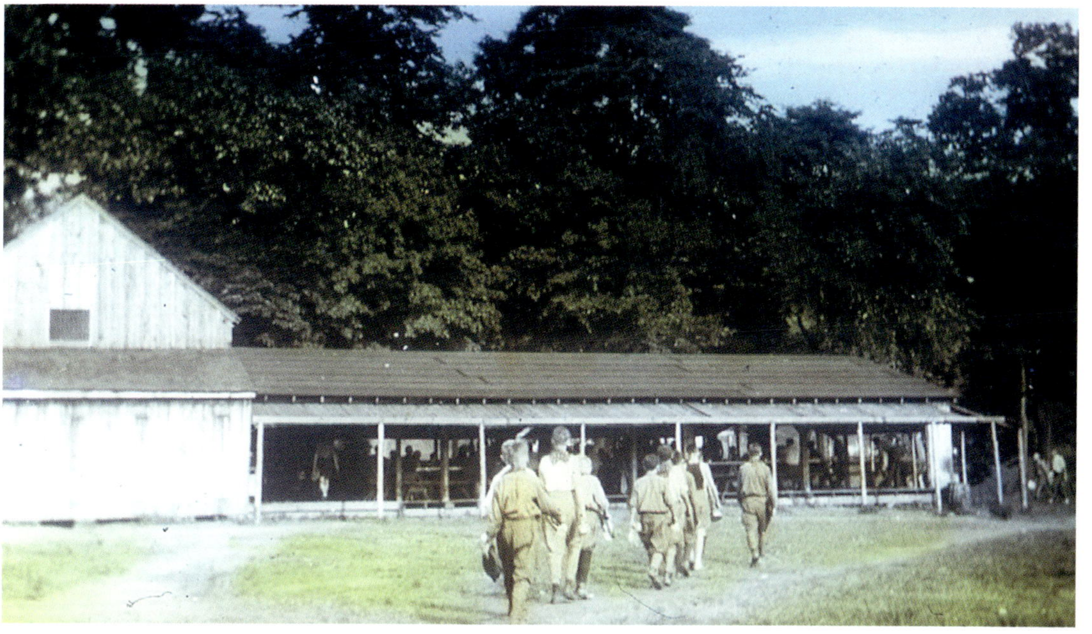

Dining Hall vs. Patrol Cooking: The two Councils that made up the North Bay Council, BSA had different camp traditions. Indian Pond's subcamp, Waskeche, was the camp predominately attended by the old North Shore Council Scouts. It operated as a separate camp across the pond. Camp Weston was used by Scouts from the old Bay Shore Council. There were noticeable differences in the culture of the two camps such as mealtime. The Waskeche units prepared their own meals at the campsites with their patrols and Weston units used the dining hall instead. To this day, several North Shore Council, BSA units retain the eat-in-site model. Troop 28 from Wrentham, formerly of both Norshoco and Indian Pond, continues this tradition by cooking in a Wah-Tut-Ca campsite.

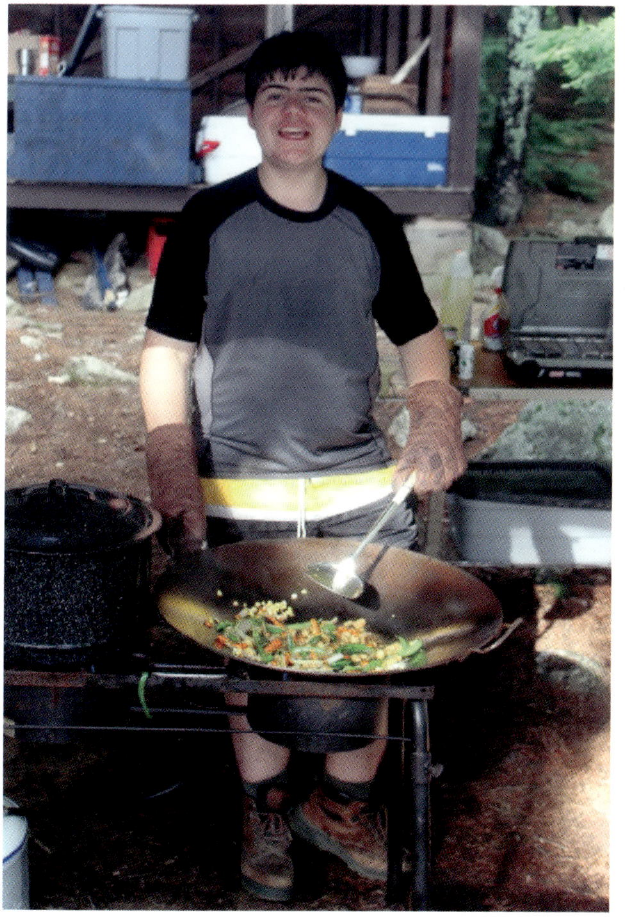

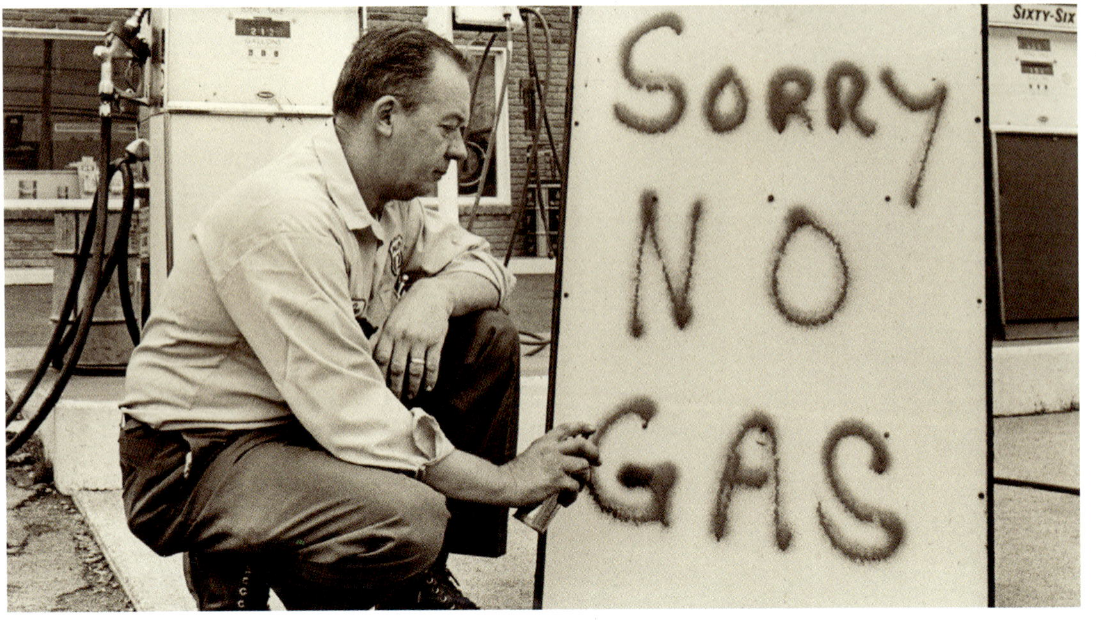

THE LONG ROAD TO INDIAN POND: The gas crisis of the late 1970s made getting to camp an expensive investment. The trip from the towns and cities of the North Bay Council, BSA was a four-hour drive. Efforts were made to provided buses to the Reservation, but attendance continued to fall. Questions about the sustainability of Indian Pond began to be asked. As a result, Camp Waskeche was closed in 1977 due to poor attendance. The Council Executive Board then voted, in 1979, to close Indian Pond.

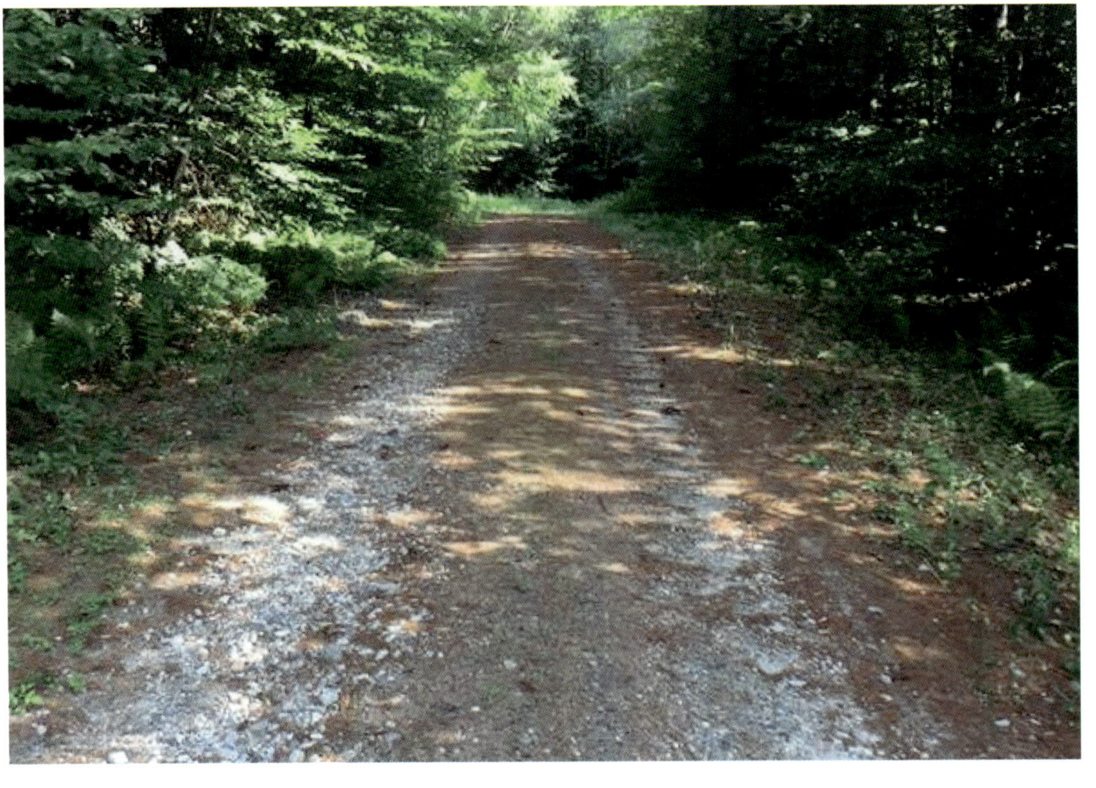

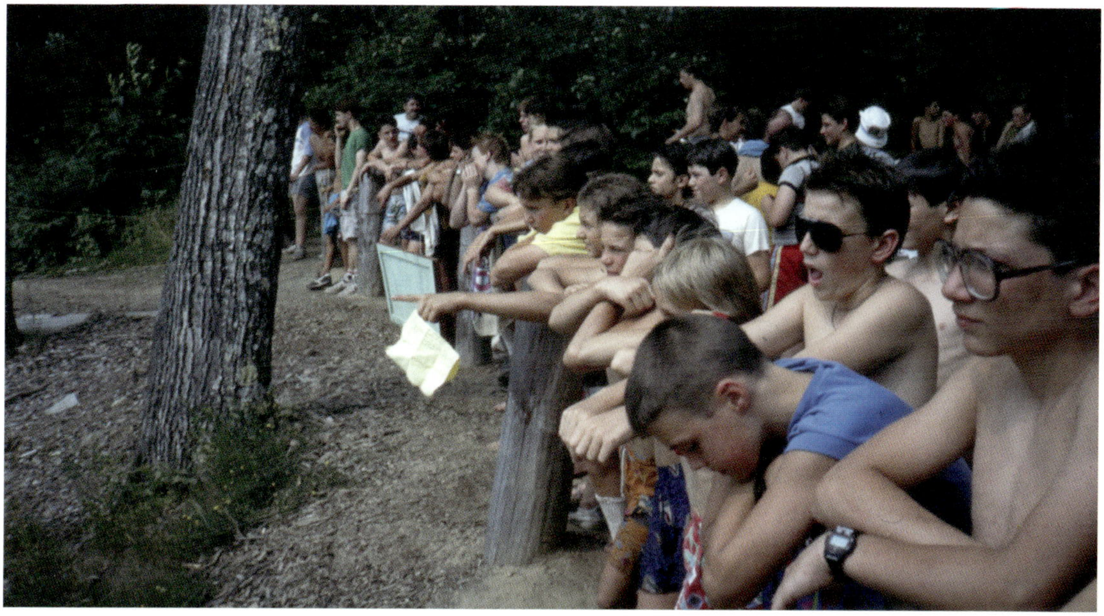

MIGRANT BUNGANUTS: In the 1980s the North Bay Council, BSA had no camp and instead entered into a series of camp sharing agreements. The first was with the Boston Council, BSA. Wild Goose Camp at T. L. Storer, pictured above, completed an expansion to support the North Bay Scouts. That agreement eventually failed. Another agreement was made with the North Essex Council, BSA for use of Camp Onway. With the North Shore frequently shifting camps, the Scout Troops began to make their own arrangements independent of council agreements. To this day most of them do not camp in a Spirit of Adventure Council, BSA camps. It became common for each Scout Troop in the North Shore to make their summer camping arrangements independent of the Council. Today most of them do not camp in a Spirit of Adventure Council, BSA camp. Some though, like Troop 53 in Swampscott, MA, have returned and they are now deeply rooted in the culture of Wah-Tut-Ca Scout Reservation, Northwood, NH.

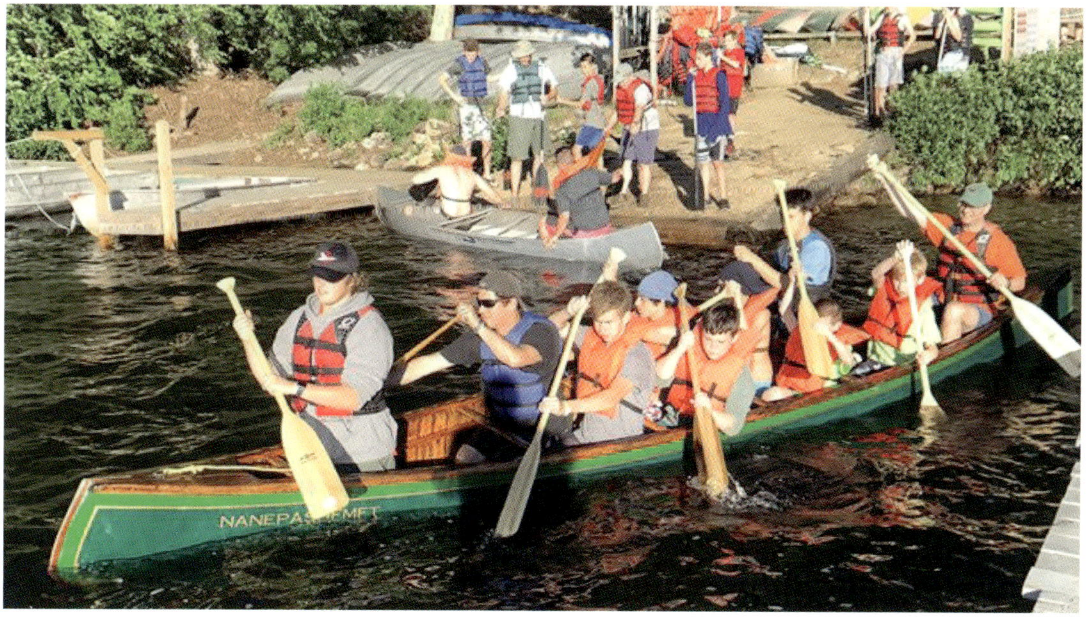

Chapter 3

Camp Onway

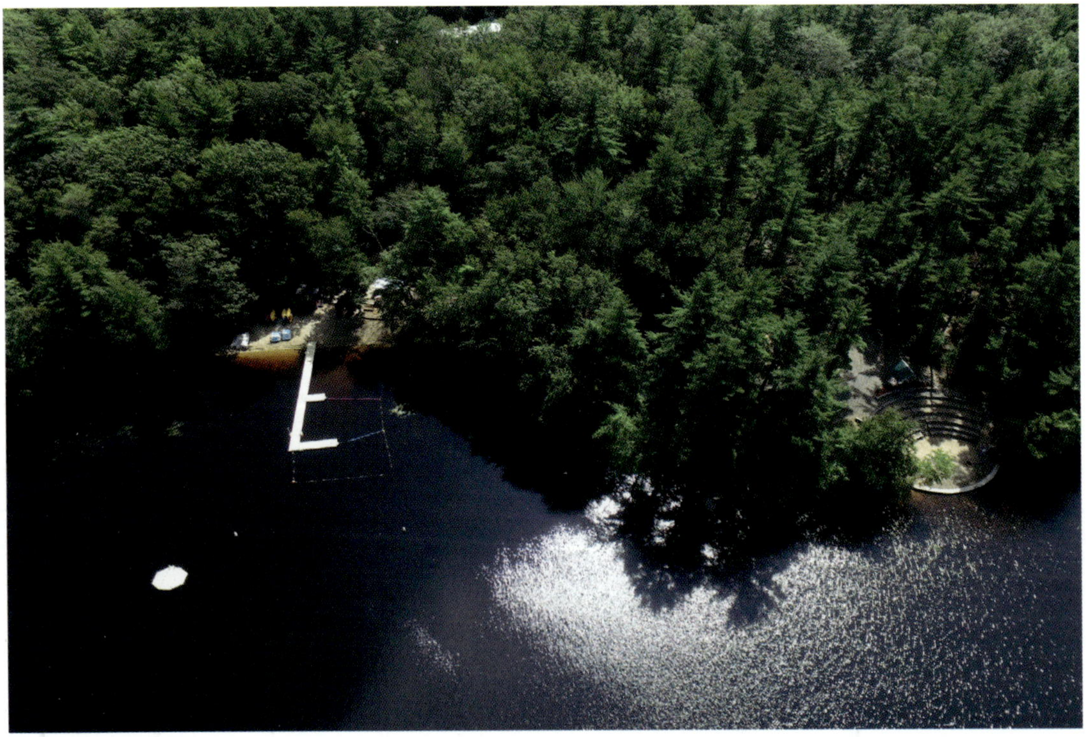

Camp Onway—Raymond, NH: Since the 1900s Onway Lake had been a camping location for the Rockingham County YMCA and the Exeter Community Council for Girls. In 1929 the North Essex Council, BSA purchased Camp Onway to serve Scouts in Lawrence, Methuen, North Andover, and Andover, MA. Harvey "Pop" Bacon, the Scout Executive, served as the first camp director. The purchase of the property was financed by the Lawrence Lions Club and the personal contributions of Burchard E. Horne, Council President from 1930-1932. Sadly, the Yankee Clipper Council, BSA, the successor of the North Essex Council, BSA, sold the camp in 2007 to grow their endowment. The need to sell Camp Onway, still today, is bitterly contested by its supporters.

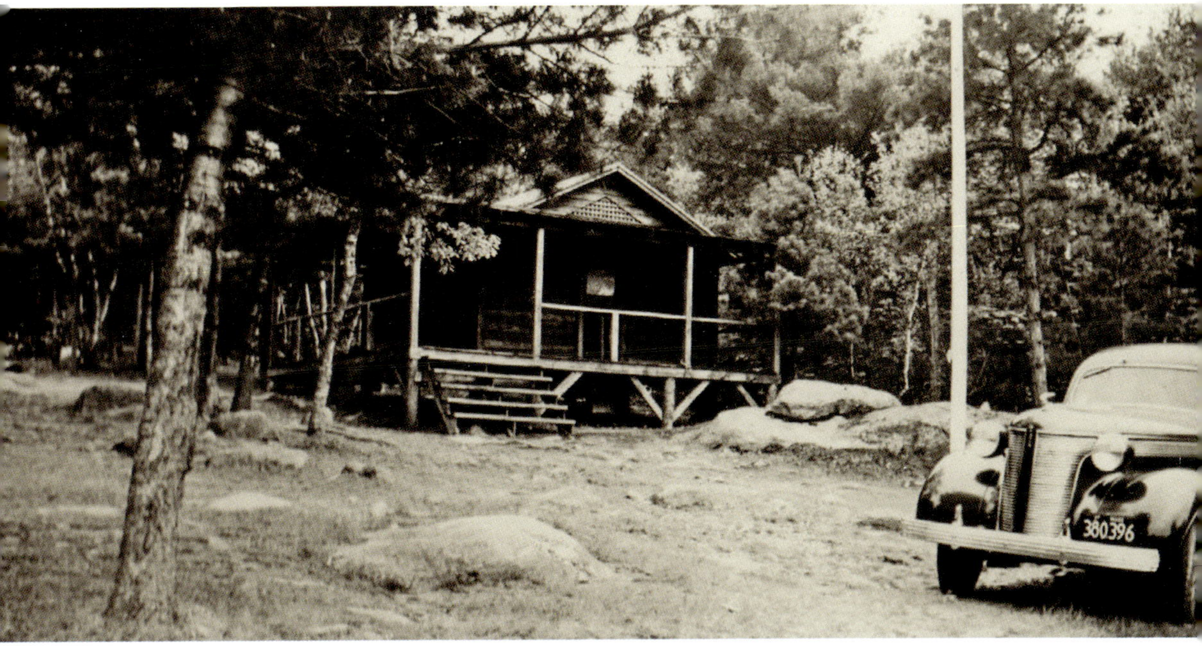

ONWAY HEADQUARTERS: The Headquarter Building was one of the original buildings on the property. Pictured above in 1936, the front and side porches were added in 1930. The building served as the camp Office and winter cabin for many years. As Camp Onway grew the building would later be known as the CIT Cabin when it was used as the living quarters of the camp's Counselors in Training. In later years the building was known as Cabin 7 and was used for storage and as the Camp Commissioners office. Pictured below is the building in 2007 with the final Camp Onway Staff.

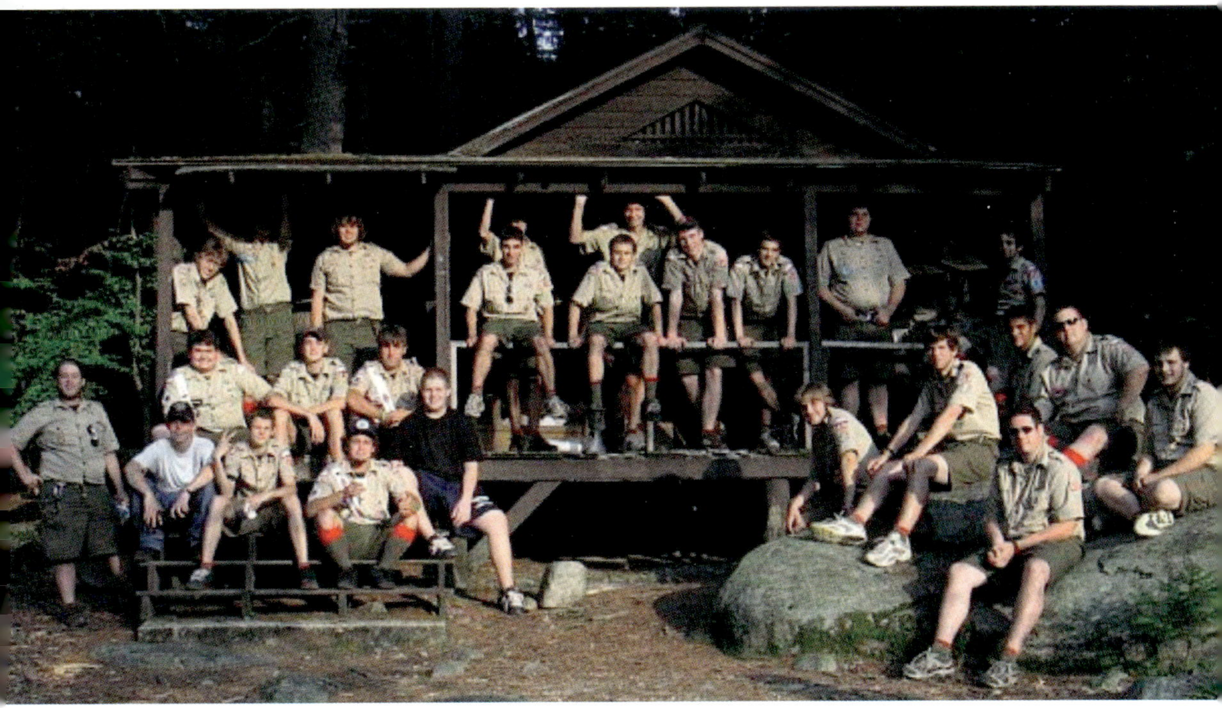

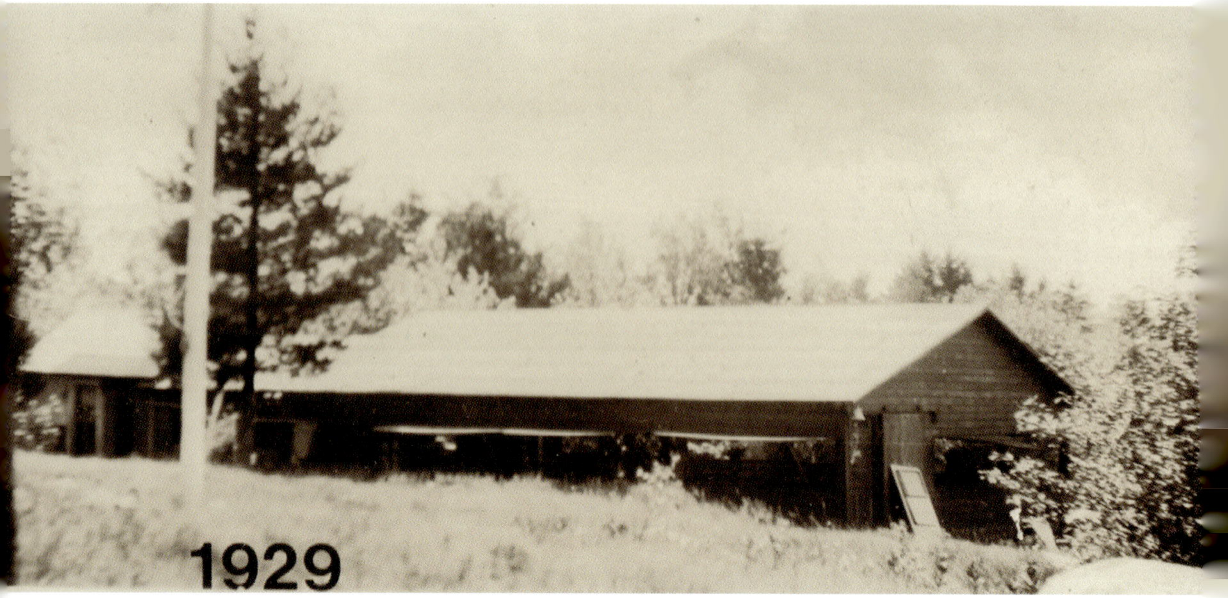

HORNE DINING HALL: The Dining Hall was another original building on the property. It was named in honor of Burchard E. Horne, Council President and camp benefactor. Mr. Horne took a mortgage on the property in 1930 and paid off the entire amount over a ten-year period. In 1931 a porch and fireplace were added to the building. The Burchard Horne Dining Hall partially burnt down in 1943 and was rebuilt with an enlarged kitchen. Another fire destroyed part of the building in 1971. The Horne Dining Hall was completely rebuilt and restored in 1972. In the 1990s a full basement was constructed under the Dining Hall after it was elevated several feet. Pictured below is the dining hall in 2016.

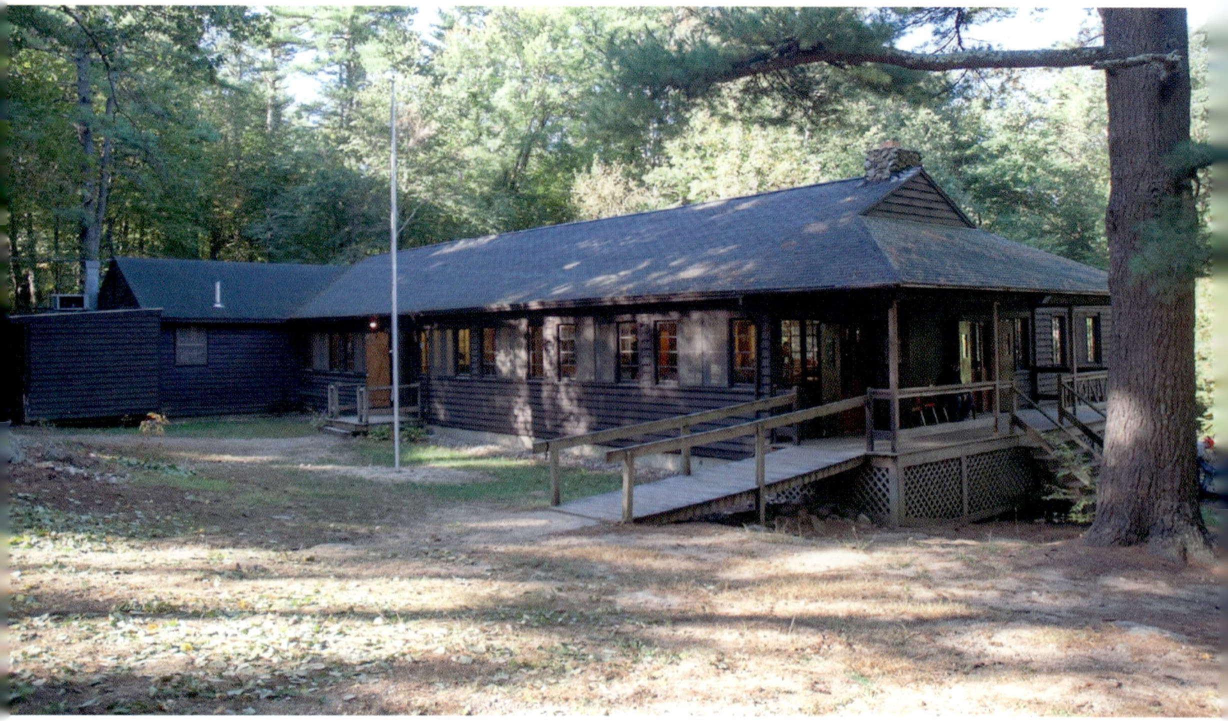

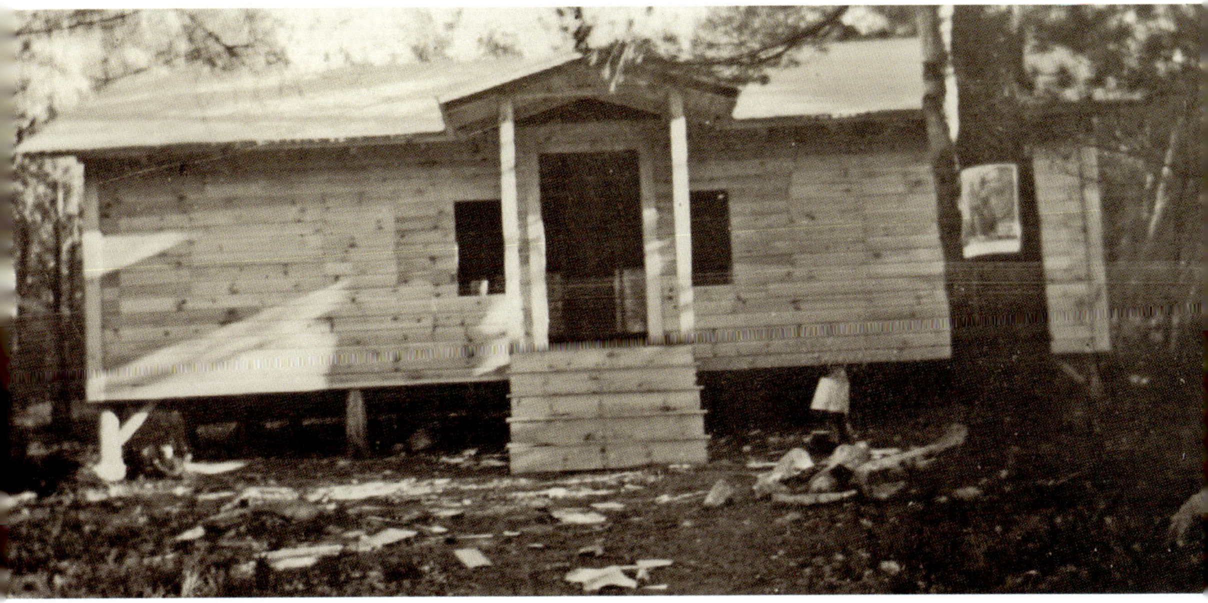

THE INFIRMARY: A canvas tent served as the infirmary until, in October of 1939, the Lawrence Lions Club announced its intentions to the North Essex Council, BSA that they wanted to build an infirmary for Camp Onway. Above is a partially finished photo of the building constructed by Lewis E. Griffin of Raymond, NH between 1939 and 1940. The building was dedicated on July 21, 1940 while celebrating the tenth anniversary of Camp Onway. The building was named the George Wilson Infirmary, in memory of a Lions Club member who had died in 1938. Pictured below is the cabin in 1998, which was the last summer it was used for an infirmary.

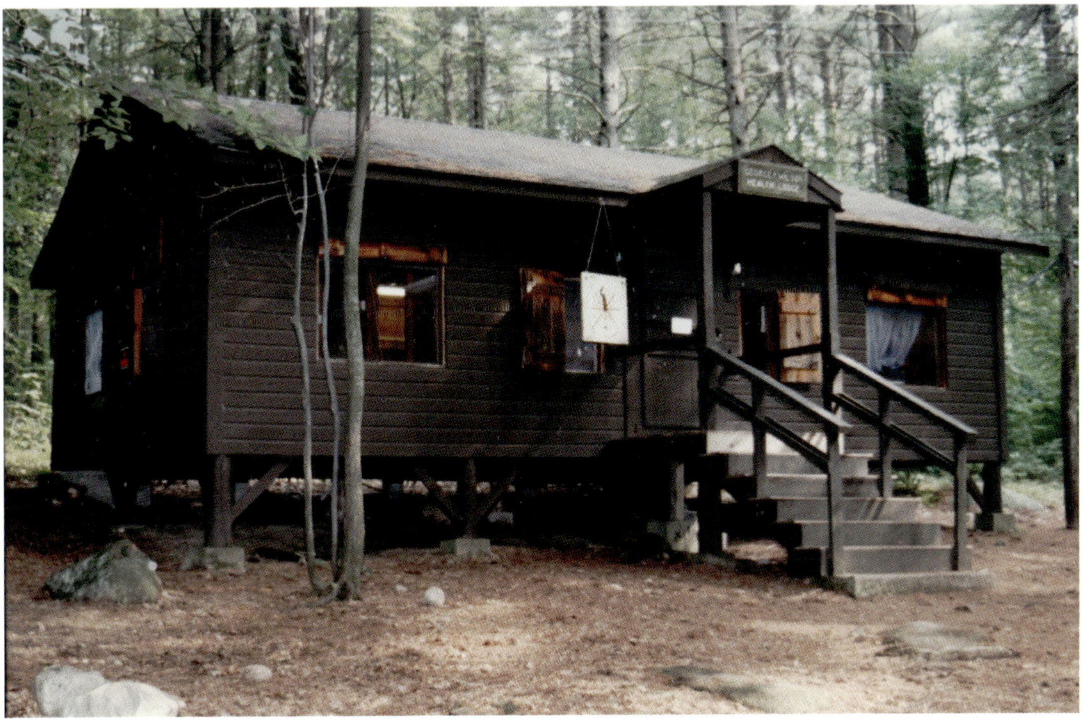

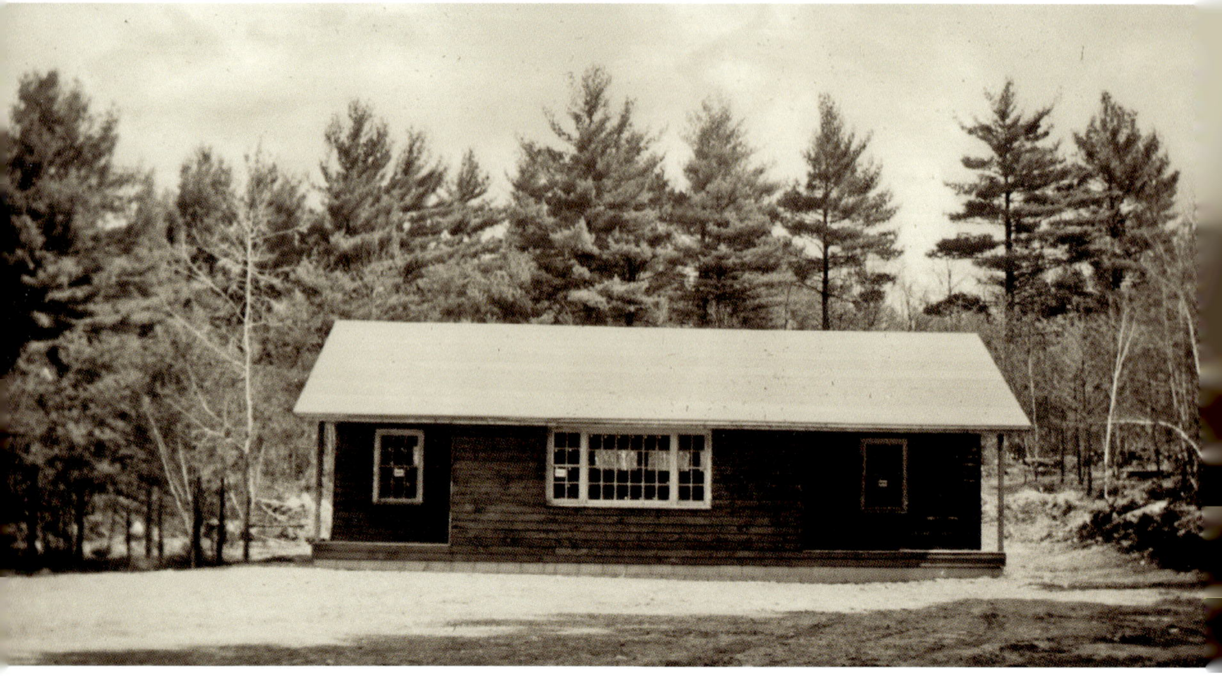

MAGEE LODGE: This building was built in 1956 with funds from the George W. P. Magee Fund. This building was originally used as the camp Office and later the camp Trading Post and Scoutmaster lounge. A fireplace was added in 1957 with funds donated by the Lawrence Lions Club. Magee Lodge was situated across from the parade field. Construction of this building relocated the center of camp from the pine grove, outside the dining hall, further into the center of camp. Pictured below is the cabin in 2018.

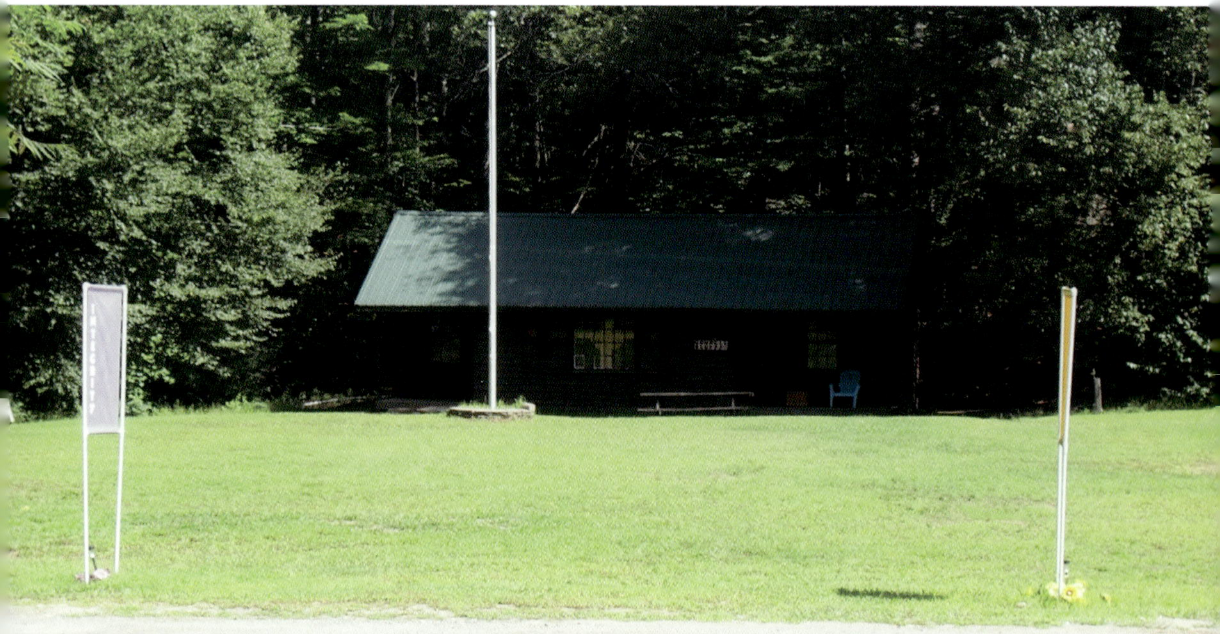

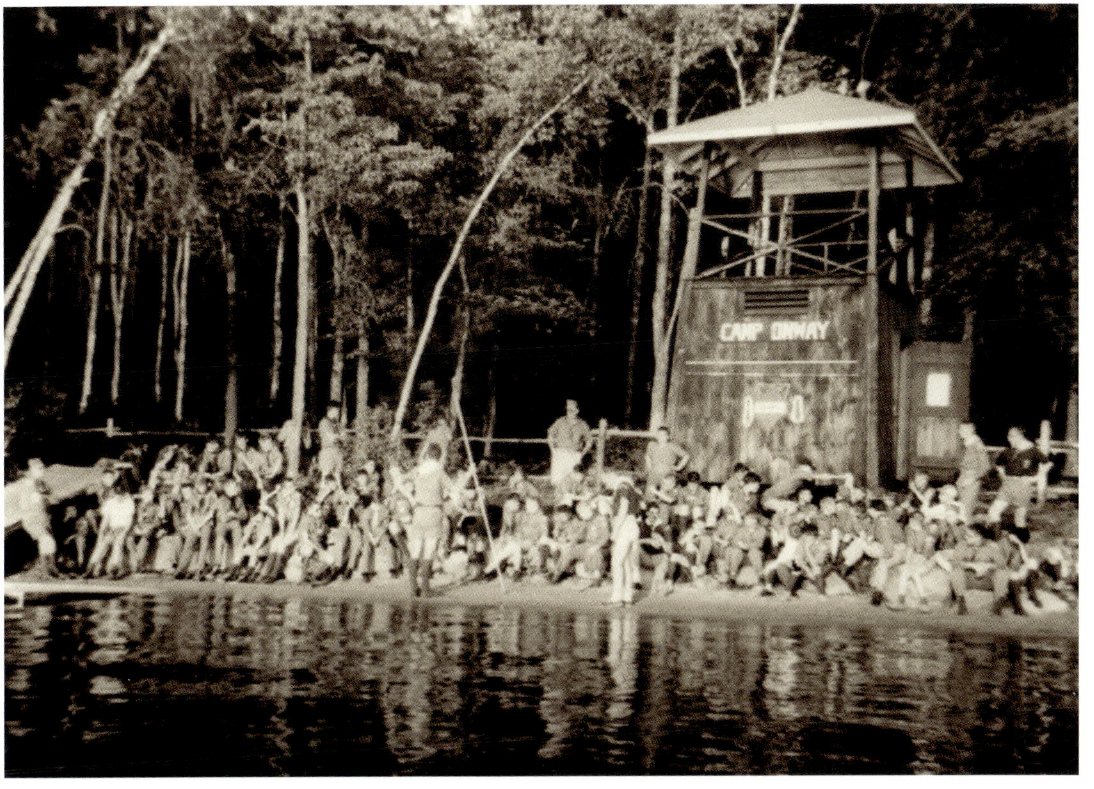

THE WATERFRONT: One of Camp Onway's best features was its extensive waterfront that has been in use since the Camp was purchased in 1929. The tower on the beach was built in 1946 with money from the George W. P. Magee Fund. Over the years, the waterfront was expanded, and the docks were upgraded. The original tower was renovated in 1975 with more storage in the rear and a redesigned tower. Pictured below is the waterfront today. While many trees have been removed, the original tower remains.

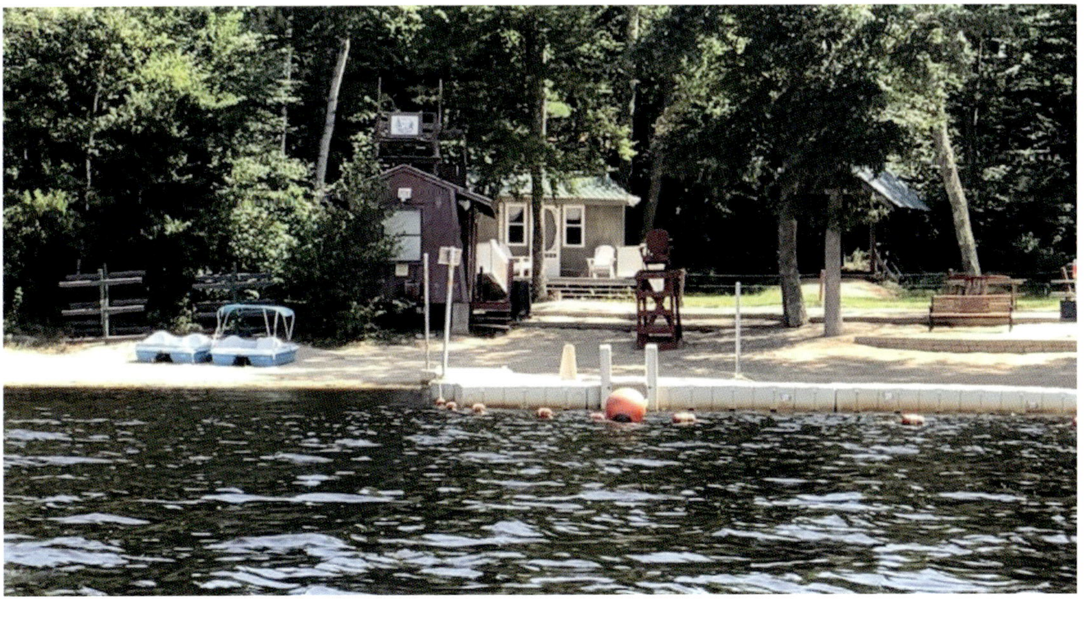

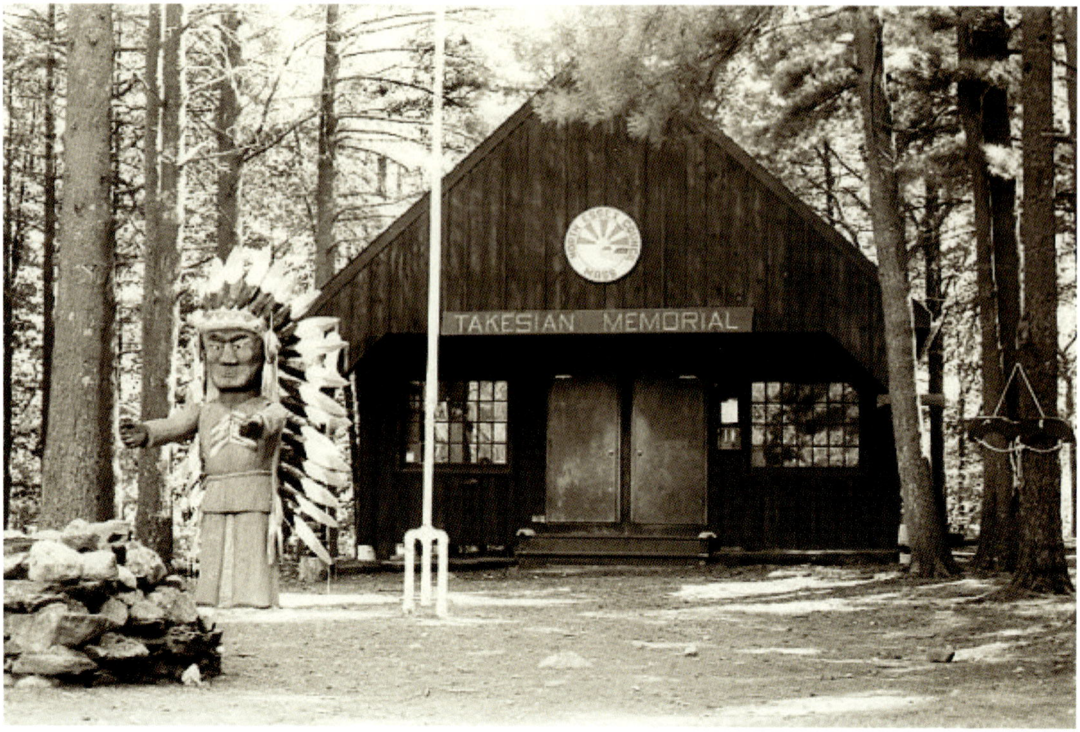

TAKESIAN MEMORIAL ADMINISTRATION BUILDING: Built in 1973 and dedicated on August 11, 1973 in memory of Richard Takesian. Richard was a long-time Scoutmaster of Troop 15 from the First Calvary Baptist Church. He had camped at Onway since 1929 and died in 1972. He was a strong supporter of the camp. The building was financed by the Friends of Onway, a camp alumni group, and was designed to be the camp Office and a museum for Dick Takesian's large collection of Scouting memorabilia. Pictured below is the building today where it is used as a cabin for visitors to camp and off-season housing.

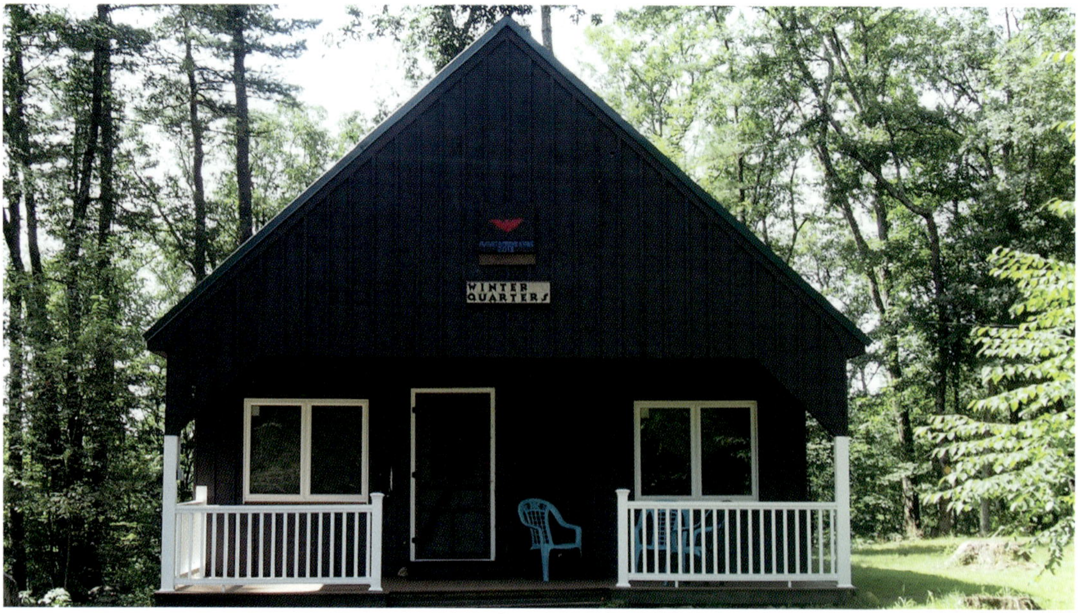

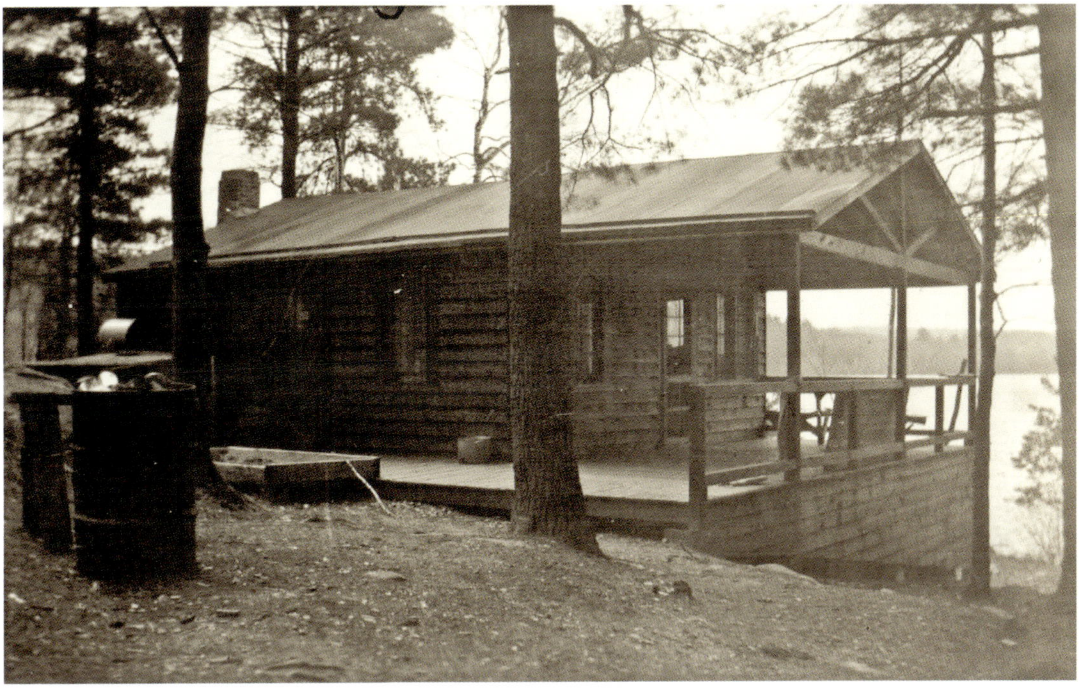

ONWAY EXPANSION: In 1946 additional land was purchased adjacent to Camp Onway with funds from the George W. P. Magee Fund. The cabin pictured above in the 1950s was on the purchased land and became the camp director's cabin. Known as the Director's Cabin, or Cabin 13, it was home to the camp director and other senior staff each summer. In the winter the cabin was a great location for winter camping. Pictured below is the building in 2018 as viewed from Onway Lake.

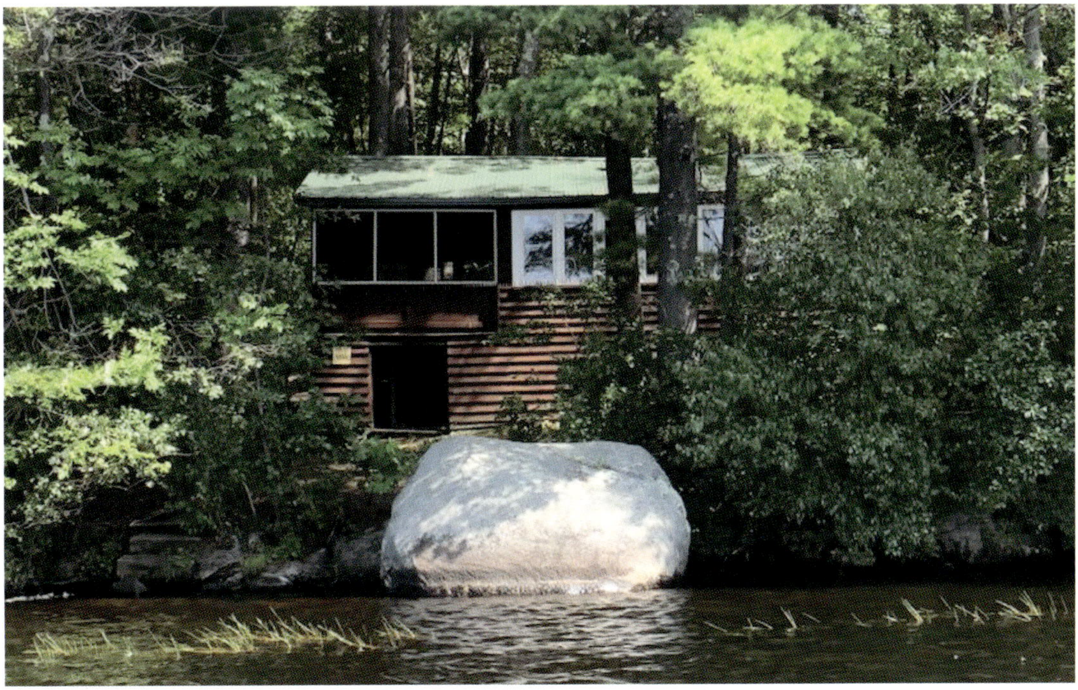

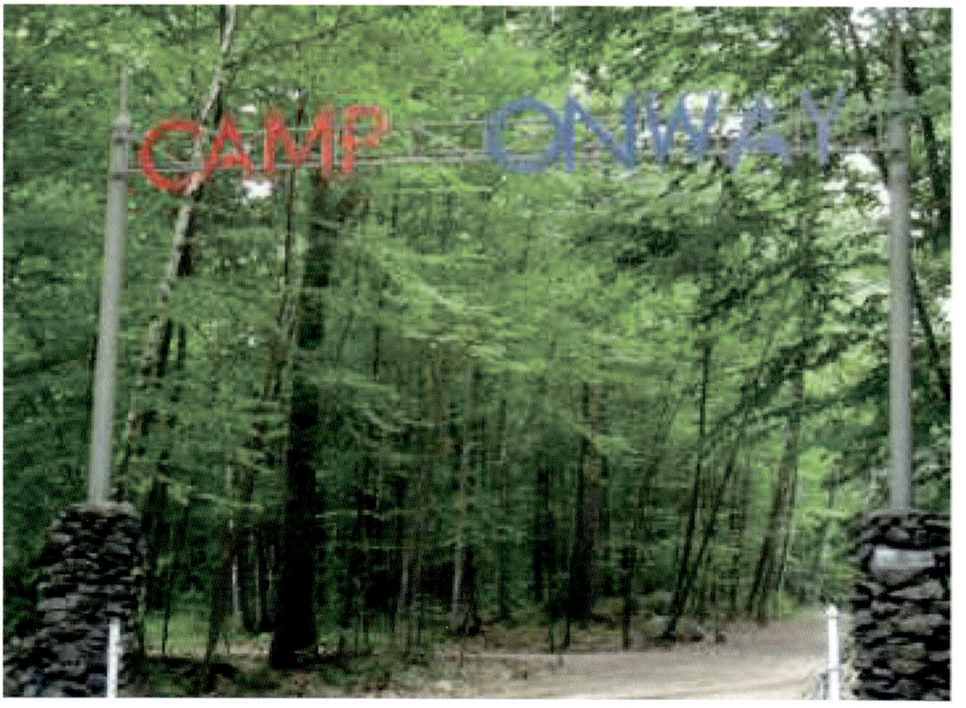

CAMP GATE: Pictured above was the main entrance gate to Camp Onway. In 1961 a new road into the camp was built by the Corps of Engineers and the US Army Reserves and was named "Pop" Bacon Road in honor of Harvey Bacon, the first Scout Executive of the North Essex Council, BSA. The Lawrence Lions Club financed the creation of the main entrance gateway for the new roadway. Pictured below is the same gateway. It is now being used for Zion's Camp which is owned and operated by members of The Church of Jesus Christ of Latter-day Saints where they run a camp for girls for eight weeks each summer.

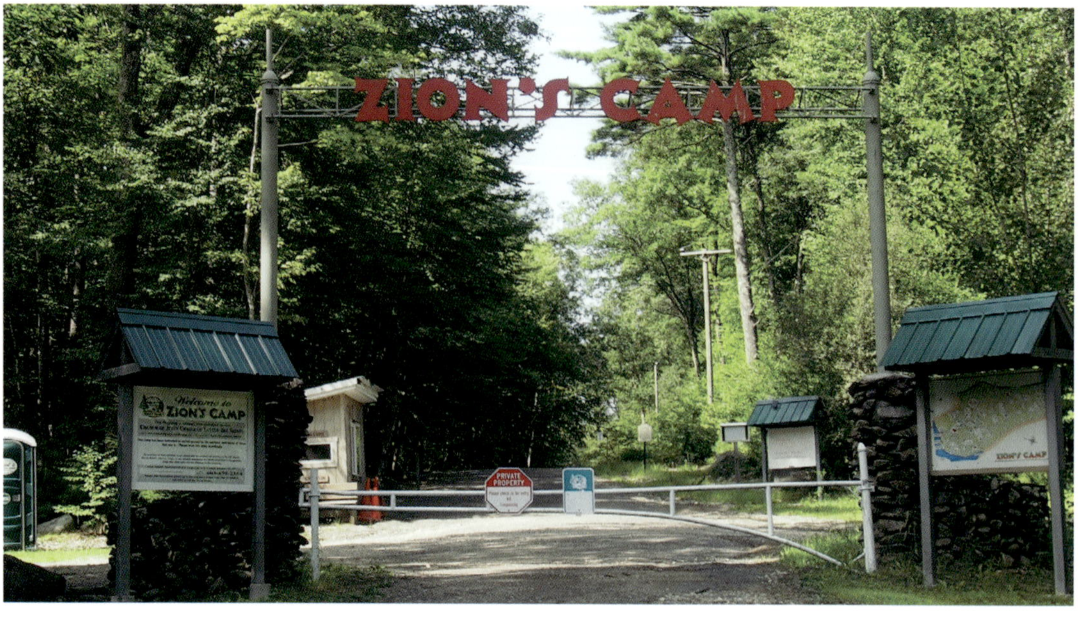

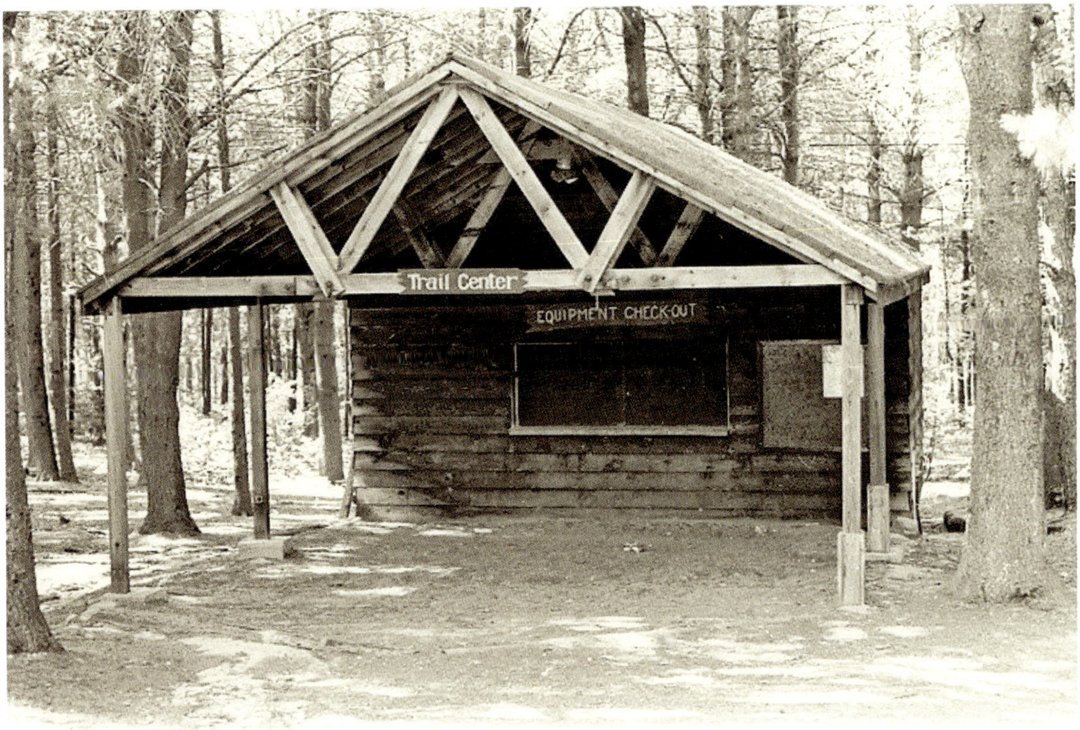

TRADING POST: No camp would be complete without a trading post. Pictured above is the original building built as a trail center. Over the years, walls and a front porch were added to make the building more useful year-round. Many campers enjoyed a cool drink, candy or slushy from the Trading Post. Located adjacent to the parade and sports field, it was a popular spot after athletic activities. Pictured below is the same building with some modifications in 2018.

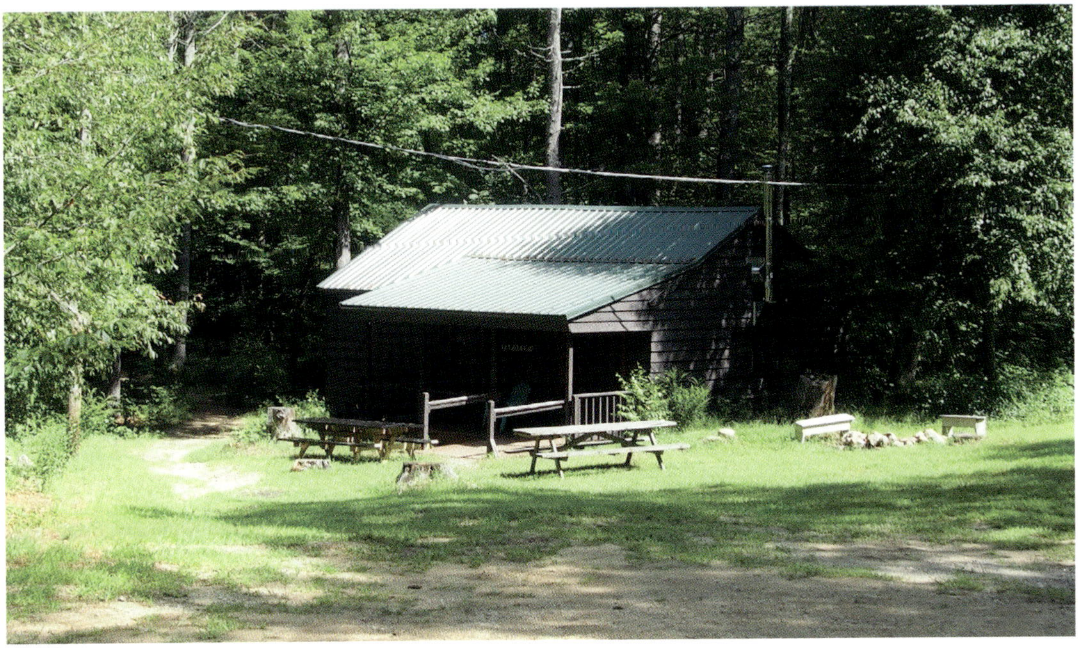

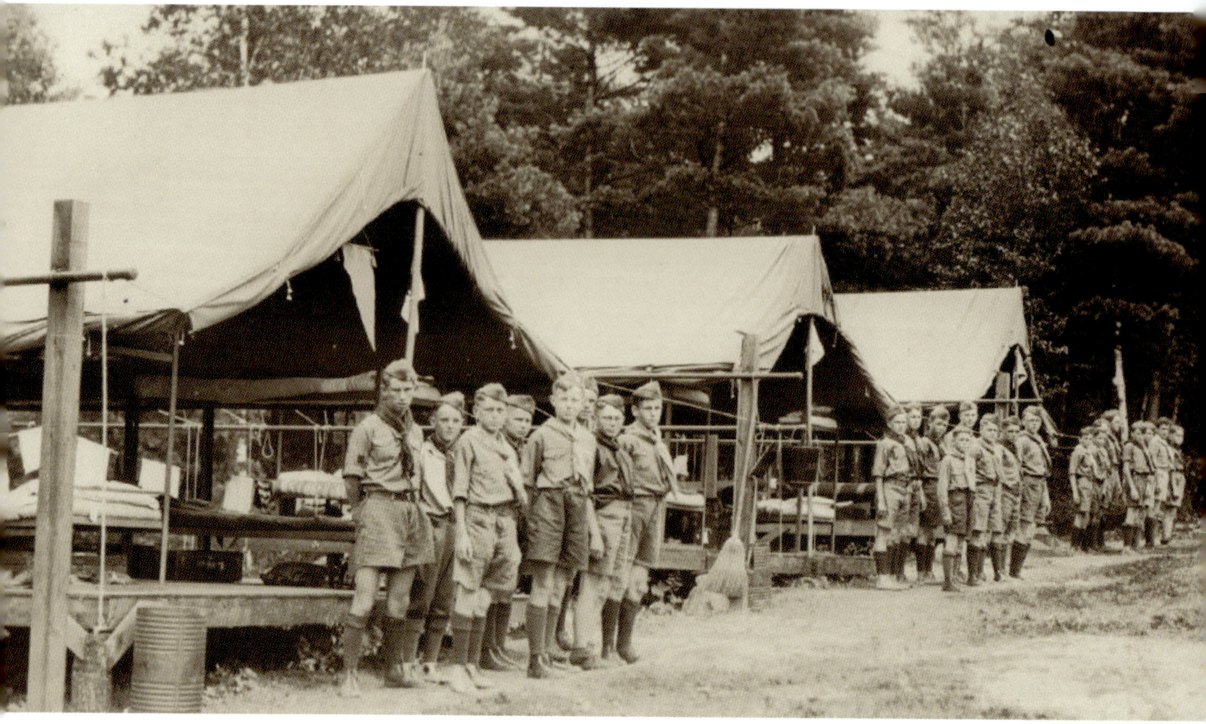

CAMPSITES AND HOUSING: Pictured above are a row of tents circa 1930. In the camp's early years there were two campsites: Abnaki and Pedhela, each containing around four 8-man tents. Each tent housed a different patrol. The two campsites would compete during the week for different athletic and skills-based awards. The 8-man tents were eventually replaced with the now standard two-man tents. In recent years the camp's new owners, The Church of Jesus Christ of Latter-day Saints, have replaced canvas tents with small cabins pictured below.

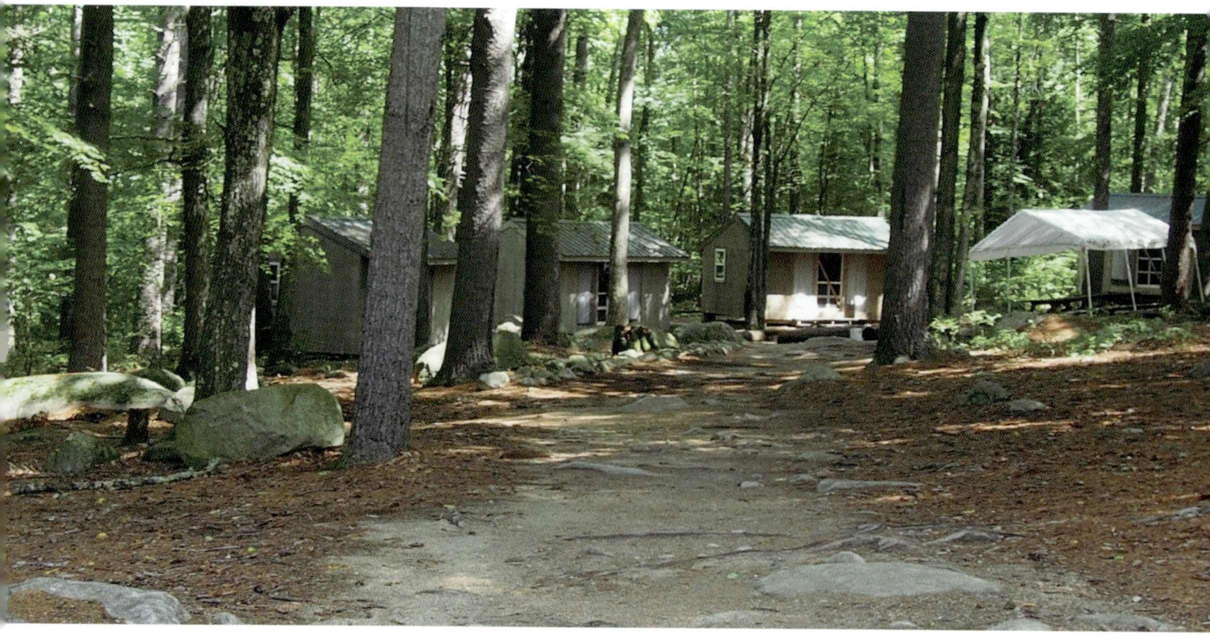

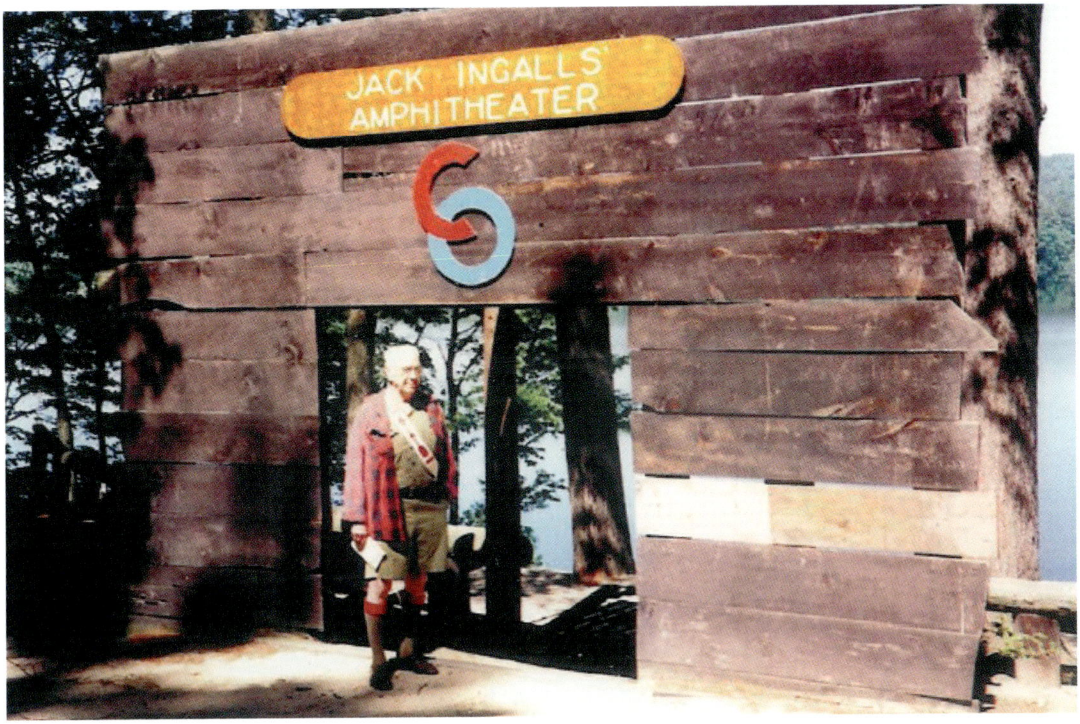

THE AMPHITHEATER: Pictured above is the Jack Ingalls Amphitheater, named after a long time Scouting volunteer and Order of the Arrow Adviser, Jack Ingalls. The original Amphitheater was built on the banks of Onway Lake using railroad ties from the Boston and Maine railroad which passes along the western part of the lake. Weekly opening and closing campfires were held in the Amphitheater each summer. During the final summer at camp, in 2007, campers and Onway Alumni gathered for the final. Pictured below is the Amphitheater in 2018 where it has been beautifully renovated by The Church of Jesus Christ of Latter-day Saints, where it still offers a beautiful lakeside space for camaraderie and reflection.

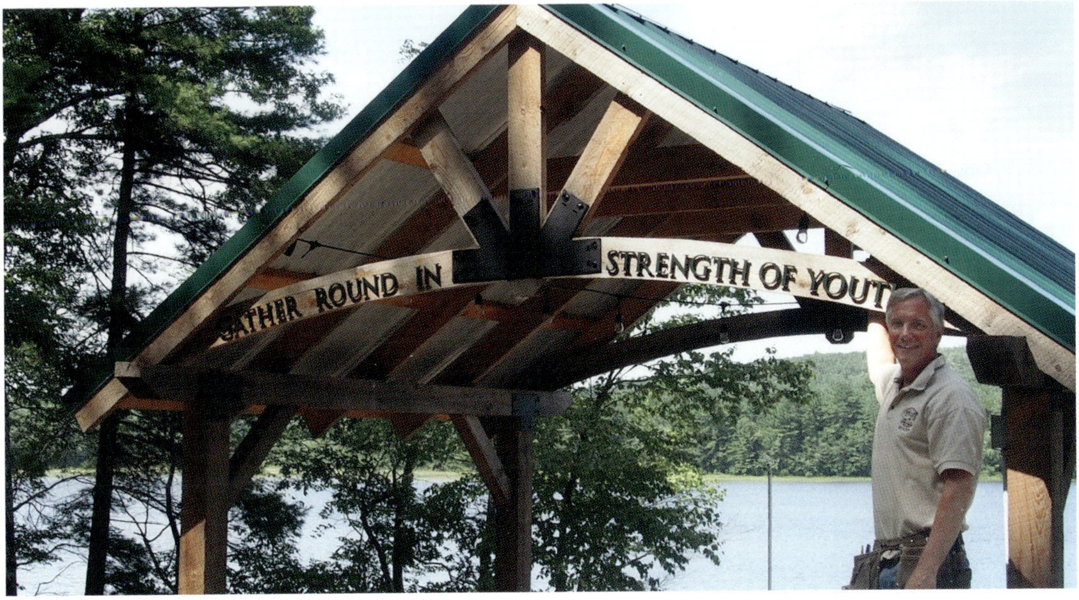

CHAPTER 4

SECOND ACTS FOR BOSTON MINUTEMAN COUNCIL CAMPS

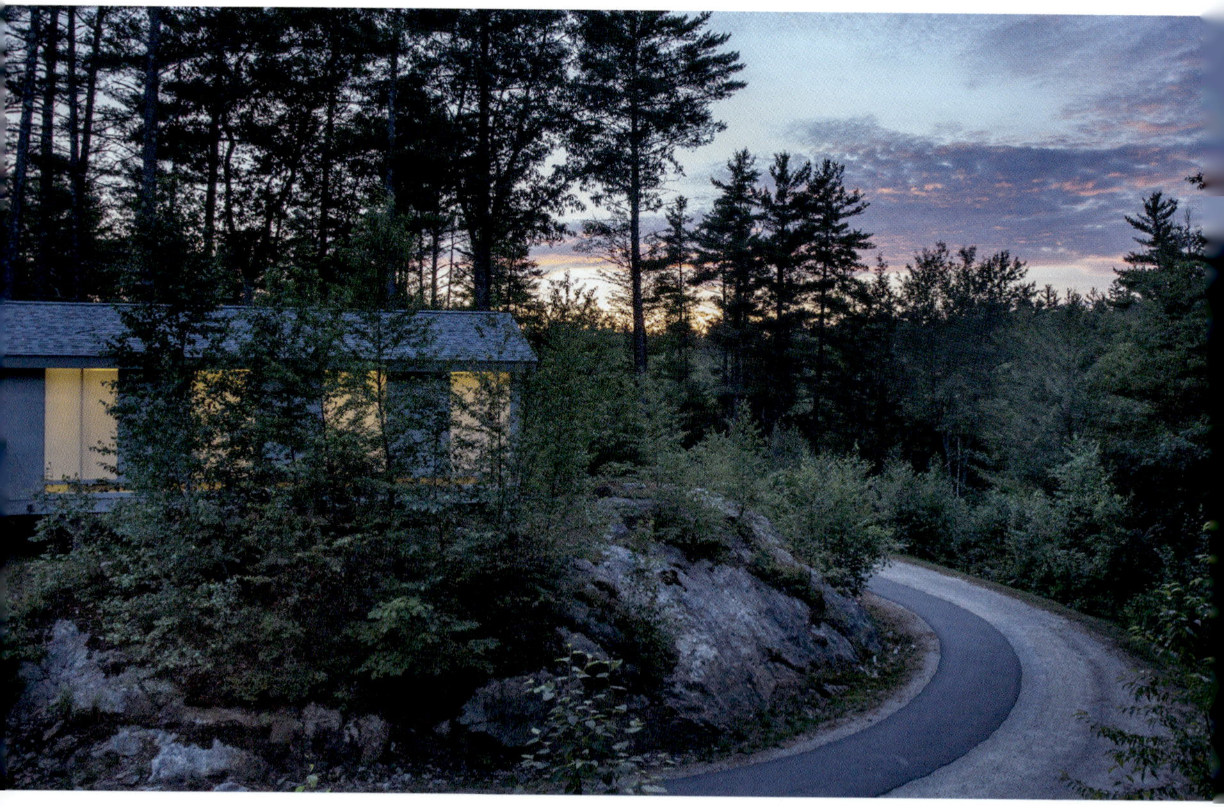

BEAM CAMP AND PARKER MOUNTAIN SCOUT CAMP—STRAFFORD, NH: In this chapter we take a few brief glimpses into major predecessor camps of the Spirit of Adventure Council, BSA. Parker Mountain Scout Camp is still owned by the Spirit of Adventure Council, BSA but is leased to Beam Camp. Each summer Beam Camp holds two three-week seasons for New York City youth. They work in partnership with public schools and community partners, focusing on skill-building, collaborative challenge, responsibility, and mentorship.

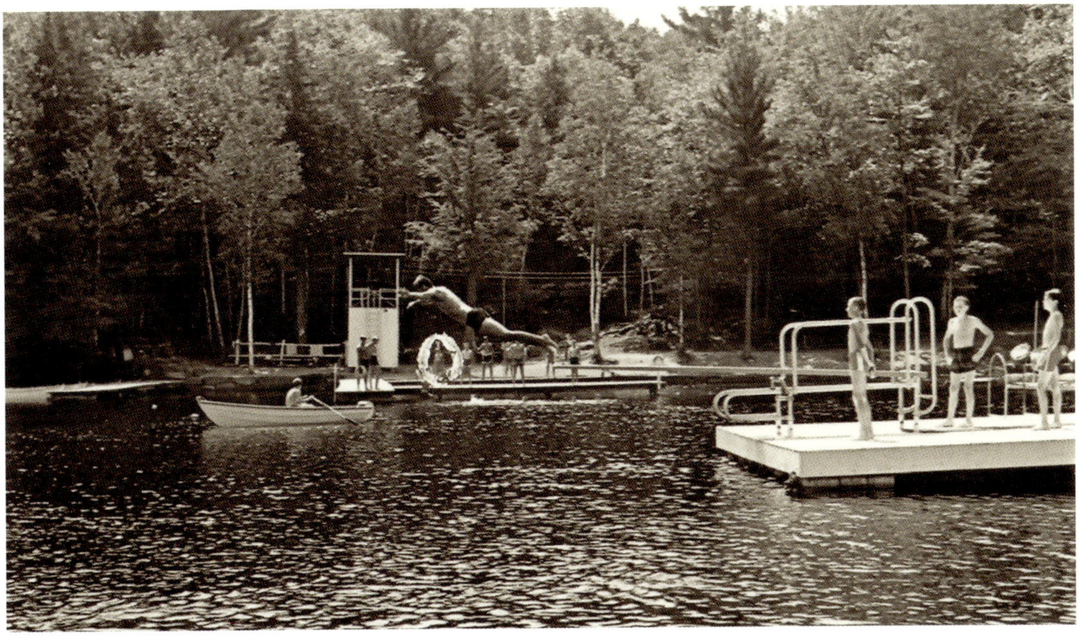

PARKER MOUNTAIN BEAMS: Parker Mountain opened in 1948 on Big and Little Willey Ponds in Strafford, NH. This land was donated by Theodore L. Storer. Parker Mountain was originally the camp of the Quannapowit Council, BSA. In 1991 it became a Boy Scout camp of the Boston Minuteman Council, BSA and continued to operate as part of that Council until 2000. It was proceeded by several camps including; Camp Manning in Andover, MA and during World War II, Wah-Tut-Ca Scout Reservation in Northwood, NH. In 2004 Beam Camp was founded and leased by Brian Cohen and Danny Kahn. The camp provides children with creative problem-solving experiences by working with their hands and actively collaborating with others. Beam also provides traditional summer camp programs and activities.

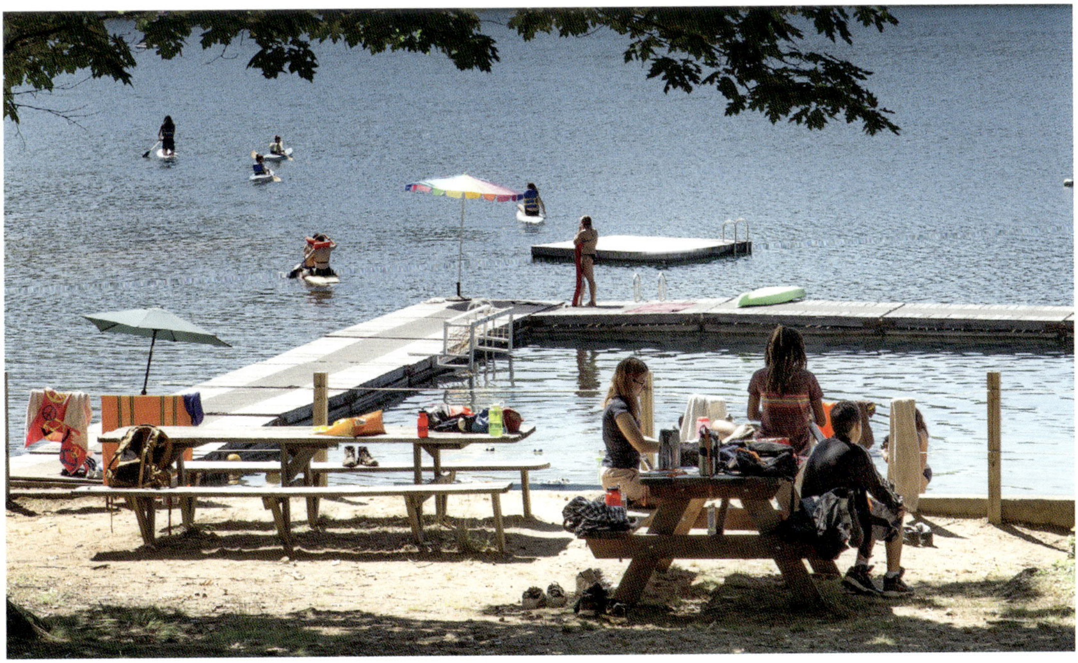

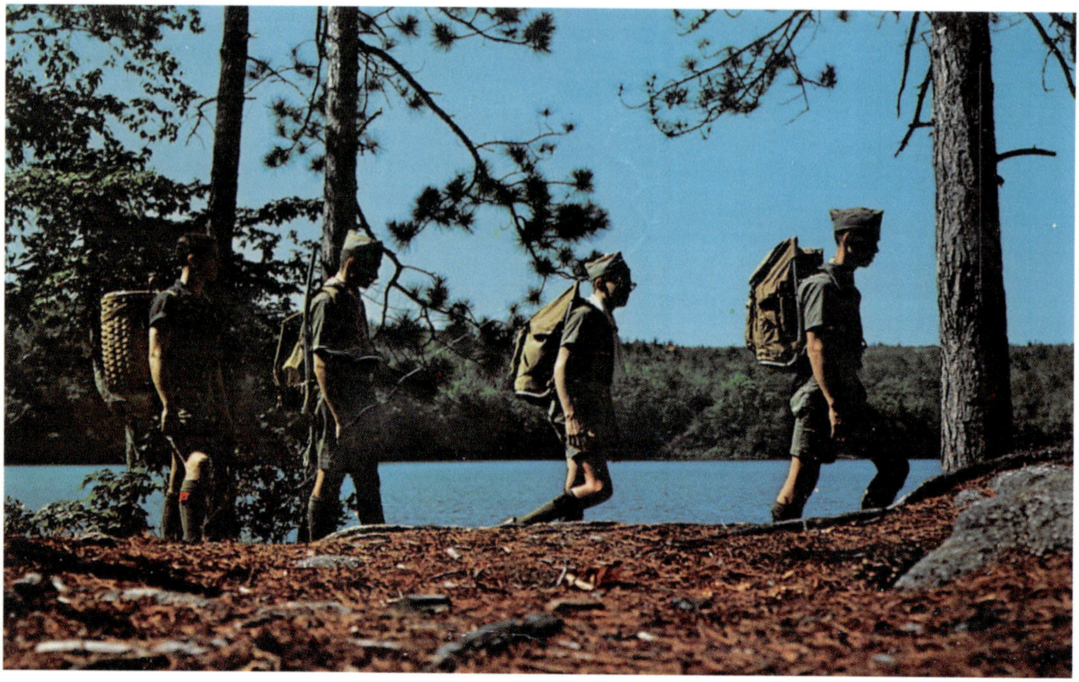

MOUNTAINS AND PONDS: Parker Mountain's location in Southern New Hampshire created a great atmosphere for a Scout camp. Nestled beneath Parker Mountain, (elevation 1,410 ft.) is an exceptional area for day hikes and afternoon climbs. These trails are still used by Scouts from Wah-Tut-Ca and T. L. Storer.

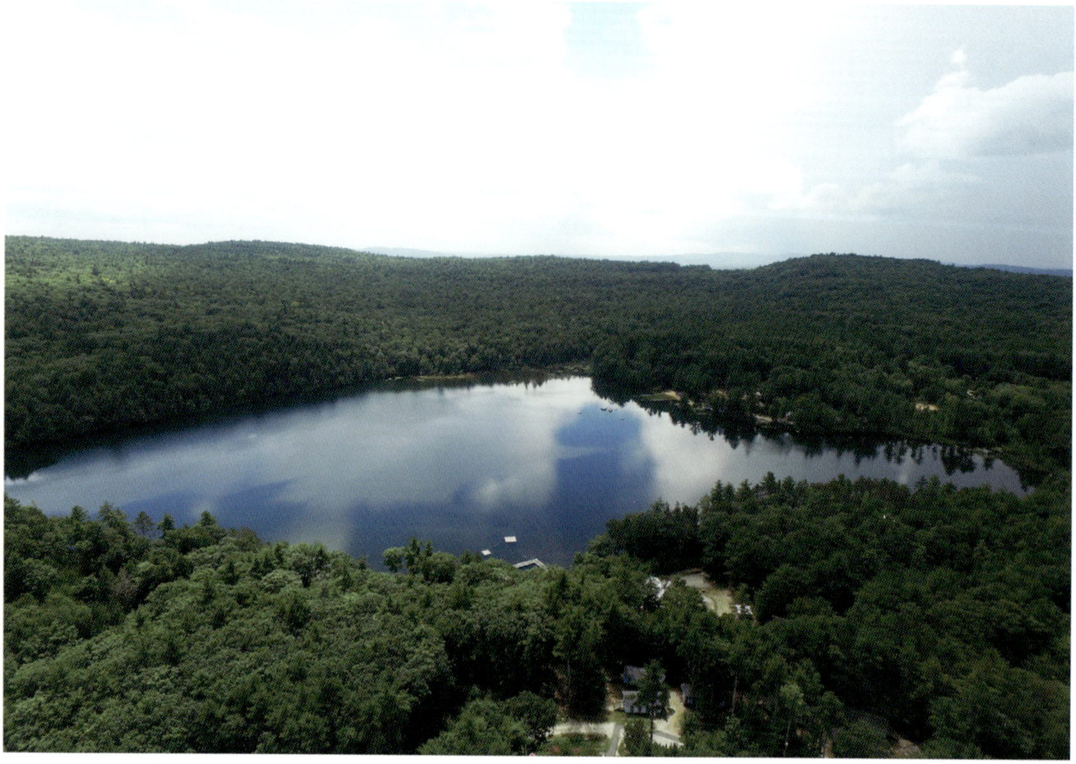

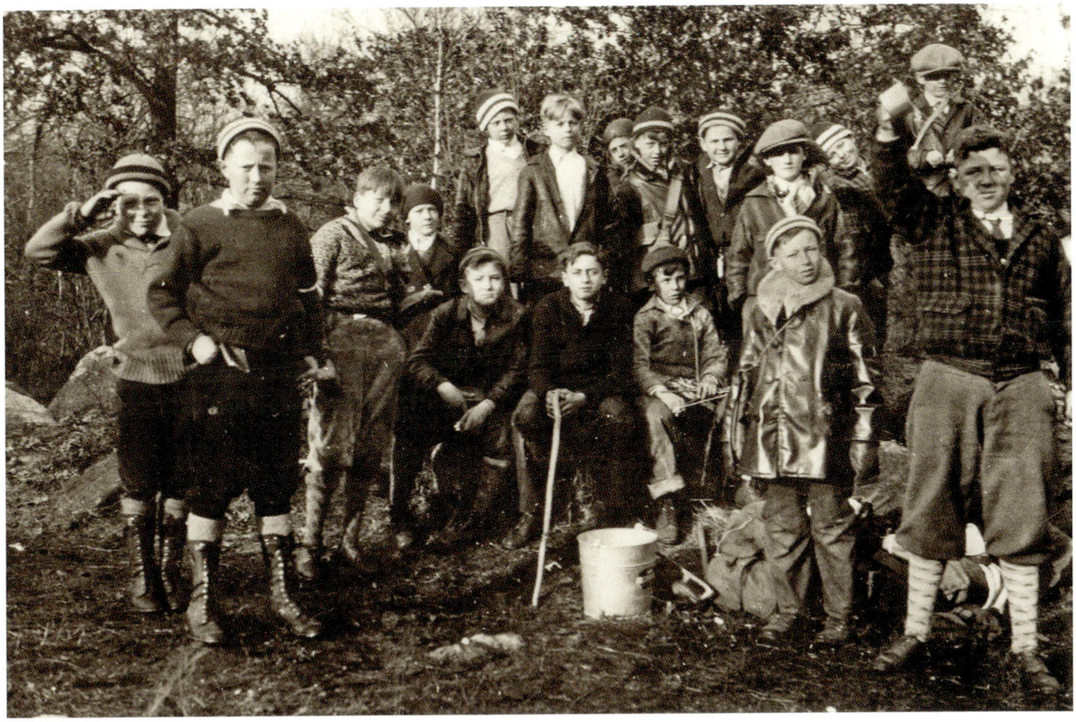

Camp Massasoit—Plymouth, MA: The Quincy Council, BSA established Camp Massasoit in 1927. The community was very proud of this camp and generations of leaders contributed to its success. In 1966 the Quincy Council was merged with the Boston Council and soon after the merger Camp Massasoit ceased operations as a Boy Scout Summer Camp, but it remained a Cub Scout camp and weekend camp for several decades.

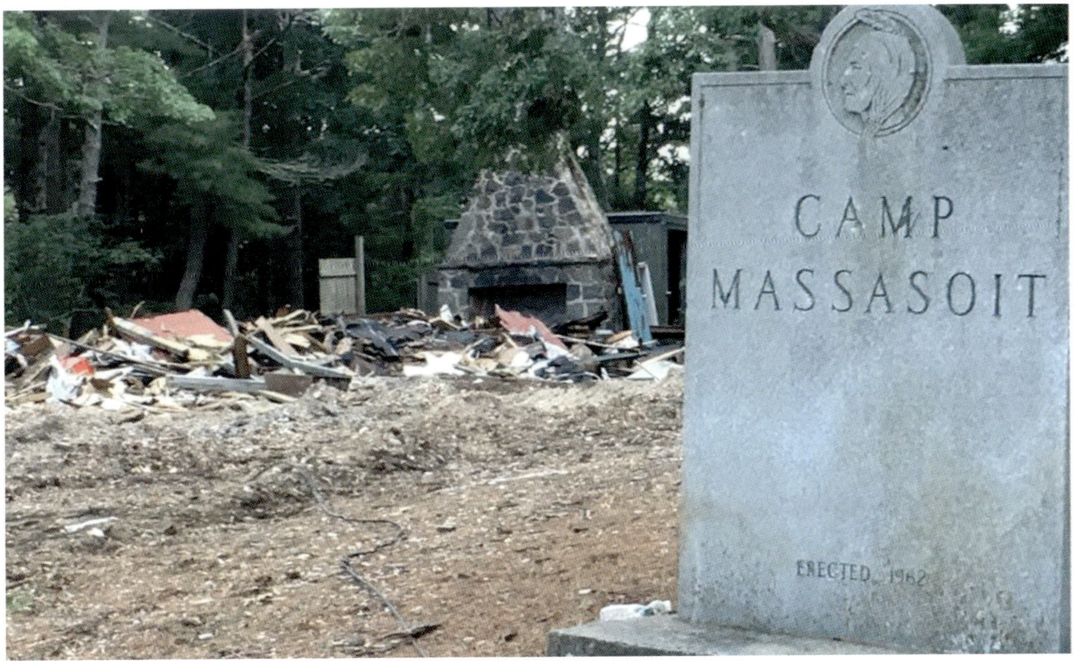

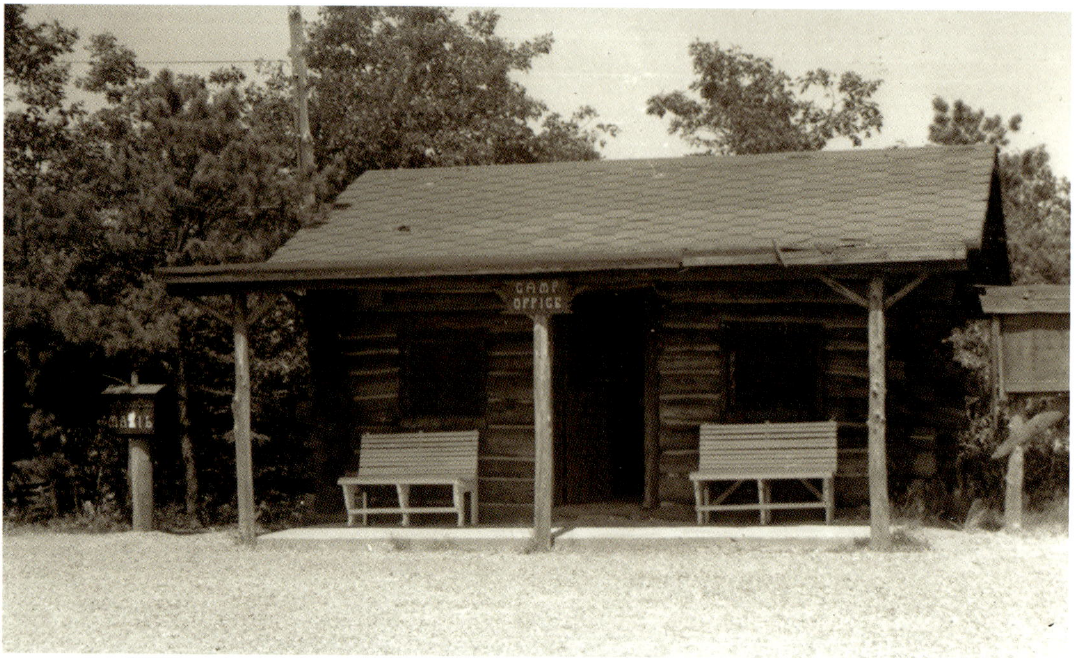

DECLINE AND SALE: The camp eventually fell into disrepair and, lacking the resources to maintain it, the Boston Minuteman Council, BSA put it up for sale in 2014. It was sold four years later, in 2018, for real estate development.

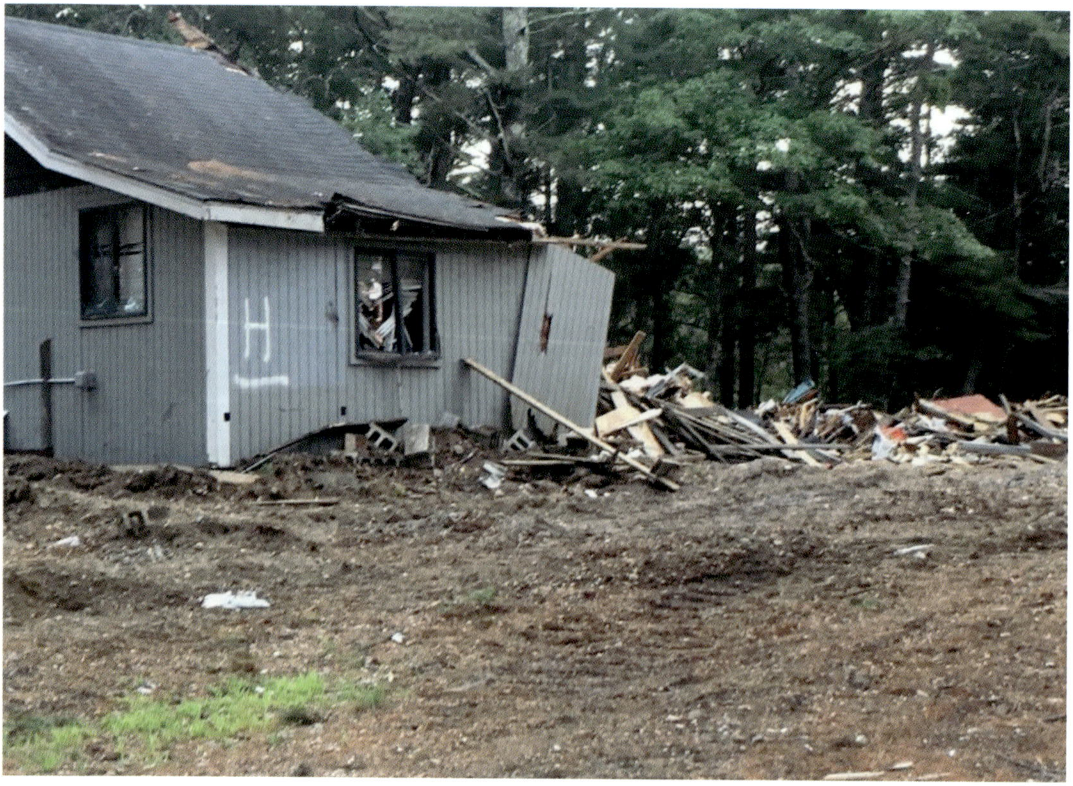

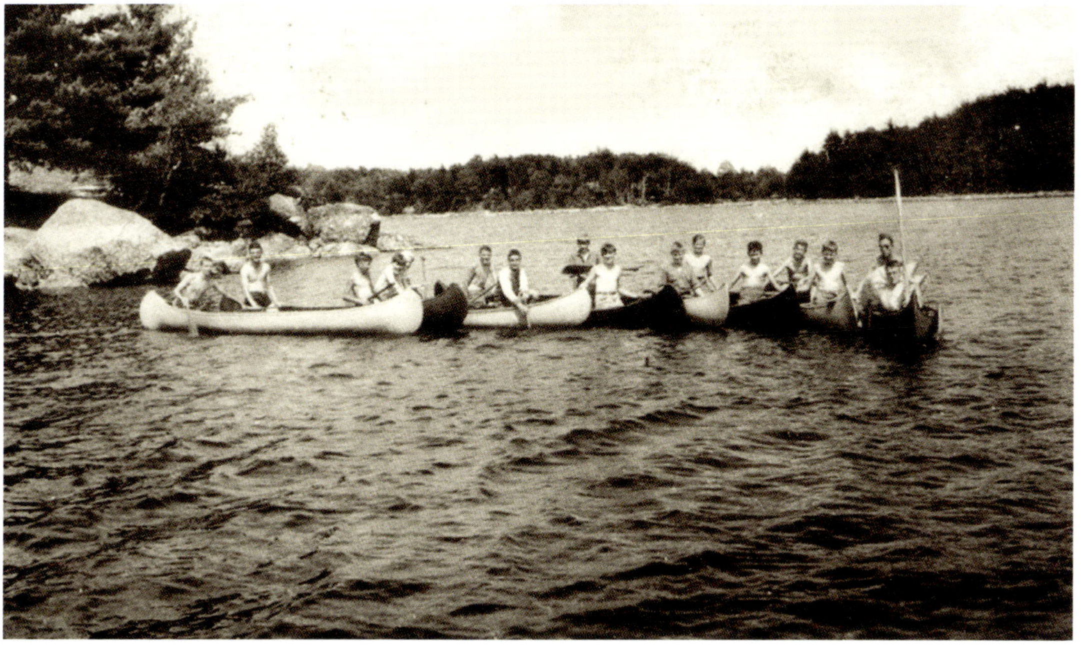

CAMP SACHEM—ATRIM, NH: The Sachem Council, BSA, established Camp Sachem in 1928 on Gregg Lake. The camp operated until 1991. It was sold to the Girl Scouts who invested over a million dollars in facility improvements. They operated it under the name of Camp Chenoa until 2013. Today it is operated by Harbor Camps, a nonprofit organization that provides camps for youth and families of specific populations that may often feel marginalized. It is now called Camp Aranu'tiq and it specializes in serving youth who express their gender differently than others.

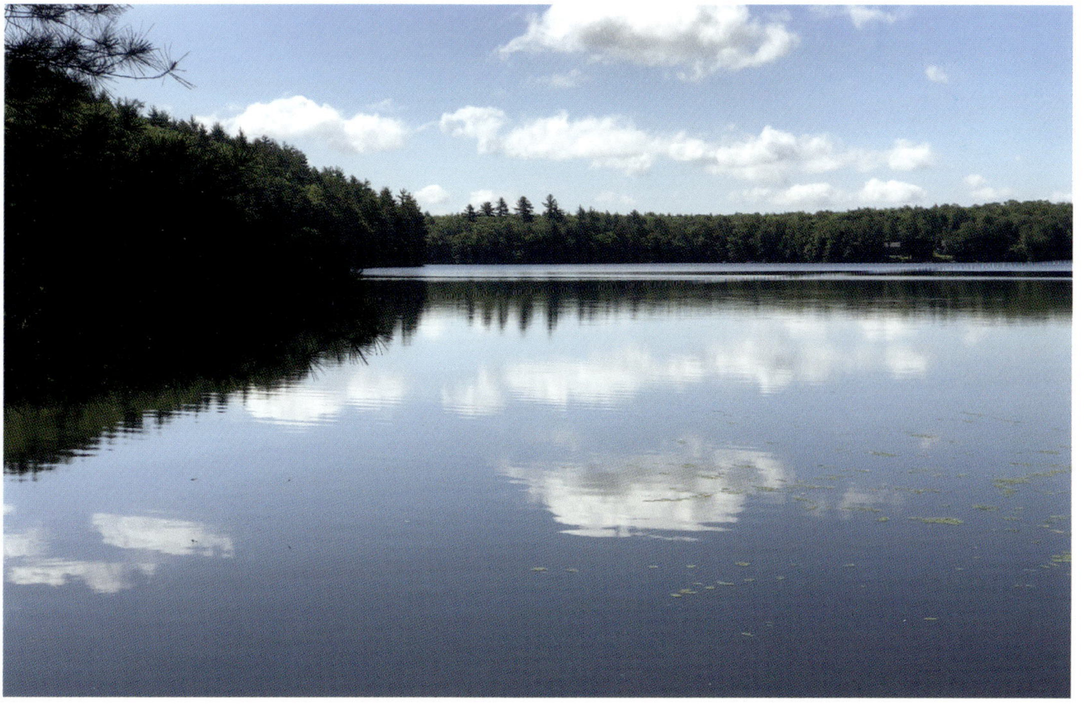

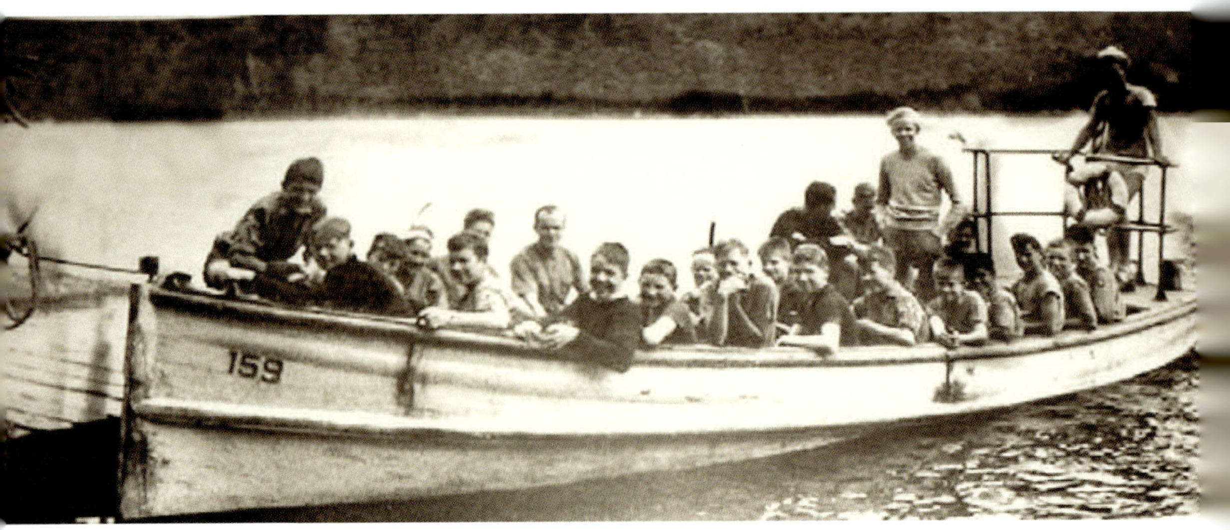

TRANSPORTATION BY FERRY: In the early years of Camp Sachem there were no reliable roads to get to the camp. Scouts would access the camp in special ferry boats made from re-purposed US Coast Guard Boats. Crossing the waters in boats like these are a tradition still carried on at Wah-Tut-Ca Scout Reservation.

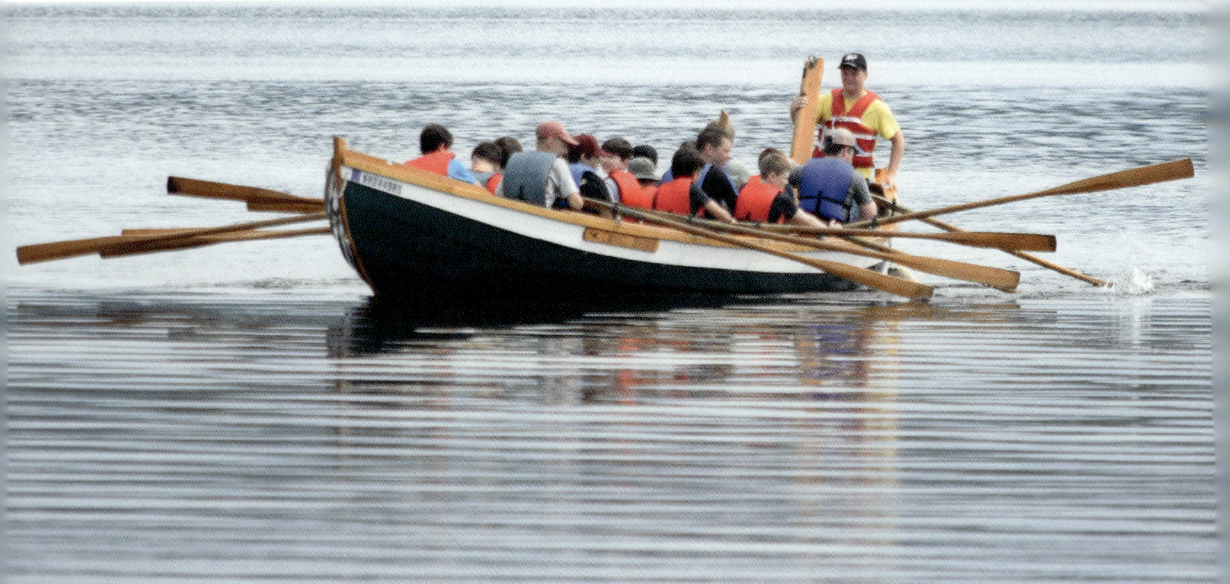

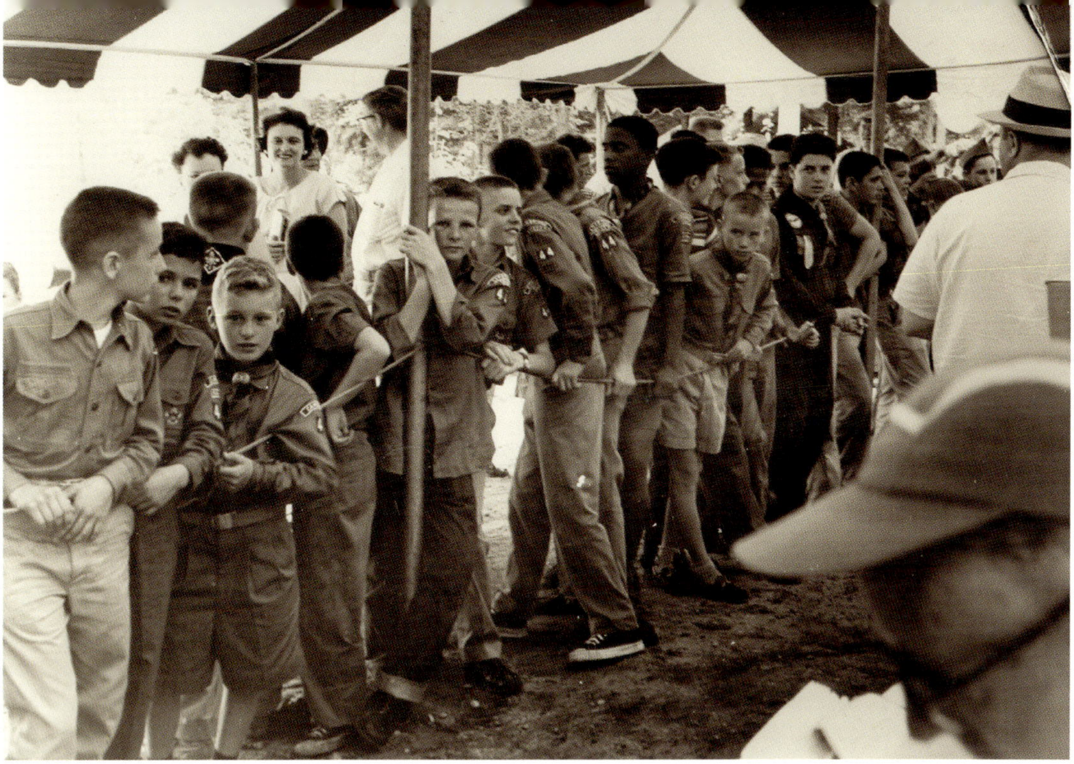

CAMP QUINAPOXET—RINDGE, NH: From 1925 until the summer of 2001, Scouts of the Cambridge Council, BSA camped on Hubbard Pond. The 300-acre property was sold shortly before the Cambridge Council was merged into Boston Minuteman Council, BSA. Purchased by the Massachusetts Audubon Society they renamed it Wildwood Camp. Eight weeks of programs are held each summer with a focus on gaining a greater respect for nature as well as teaching campers their role in protecting it.

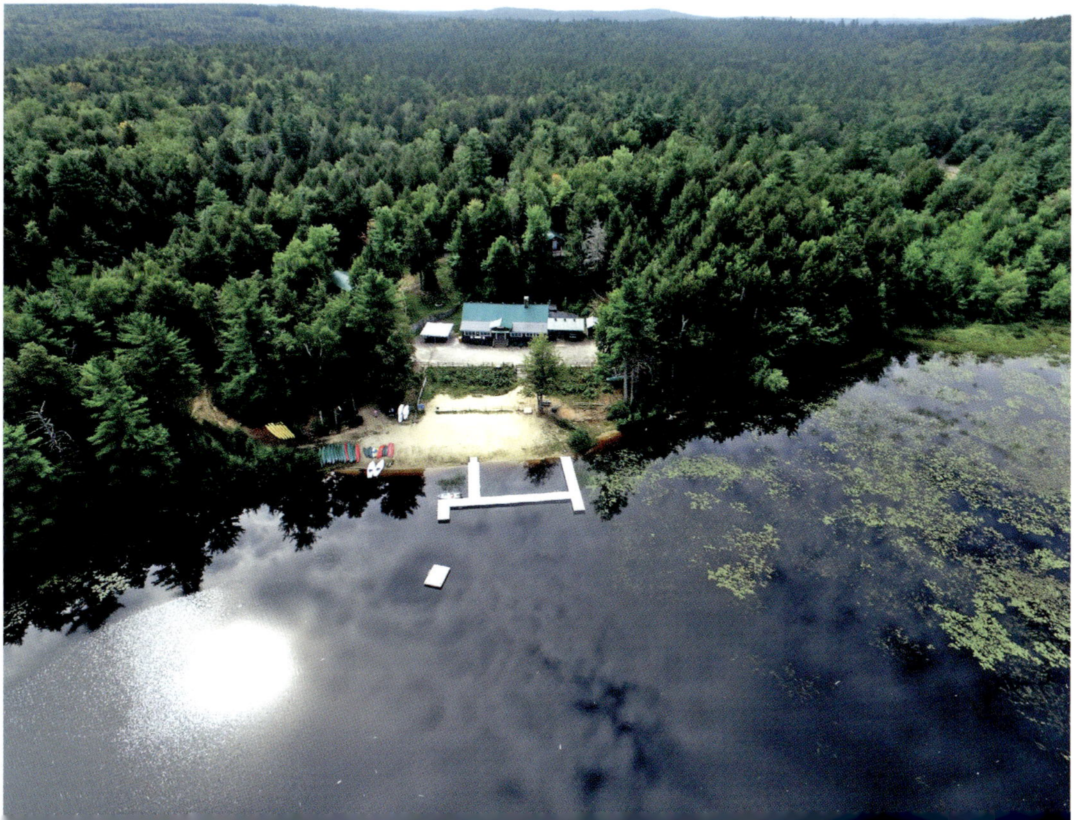

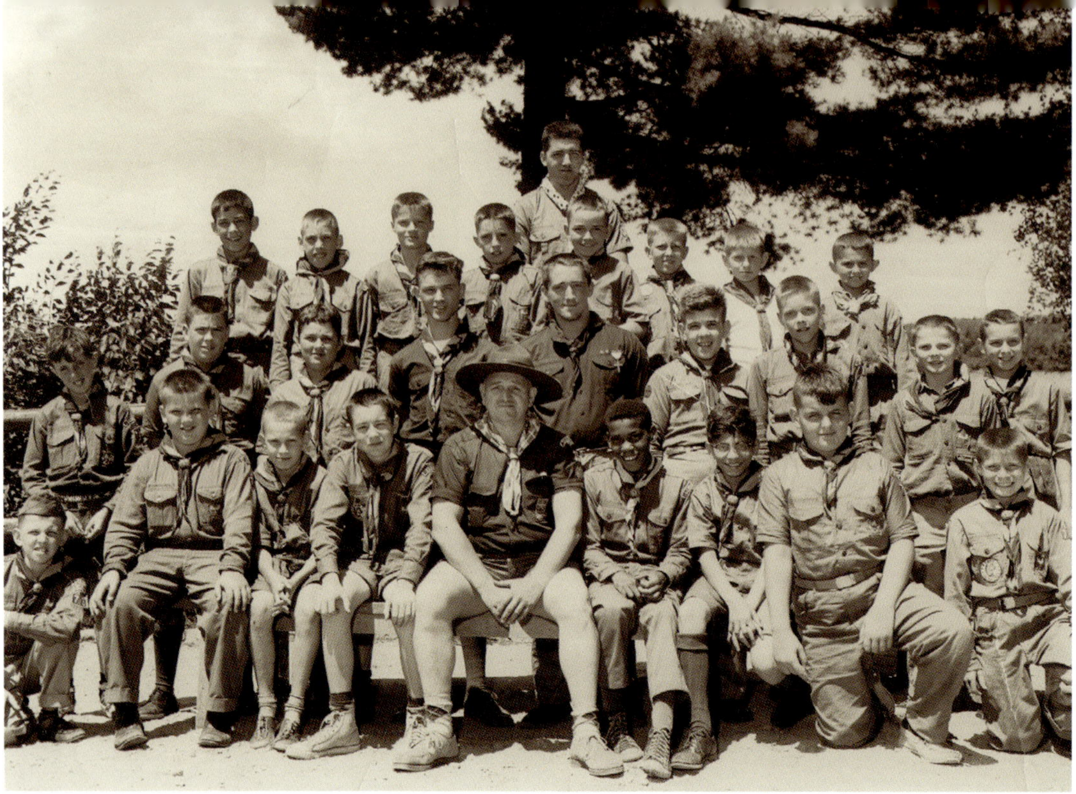

STILL SERVING YOUTH: Camp Quinapoxet was the pride of Cambridge, MA Scouting. Today at Wildwood Camp, hundreds of young people enjoy the benefits of that legacy. Most of the old buildings have been beautifully restored. New facilities have been added including small cabins that have replaced the old canvas housing. By all measures, Wildwood is both a program and economic success, impacting the lives of children and young adults.

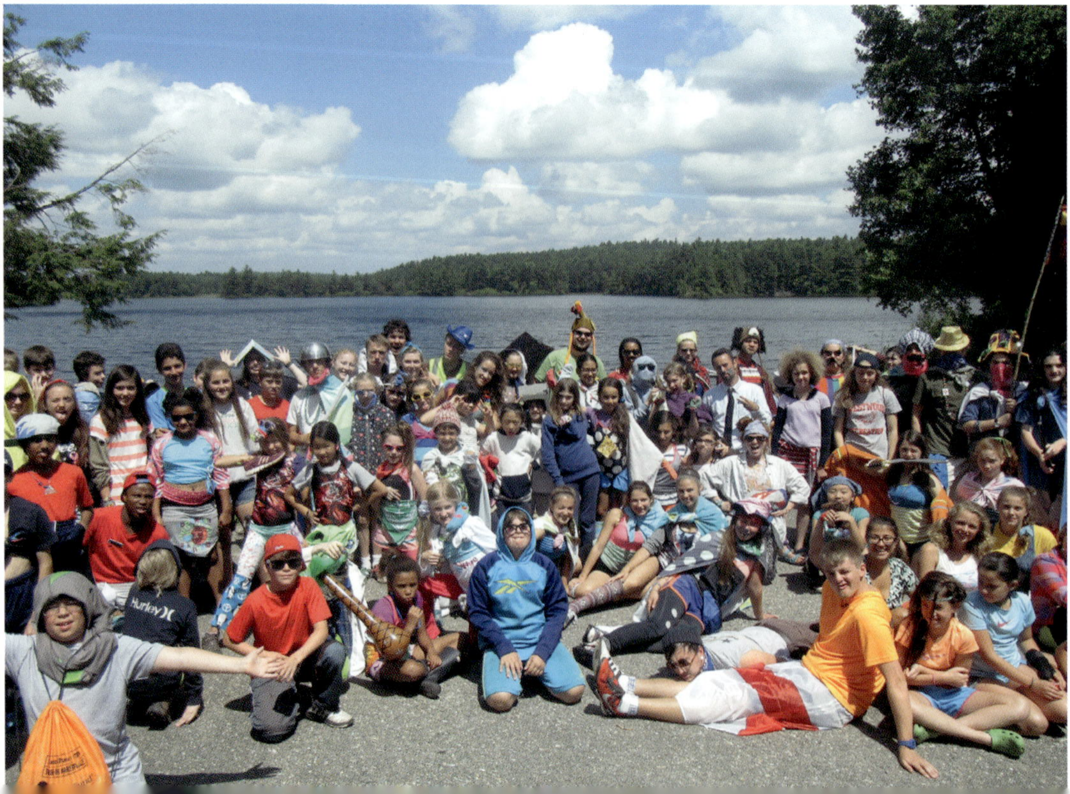

Chapter 5

Lone Tree Scout Reservation

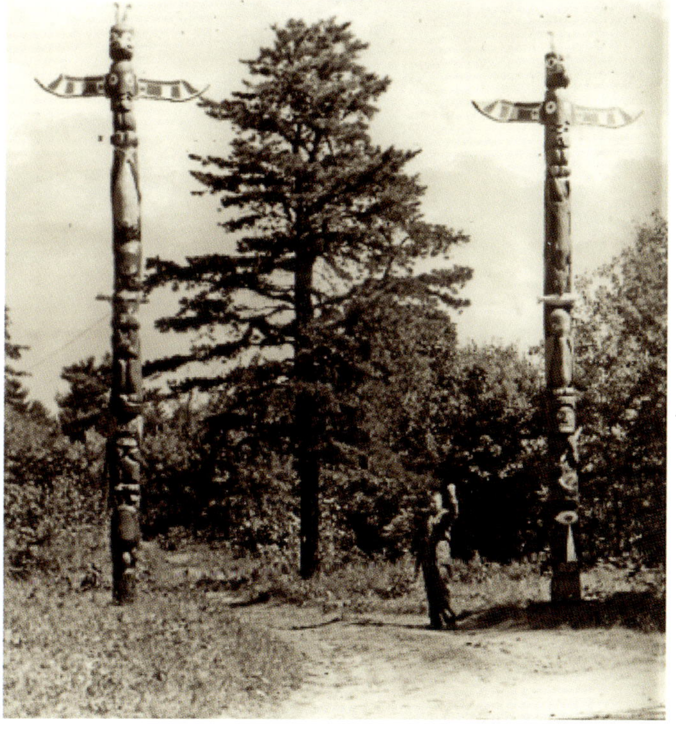

Lone Tree Scout Reservation: Since its founding in 1946 Lone Tree Scout Reservation has been a year-round outdoor facility hosting Scouts and campers all twelve months of the year. From 1947 until 1994 it served as a summer resident camp for Boy Scouts and later for Webelo Scouts. Cub Scout summer day camp programming began in 1978 and continued through 2017. The camp continues to host Scouts, Cubs, and Venture Scouts year-round offering staffed programming on weekends in the spring, winter, and fall. Scouts, units, and families can participate in open programs, for the day or the weekend, testing their skills on the challenge course, at the shooting ranges, or on the waters of Country Pond.

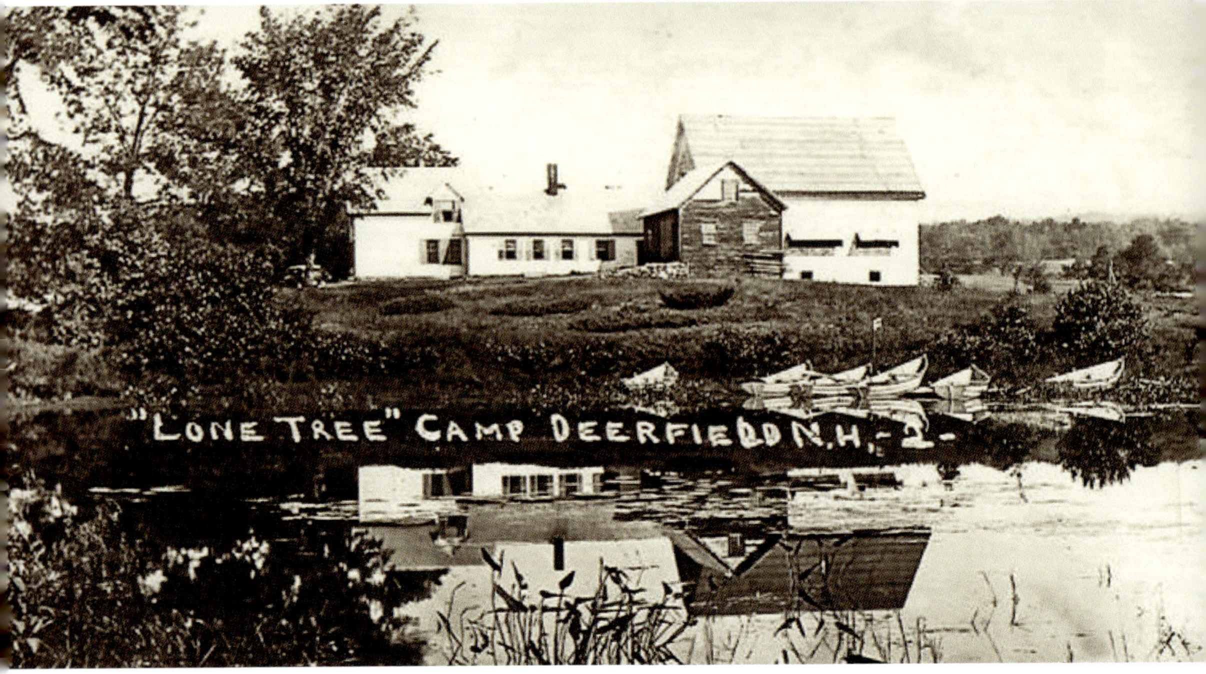

LONE TREE CAMP—DEERFIELD, NH: In 1926 Scout leaders of the Lower Merrimack Valley, from around the Amesbury and Newburyport, MA areas, formed the Lone Tree Council, BSA. Three years later they purchased 150 acres of land in Deerfield, NH upon which they built Lone Tree Camp. The property was a former farm that straddled State Route 107 and encircled the small Freese's Pond. Sixty volunteers and thirty truckloads of equipment and materials traveled from Haverhill and Amesbury, MA to Deerfield, NH to build five cabins and make the farmhouse and barn suitable to serve as camp headquarters and mess hall prior to the opening of camp in July 1929.

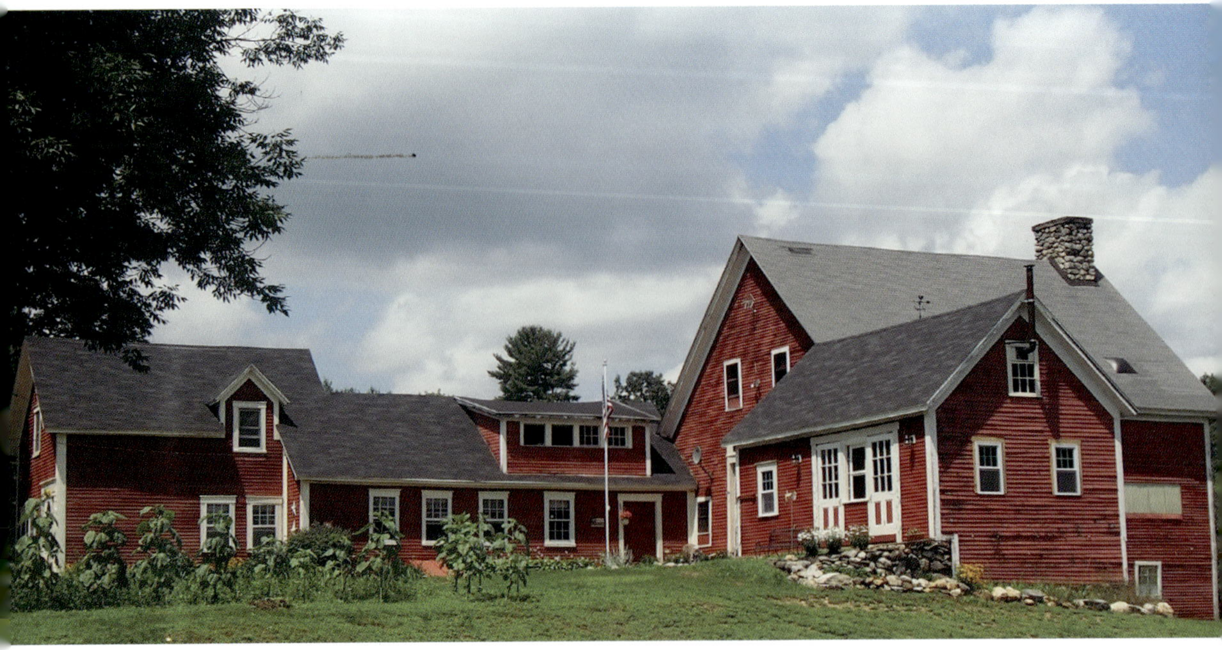

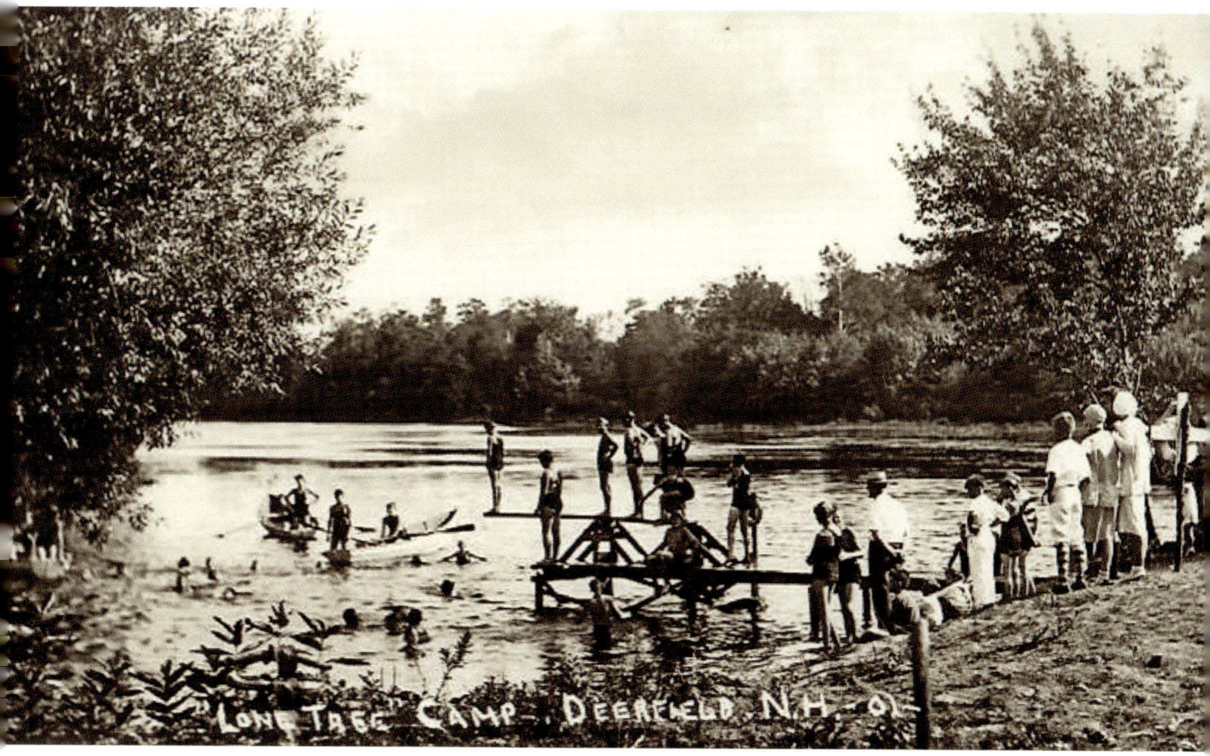

FREESE'S POND—DEERFIELD, NH: With the widening of the state highway dividing the property, and advice from the National Council of the BSA that the property would not meet new standards being developed for Scout camps, the location was abandoned as a summer camp after the 1941 camping season. Scouts from the Lone Tree Council, BSA would then attend North Essex Council, BSA's Camp Onway until the conclusion of World War II.

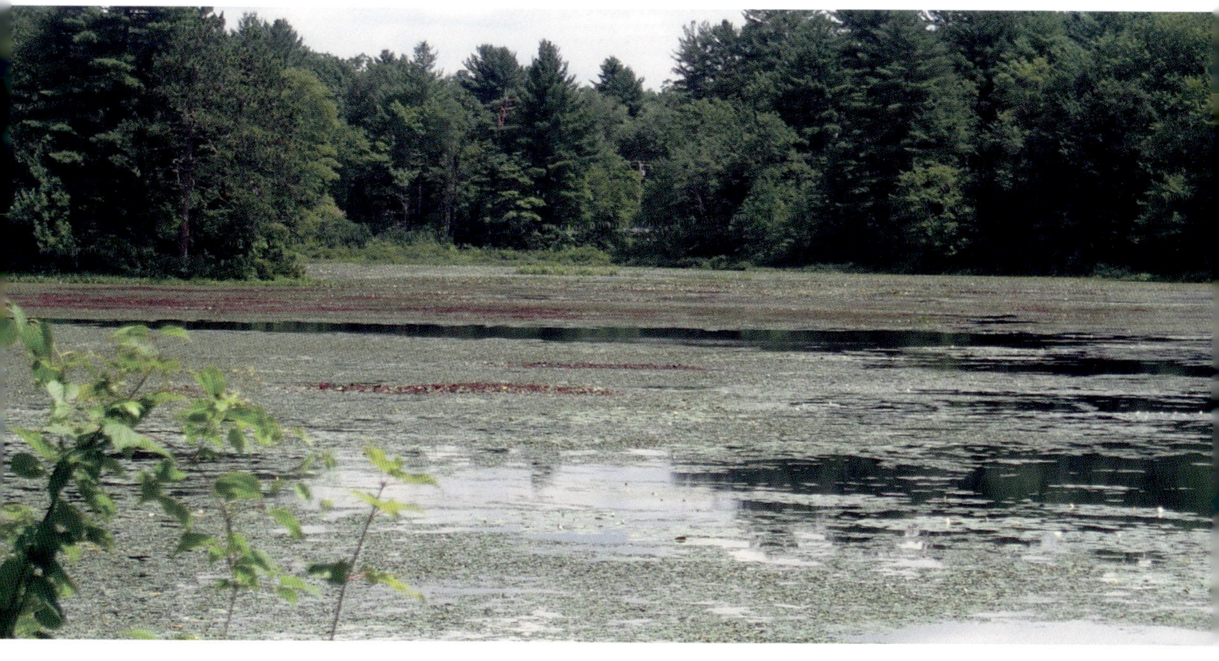

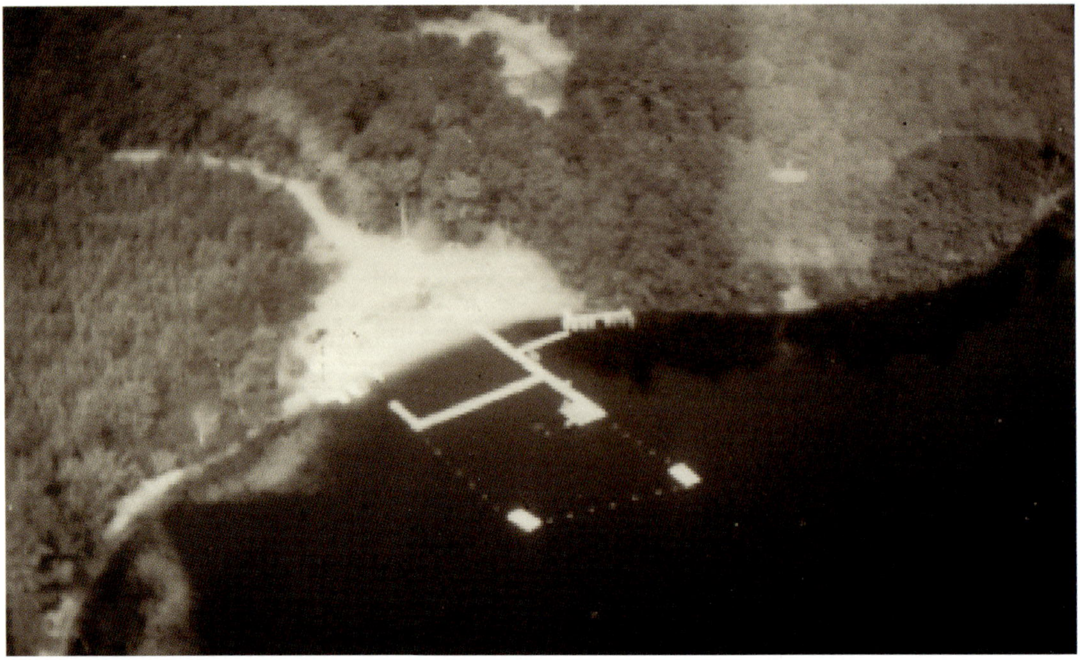

A NEW BEGINNING ON COUNTRY POND—KINGSTON, NH: Led by Council President Lewis R. Hovey, Scout Executive George T. Laing, Property Chairman George Briggs, and Camping Chairman Earl Moses, the leaders of Lone Tree Council, BSA again began a search for a property more suitable to serve as a Scout Reservation for the generations to come. In September 1946, they purchased 125 acres on the shores of Country Pond in Kingston, NH which would become Lone Tree Scout Reservation. More than $15,000 was earned by Scouts in Haverhill, Merrimac, Groveland, Georgetown, and Newburyport, MA through war time newspaper and scrap drives. The land was purchased for $10,000. Initial improvements of another $11,000 were undertaken in the first eighteen months using the additional funds received from the sale of the Deerfield, NH property and donations from community organizations.

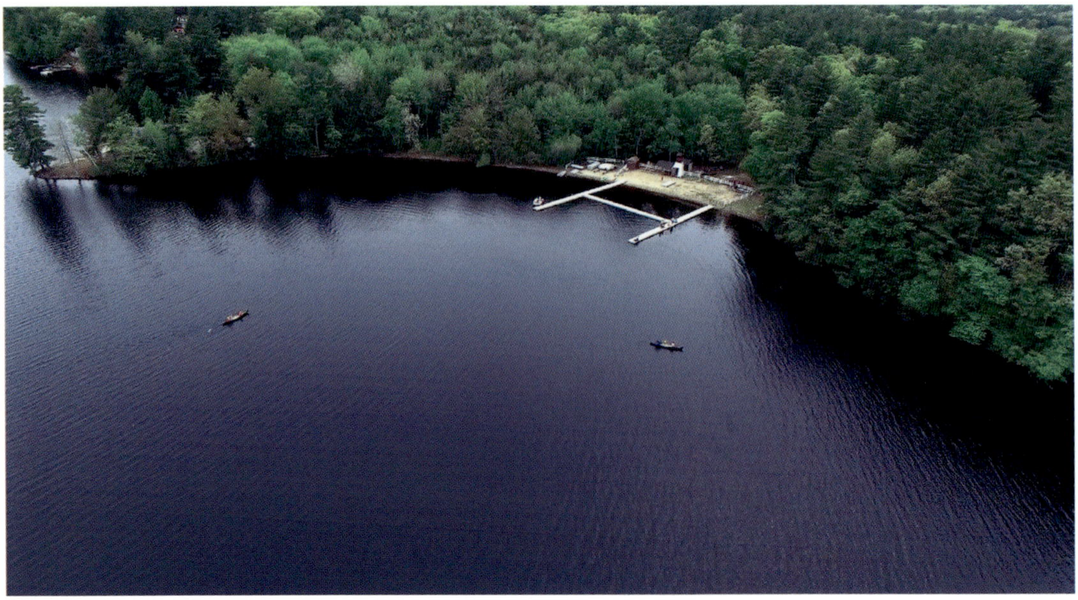

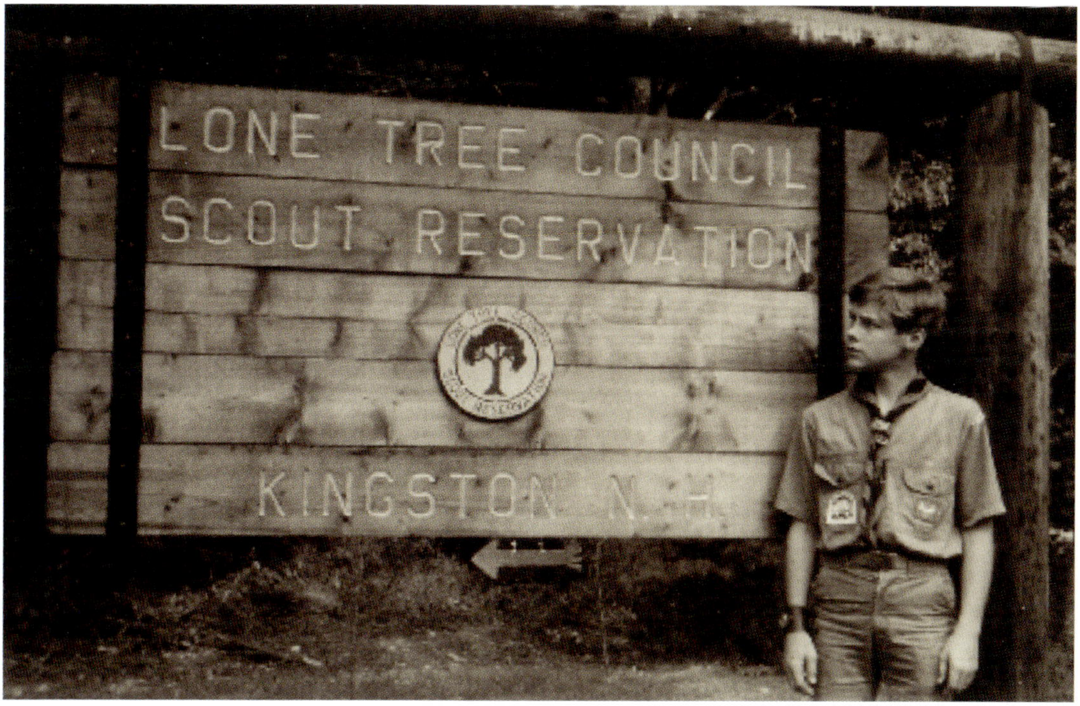

BUILDING LONE TREE SCOUT RESERVATION: The building of this Scout Reservation was a major undertaking. Scout Executive George T. Laing wrote in his 1947 annual report, "We have the start of a wonderful camp, one that will compare well with any in New England. One that you can well be proud of, one that we are proud of. It took time, effort and devotion. It took blood, sweat, and tears." Troops from throughout the council quickly made Lone Tree Scout Reservation their home.

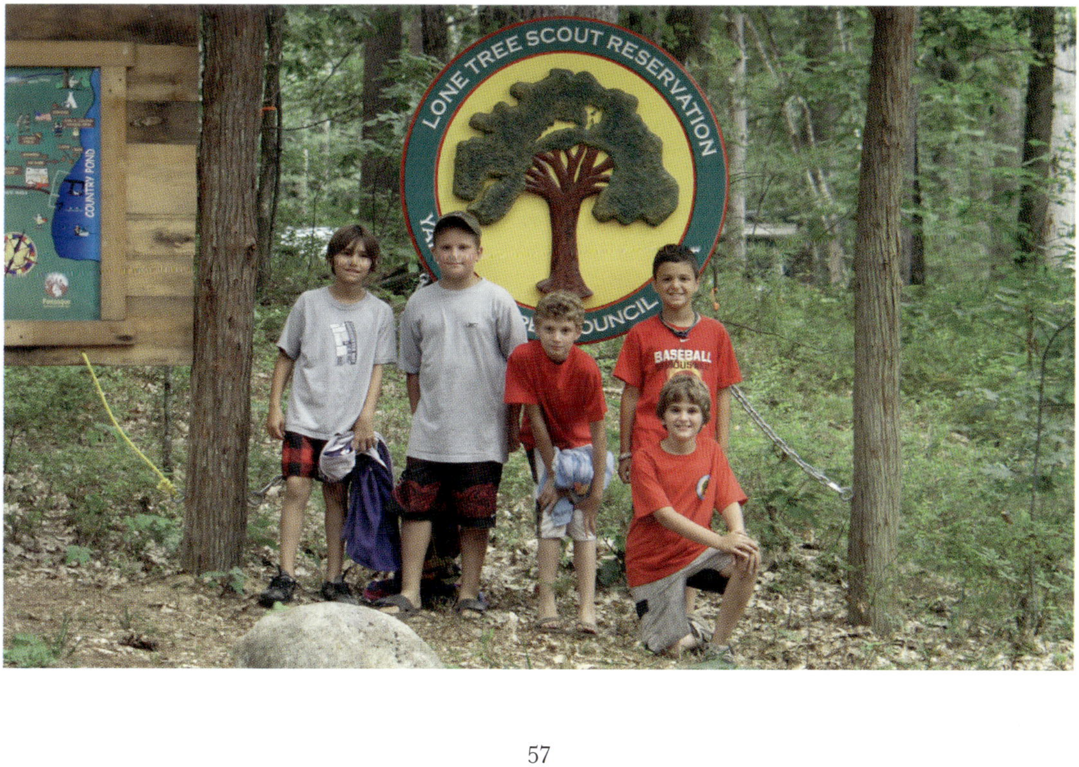

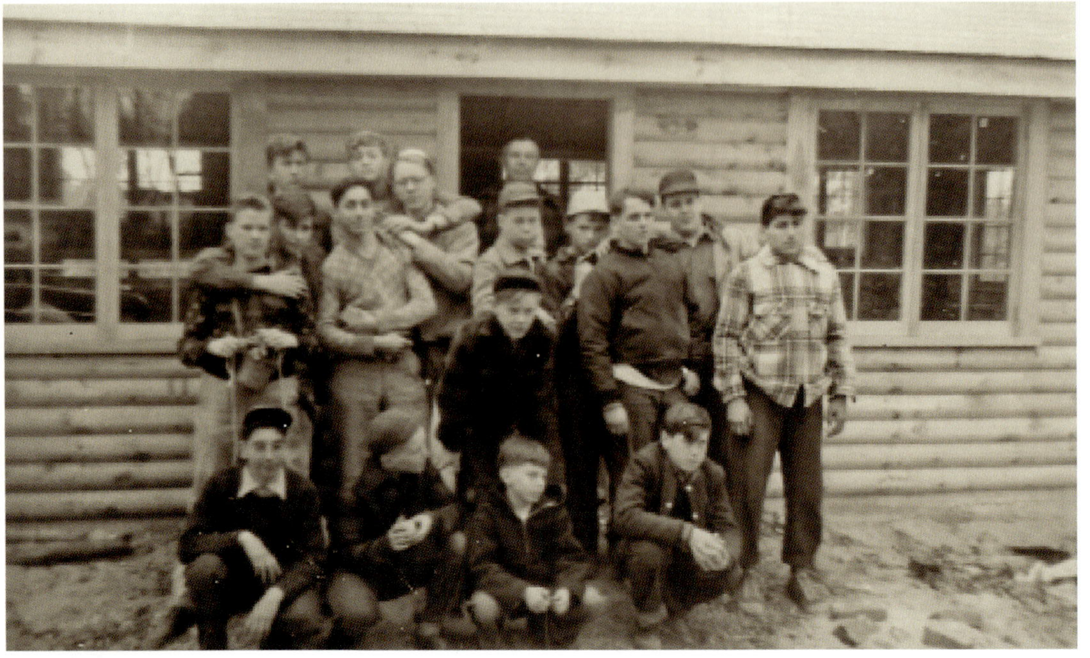

GROWING LONE TREE: By 1950, the reservation had all the amenities and facilities found in a Boy Scout camp. In the years that followed the reservation would add a chapel, nature lodge, office and trading post, a challenge course, rappelling tower and several pavilions. In 2012 an additional thirty acres of abutting land was purchased along the Reservation's Northwestern border to protect against encroachment.

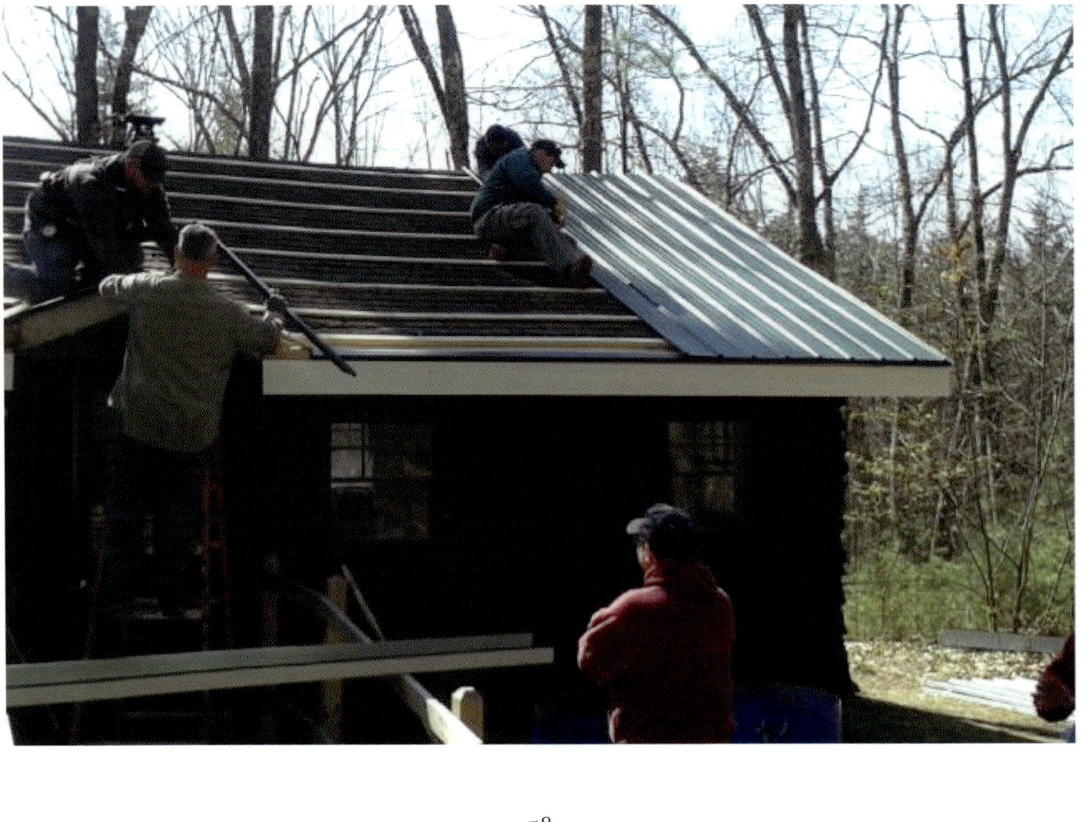

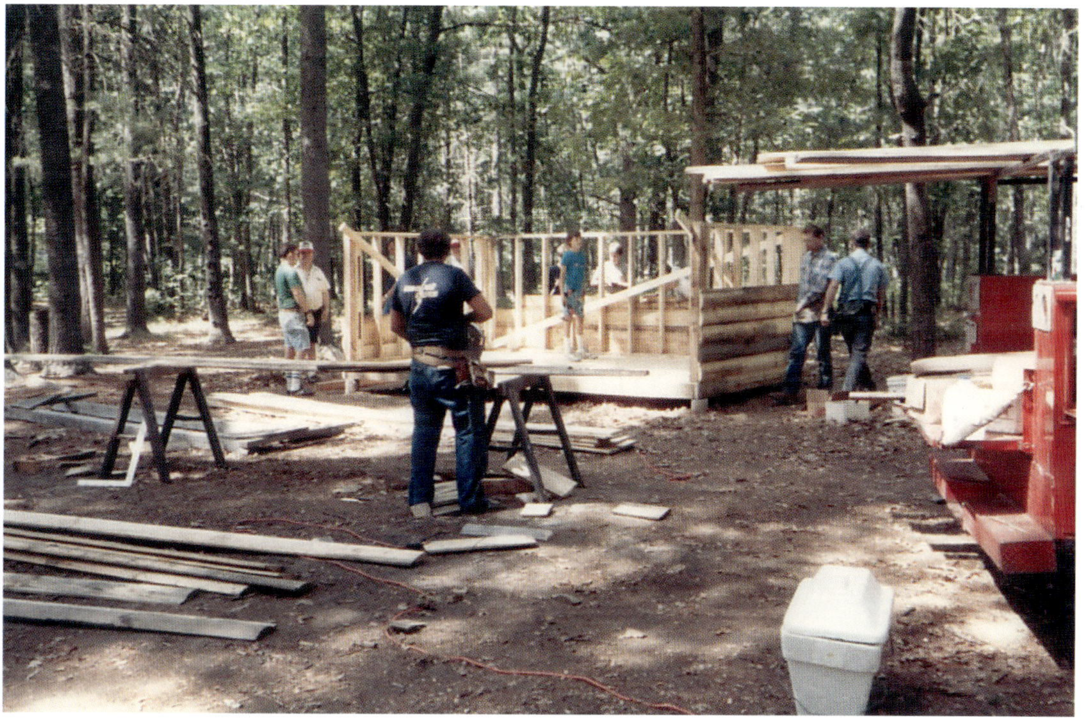

MANY HANDS: A Scout camp relies on volunteers for the year-round maintenance of, and improvements to, the camp. At Lone Tree these volunteers go by many names: volunteer staff, Camp Builders, Property and Maintenance Committee, The Lone Tree Spirit Foundation, and the Order of the Arrow. Much of the work that keeps a camp going is done by these volunteers. It takes a community of service-minded people committed to something bigger than themselves and with a love of Scouting to make a camp thrive. That level of commitment and service is something money cannot buy.

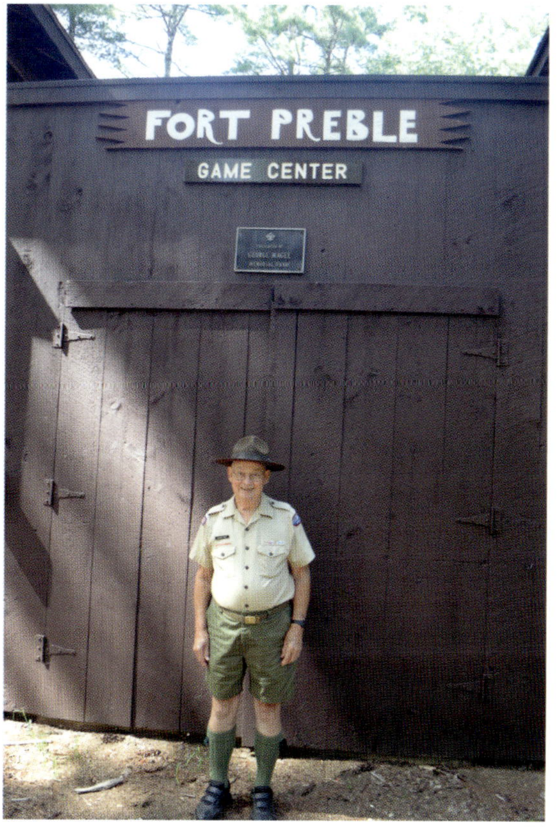

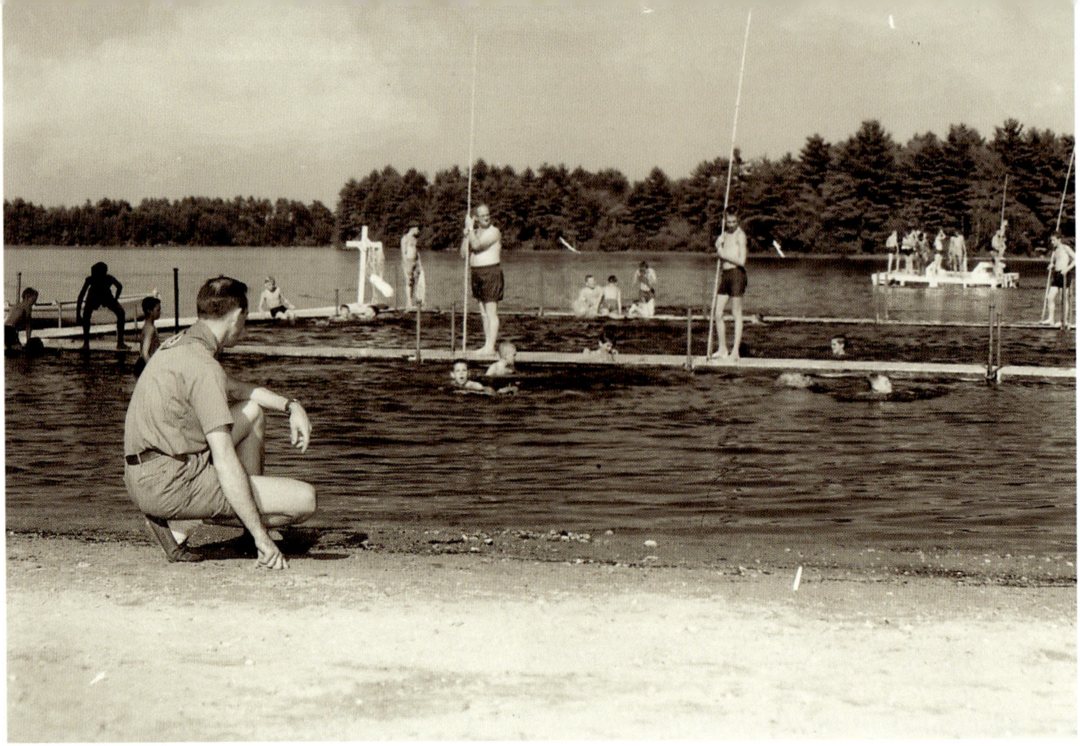

THE WATER IS FINE: The waters of Country Pond were a major improvement over the leech-filled swimming hole at the Deerfield, NH property. There was a beach and plenty of water for canoeing, rowing, sailing, and fishing. In the years that followed, motorboating and waterskiing would be added to the summer camp aquatics program. As with many Scout camps, the waterfront is a focal point of the camp. Water draws Scouts to activities that are difficult to come by in the typical daily life of a Scout. The camp continues to offer boating and fishing as part of its year-round program. Country Pond is also a popular winter ice fishing destination.

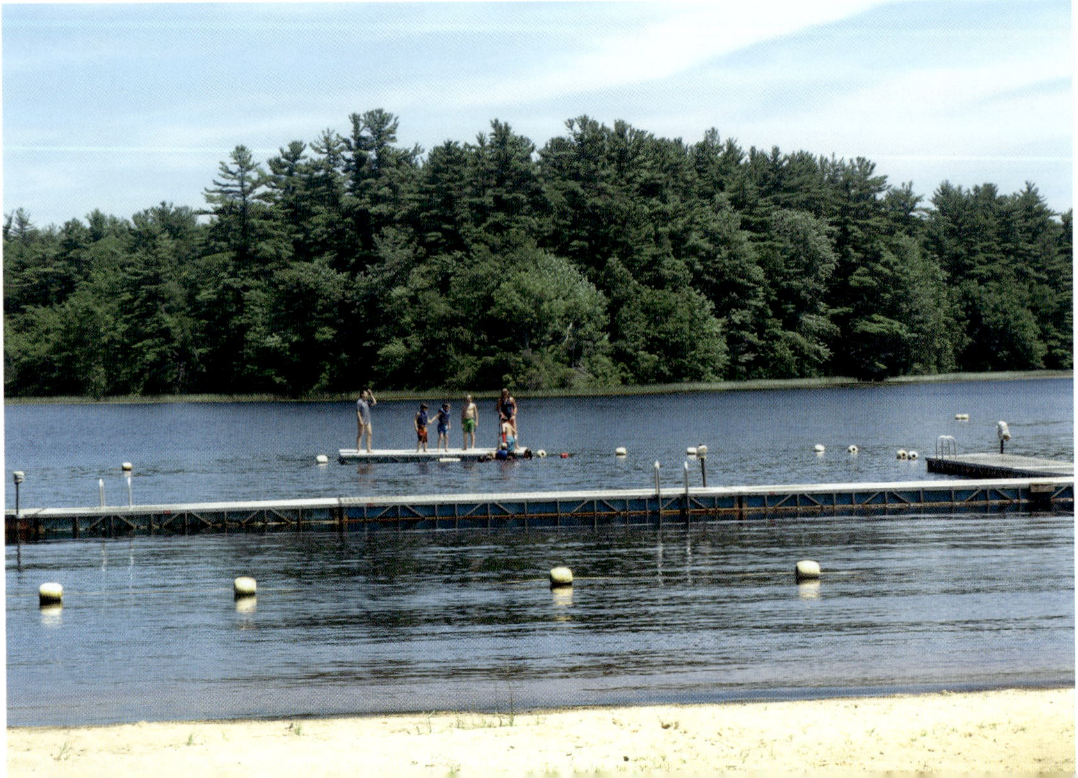

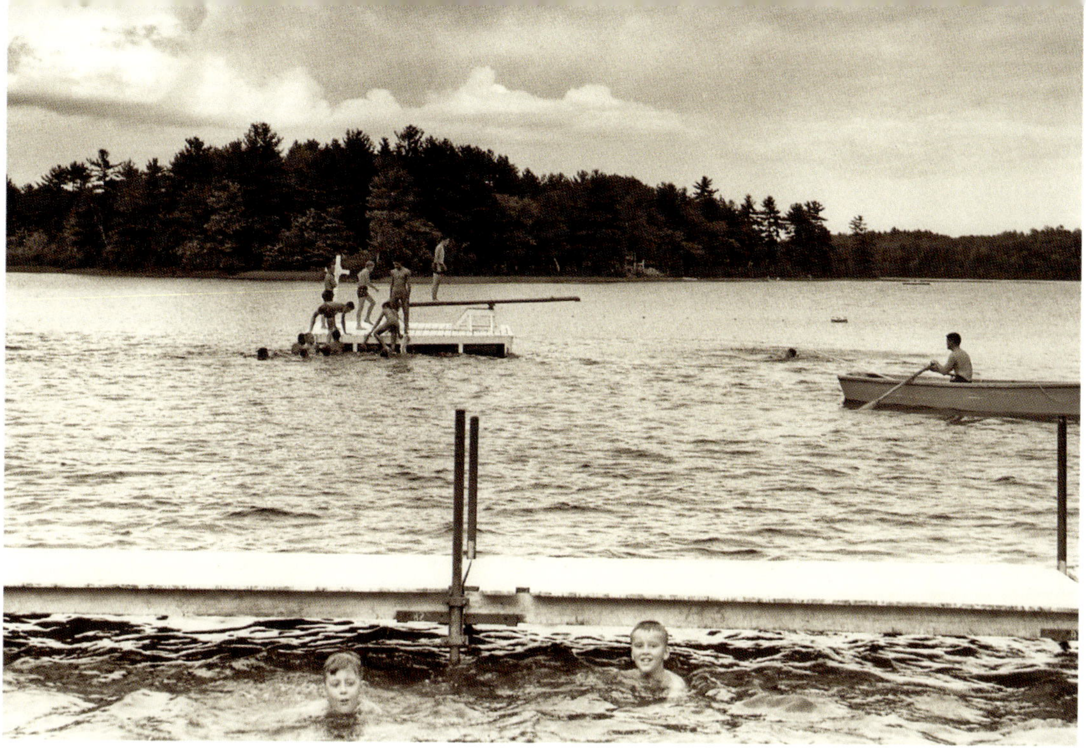

AQUATIC DIVERSITY: The waters of Country Pond offer 306 acres of fishing, swimming, and boating. The Powwow River flows through the pond and is accessible by canoe or kayak. Along the shores of Country Pond, within the camp, and along its southeastern border, lies one of the largest outcroppings of Atlantic white cedar in New Hampshire—a globally rare type of natural community. The pond contains perch, pickerel, and both small and large-mouth bass. Country Pond is also home to several species of turtles as well as loons, beavers, great blue herons, and an occasional bald eagle. A 40-acre unimproved island lies in the middle of the pond that serves as the monument upon which Lone Tree's waterfront overlooks.

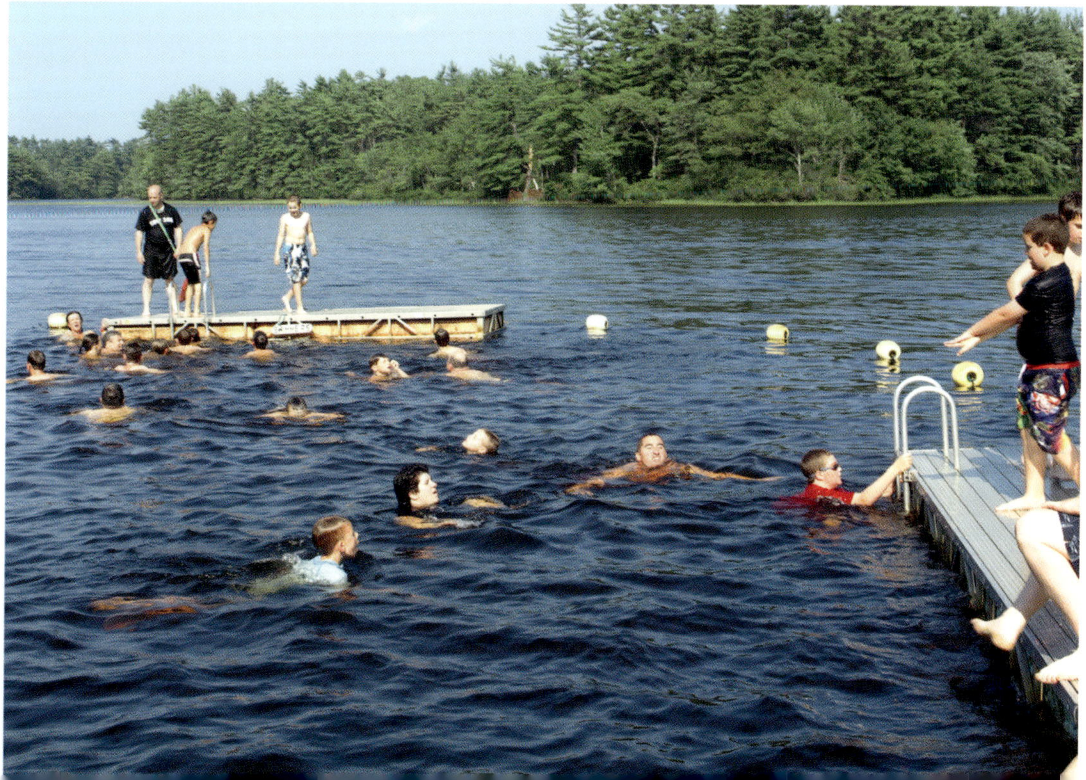

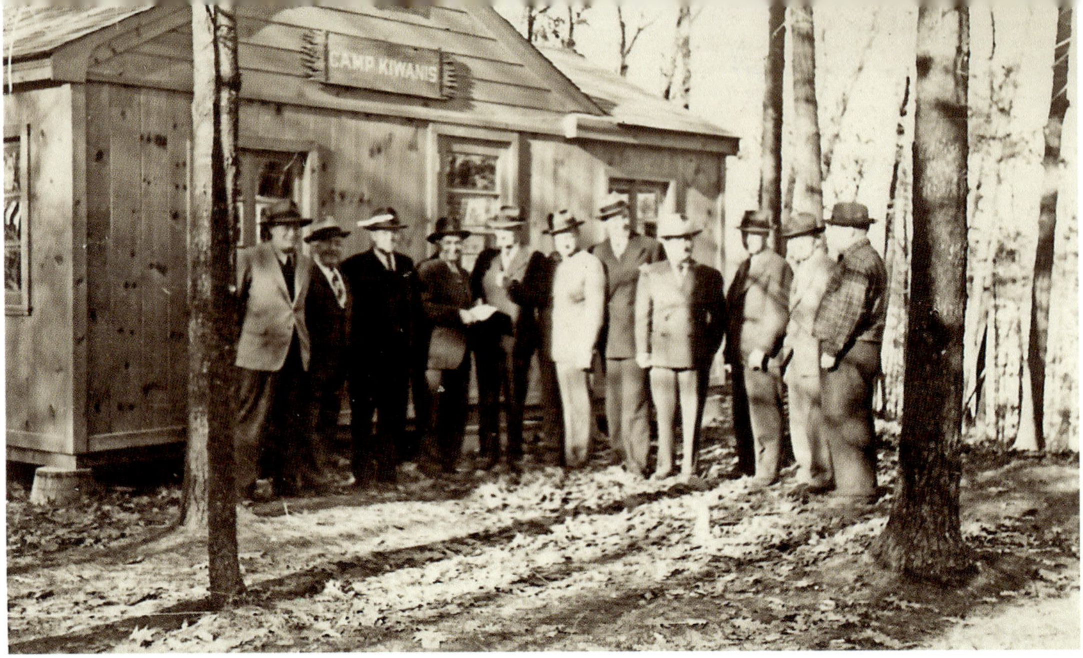

SUSTAINABILITY: The financial structure of Scouting requires that camps must stand on their own financially. To remain viable, a Scout camp cannot become a drain on council finances. To keep the promise of making the camp available to all the price of camp attendance and off-season user fees at Lone Tree are set to cover just the most basic maintenance needs of the reservation. Funding for improvements to the camp and even more costly routine maintenance often comes from outside resources. Since its founding, Lone Tree has been the recipient of many generous donations from community organizations such as area Lions, Rotary, and Kiwanis clubs. Nearly every building and major improvement in camp has been the result of targeted fundraising and donations. In recent years, the George Magee Memorial Fund, the Lone Tree Spirit Foundation, and The Key Foundation have been significant benefactors funding numerous improvement projects throughout camp. These organizations help make Lone Tree sustainable and their contributions have been vital to fulfilling the camp's mission.

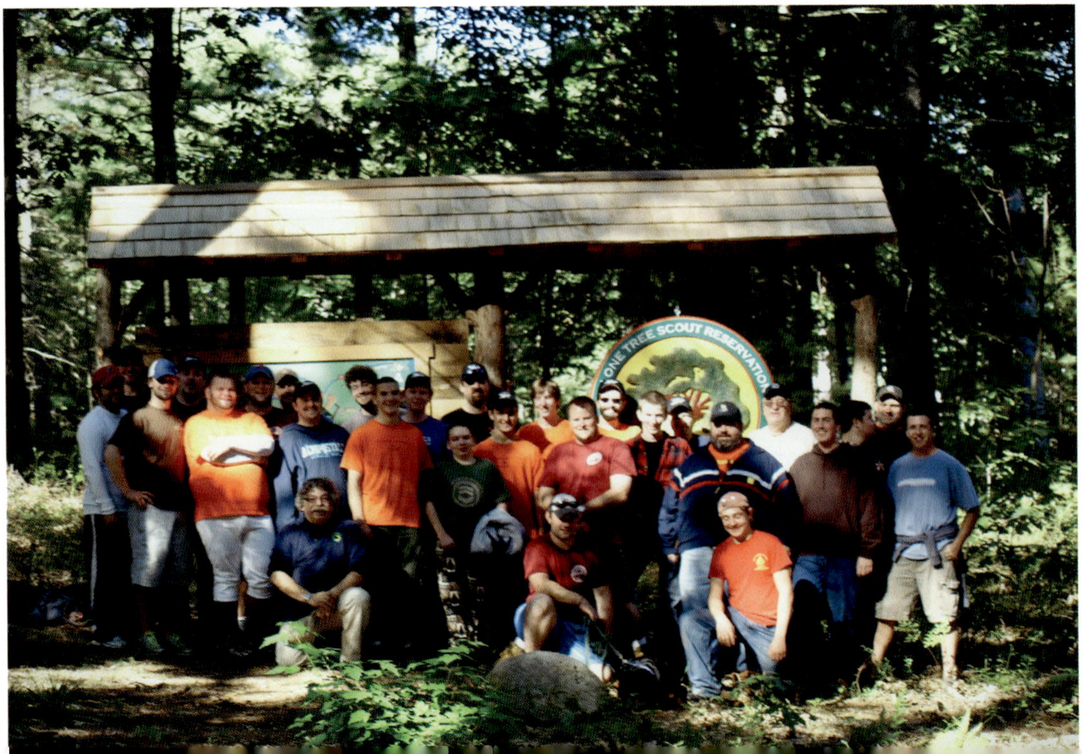

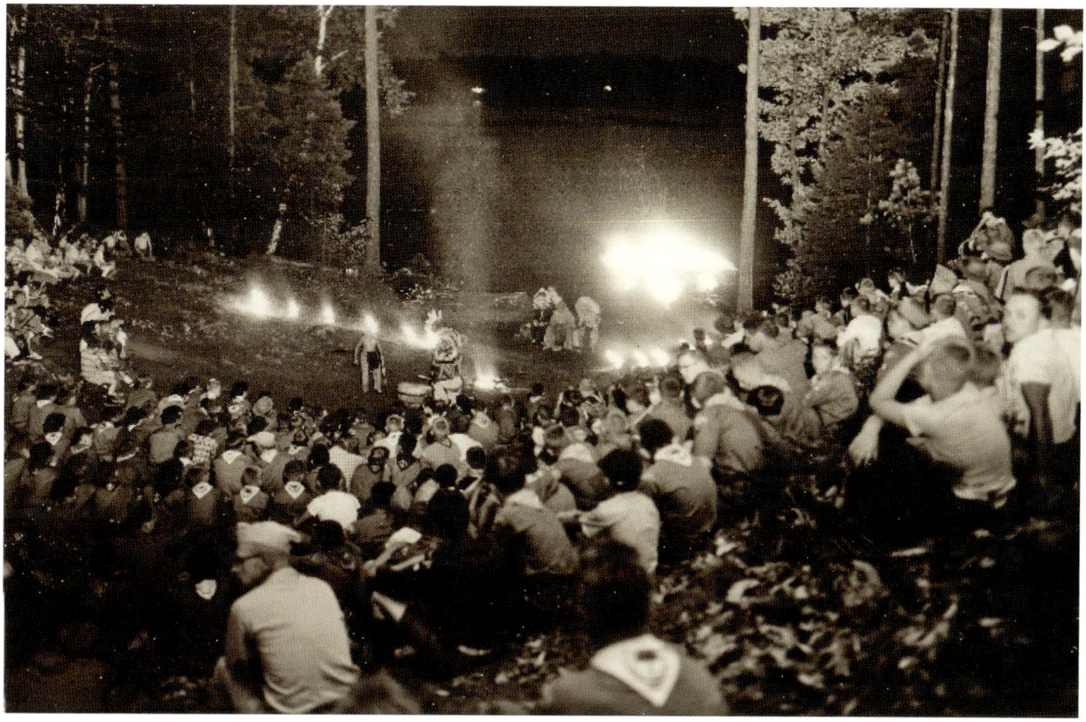

THE COUNCIL RING: At the end of a fun-filled week at camp, the closing campfire is a Lone Tree tradition. This is a time for each unit to showcase their talents and for the camp staff to say a fond farewell and "see you next summer!" to Scouts and Scouters. Lone Tree's Council Ring is named for former Order of the Arrow (OA) Lodge Adviser and District Commissioner Earl Collins. Through the years, the OA lodge has undertaken several projects to maintain and enhance the appearance of the Council Ring.

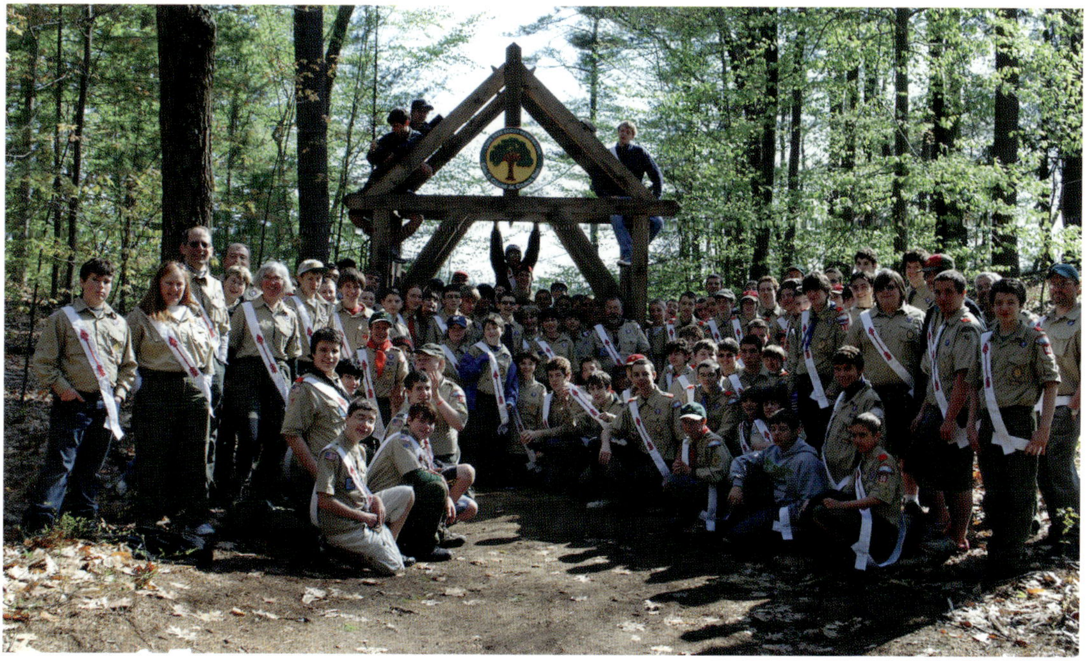

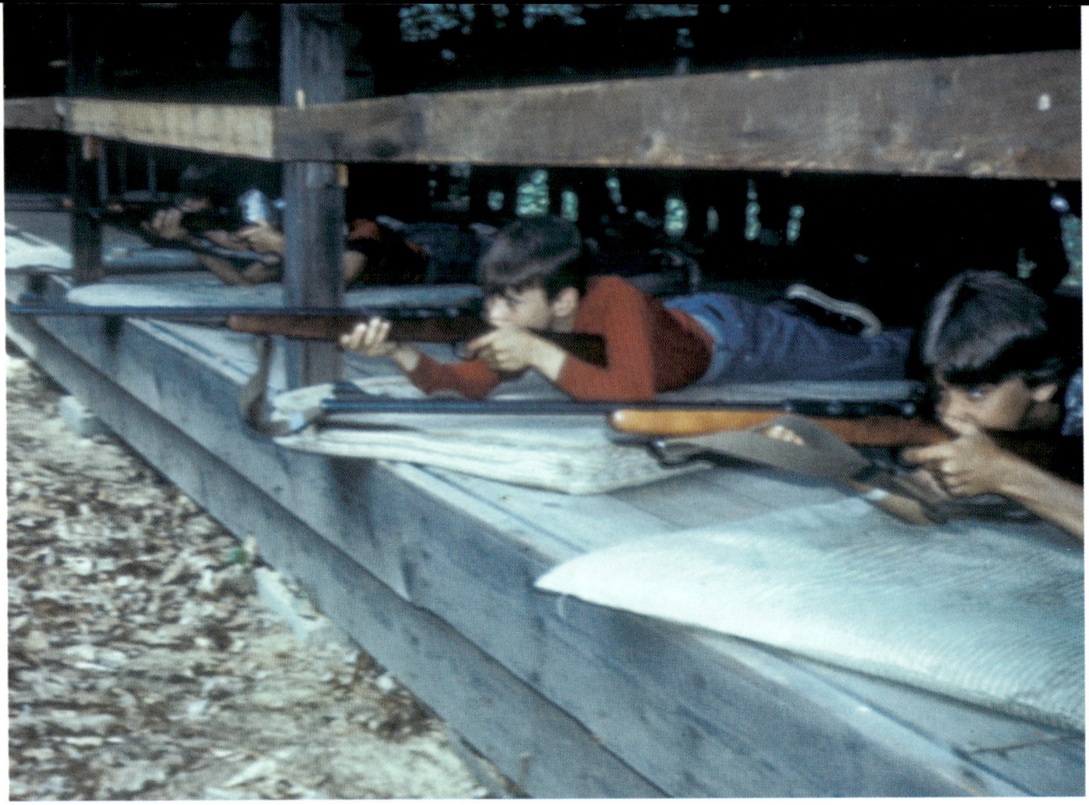

RIGHT ON TARGET: Shooting sports have a long tradition in Scouting and at Lone Tree. Scouting instills responsible handling of target shooting equipment in Scouts under the direction of certified range officers. At Lone Tree, archery is offered for youth of all ages. Cub Scouts can begin their shooting sports adventure with BB target shooting. Scouts move up to .22 rifles at the rifle range. There are other shooting sports offerings that include black powder, clay skeet shotgun shooting, .22 pistol shooting for Venture Scouts, and Tomahawk throwing.

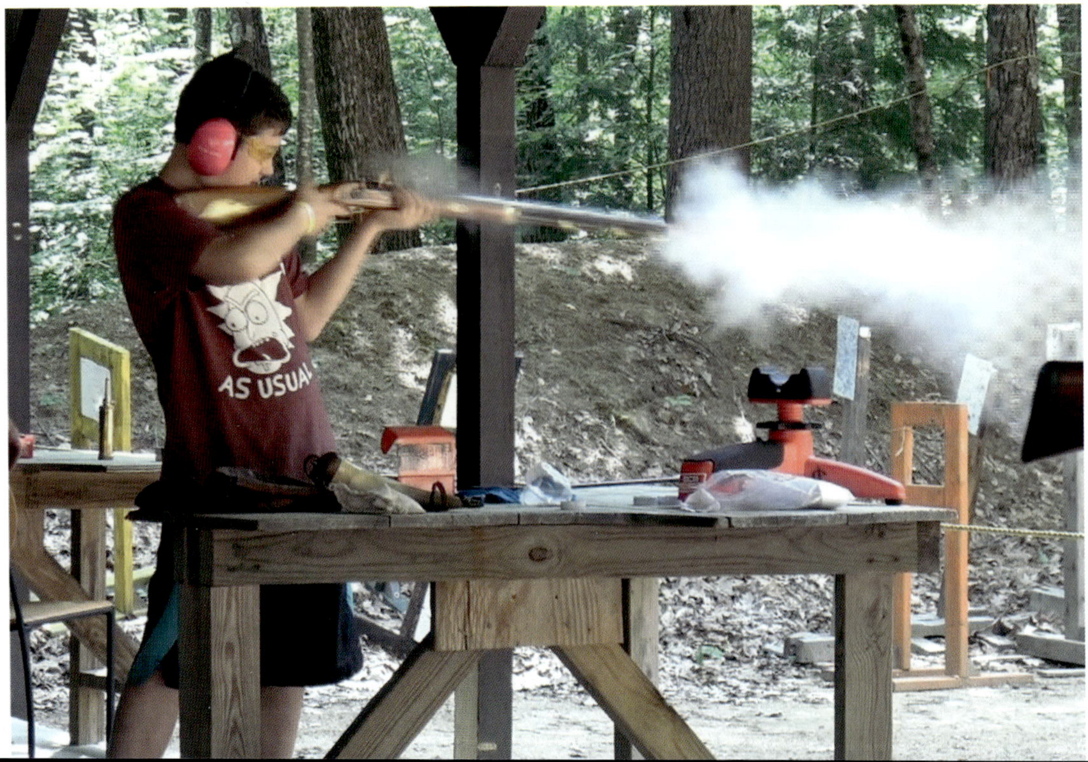

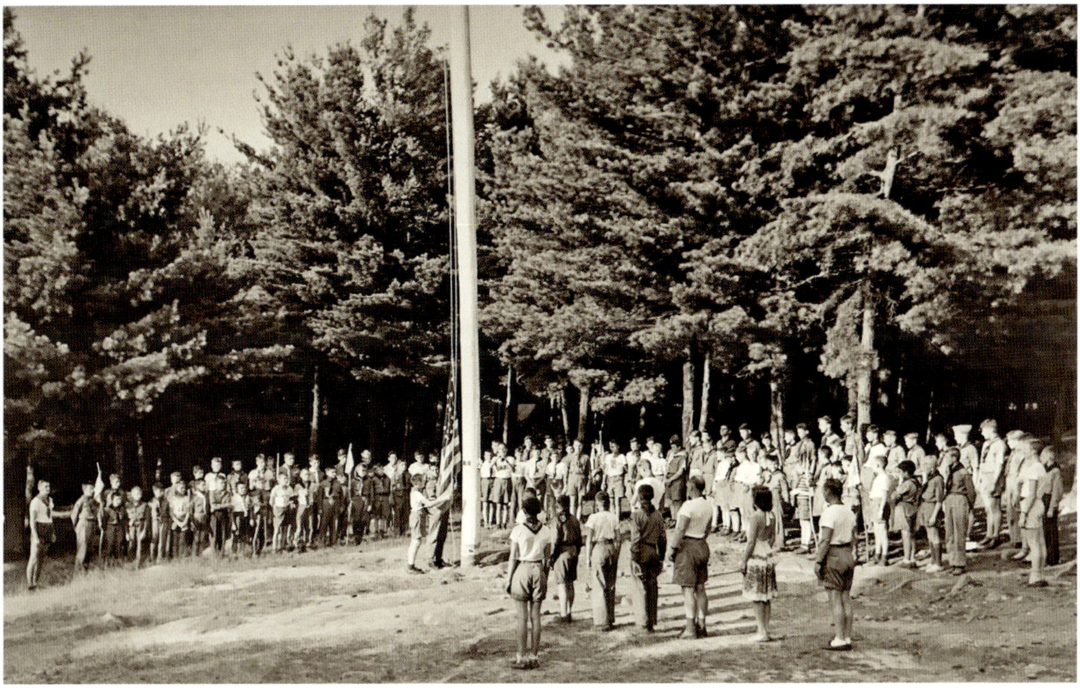

TRUE COLORS: Evening retreat, after the main program of the day is over and before dinner, is a daily occurrence during the days of Boy Scout resident summer camp at Lone Tree which continued during cub day camp. Flag ceremonies are an opportunity for all Scouts to come together as a group to show and teach respect for the symbol of our nation. Raising, lowering, and folding the American Flag is a Scout camp tradition that runs deep. That tradition endures today at Lone Tree Scout Reservation.

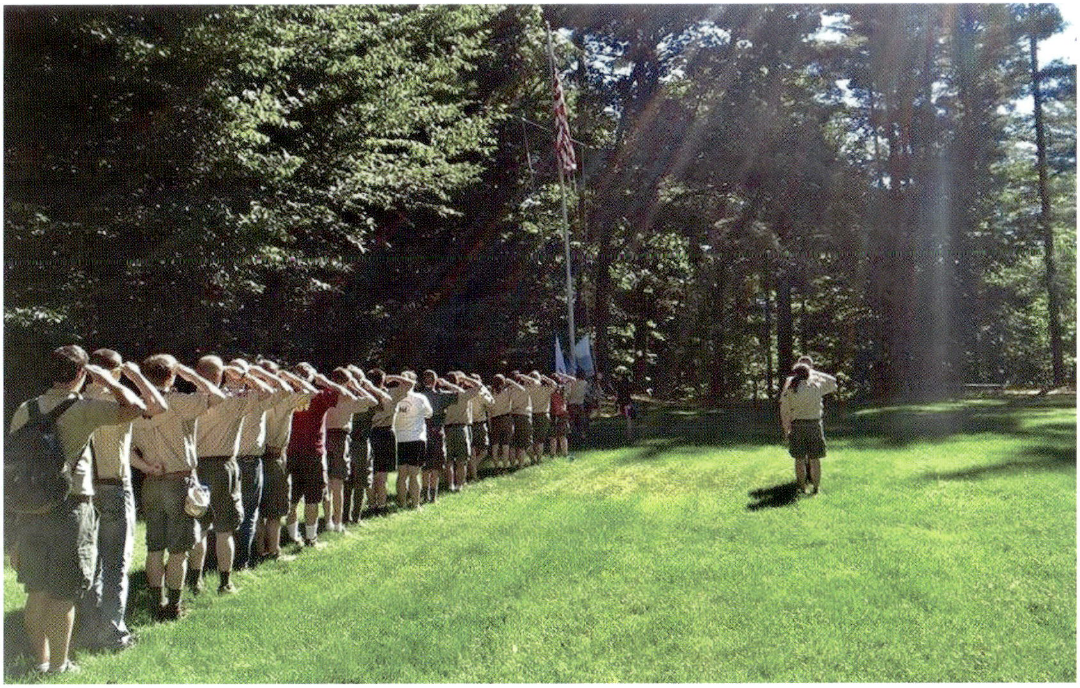

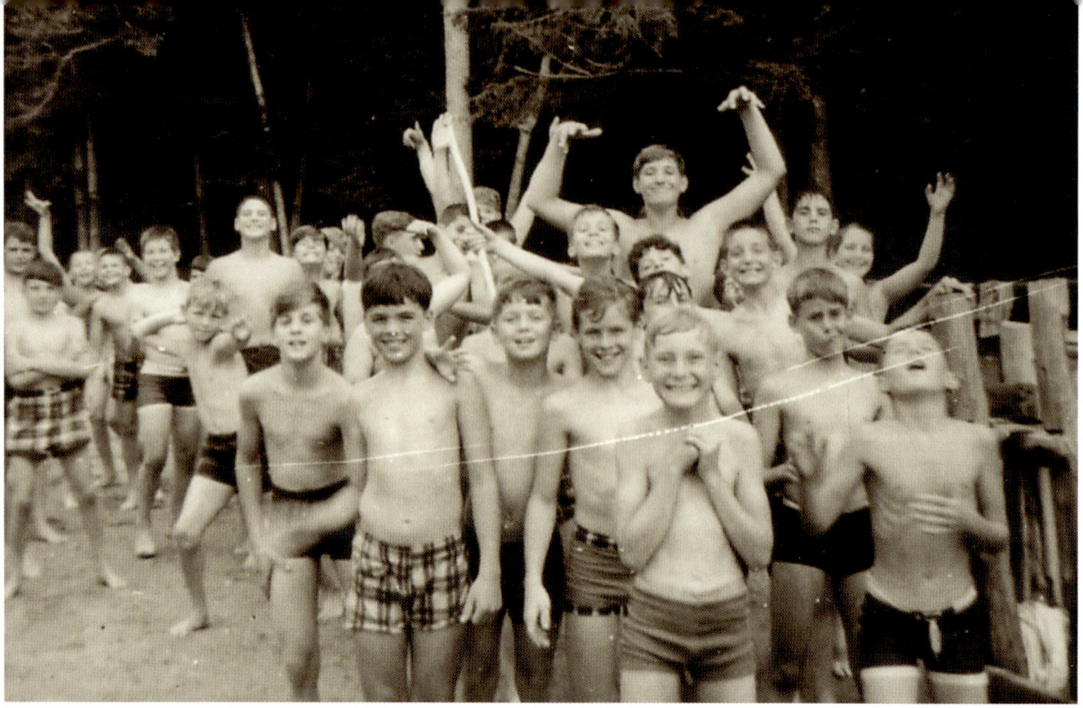

ENDURING RELEVANCE: Decreases in BSA membership, both locally and nationwide, and council mergers, led to the closing or sale of many Scout camps in neighboring or merged councils. Lone Tree has adapted its program to remain relevant to the needs of Scouting families. Lone Tree provides a wooded lakeside retreat within an hour of Boston and remains a vital Scouting resource. As the BSA enters a new and exciting time, embracing girls as part of the central Scouting program, Lone Tree Scout Reservation stands ready to continue to expand the mission of getting kids outdoors.

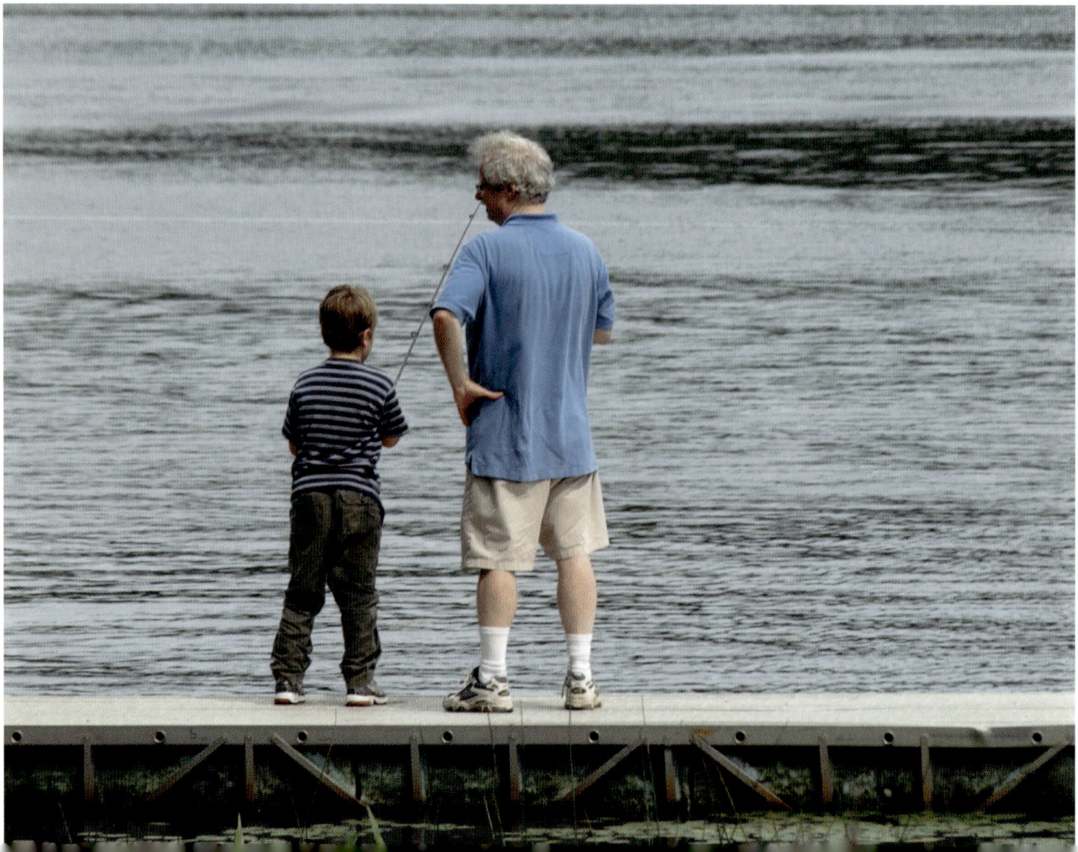

Chapter 6

Theodore L. Storer Scout Reservation

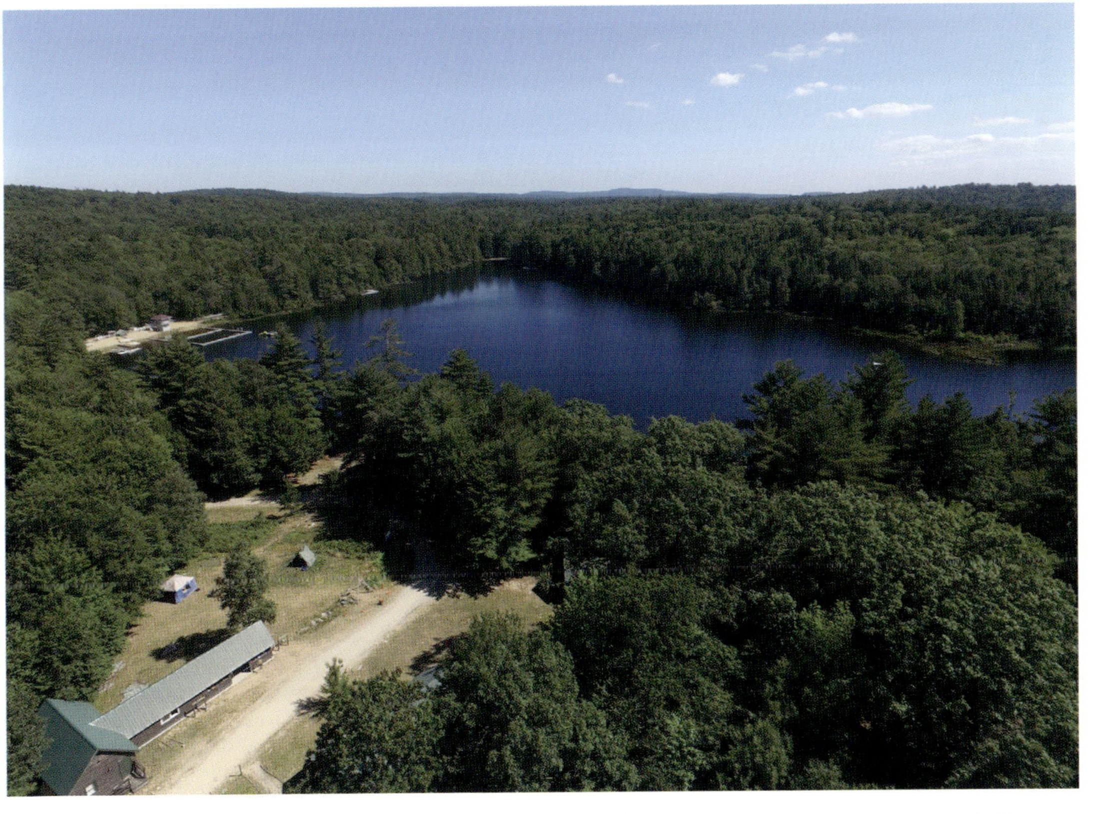

T. L. Storer Scout Reservation—Barnstead, NH: The Boston Council, BSA opened this camp in June of 1958 on land donated by Theodore Lyman Storer. T. L. Storer was a real estate executive and served on the boards of multiple Boston Metro Councils. Ten years earlier, he also donated the land for Parker Mountain Scout Reservation. The camp was opened under the name Adams Pond Camp. After the opening of Wild Goose Camp on the same property, the camp was renamed a Scout Reservation honoring its benefactor.

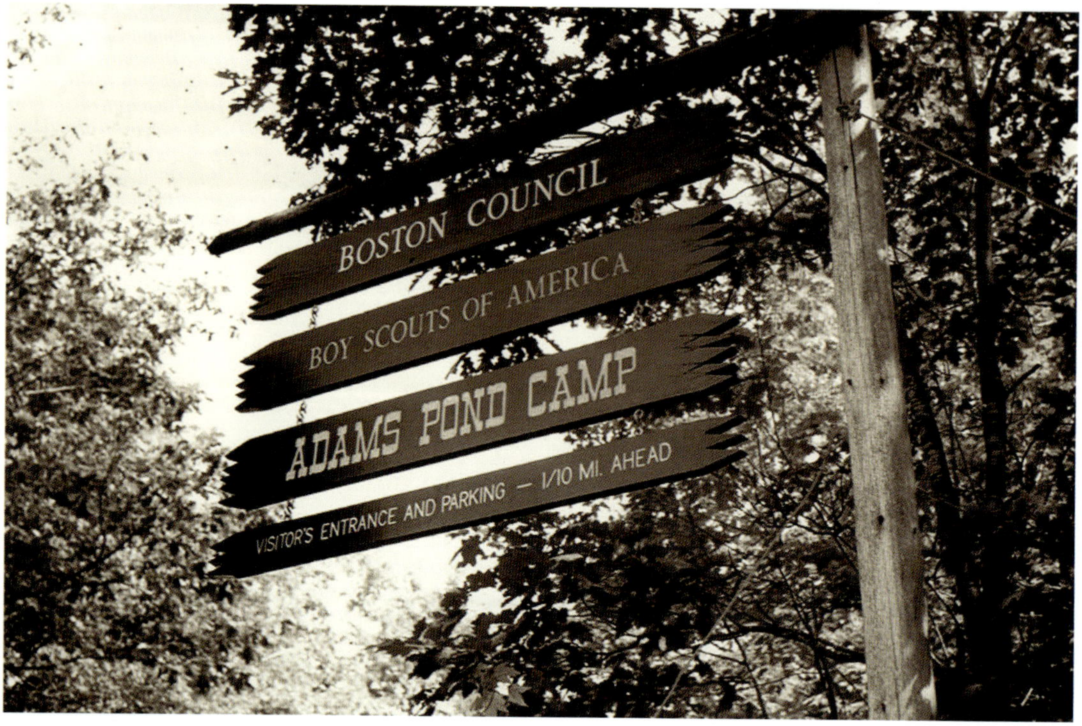

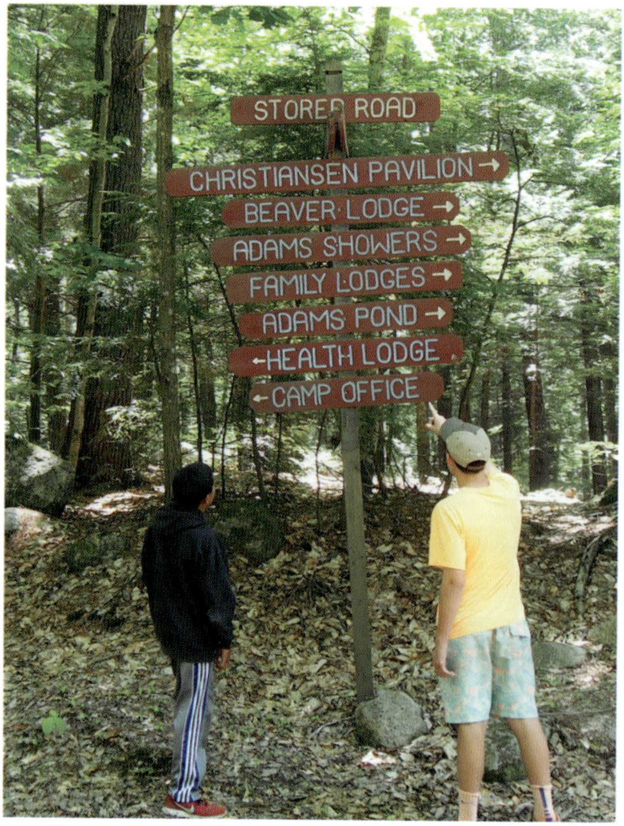

Signs of the times: Camp signage is often a reflection of the camp community. They are largely constructed by volunteers. The signs do more than just help people find where they want to go; they reflect how well the camp is cared for and maintained. It is often a demonstration of the magnitude of the operations, priorities, and procedures. They are also insightful in understanding the individual camp's culture.

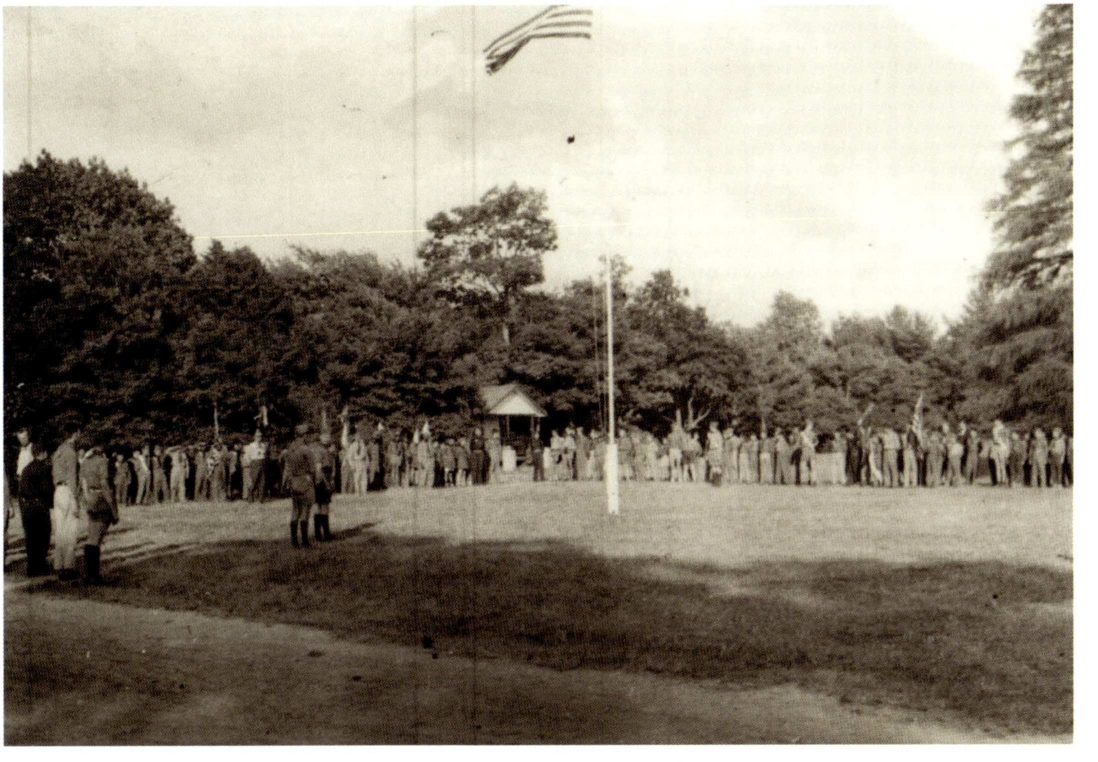

Loon Pond Scout Camp: Loon Pond, opened in 1922, was the immediate predecessor to T. L. Storer. It was located in Lakeville, MA and owned by the Boston Council, BSA. At just under 125 acres it was accessible to Boston Scouts by public transportation. The camp ran through the 1957 summer season and was then sold to sports legend Ted Williams. Williams operated a baseball camp on the property until 1985 when it was acquired by the town of Lakeville, MA. Today, the property is used as a recreational and sports center.

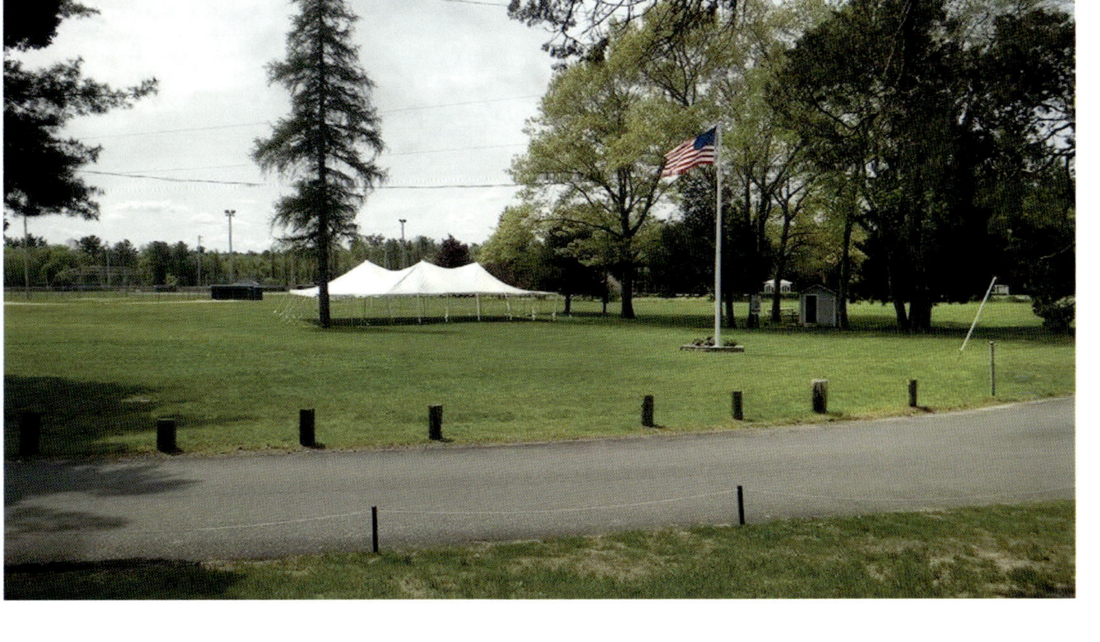

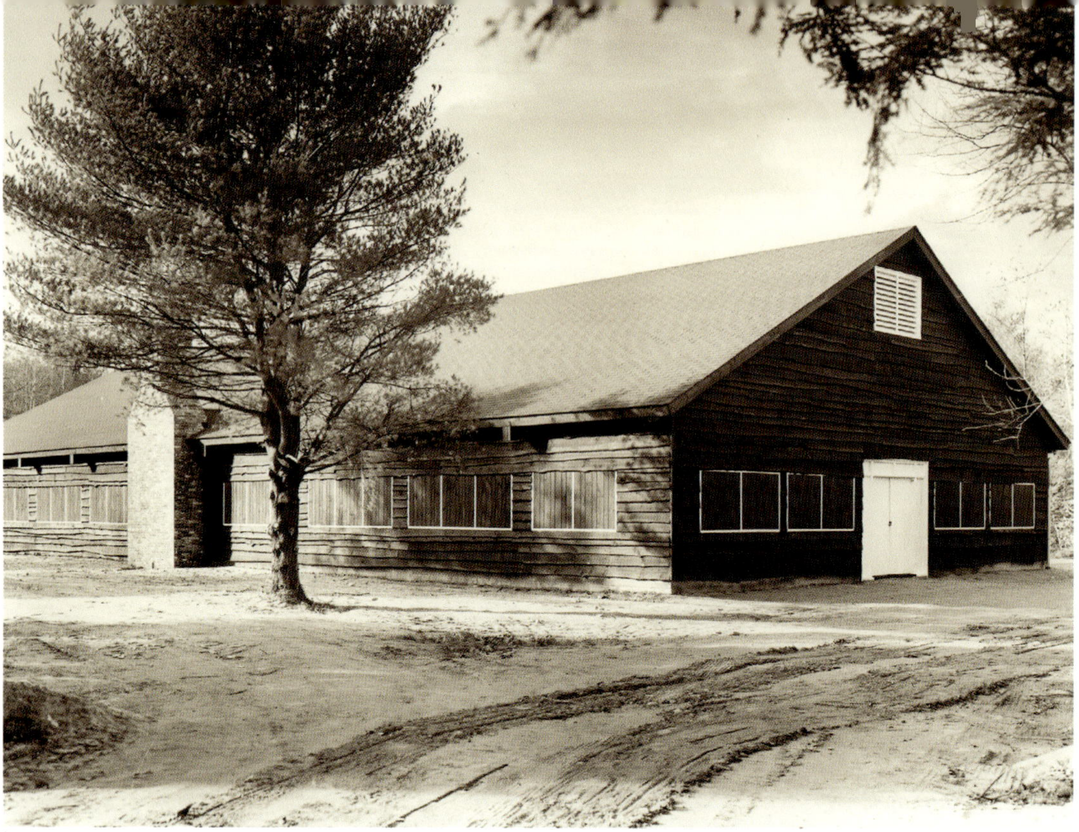

DINING HALL: Adams Pond (later T. L. Storer) Dining Hall was completed in the fall 1957 by the Harvey Construction Company of Manchester, NH. Early in the first season, (July 1958), a fire burned the building and the National Guard provided a mobile kitchen for the rest of that first season. The building was quickly rebuilt in the fall of 1958 and has been in continuous service every summer since.

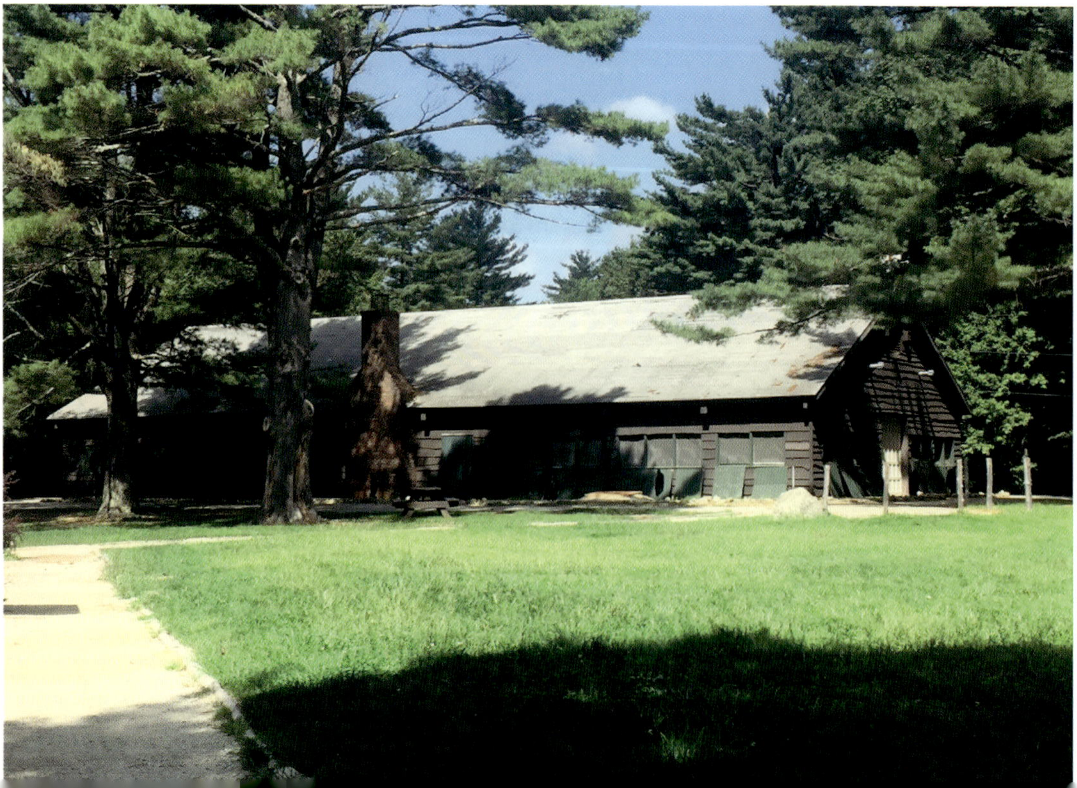

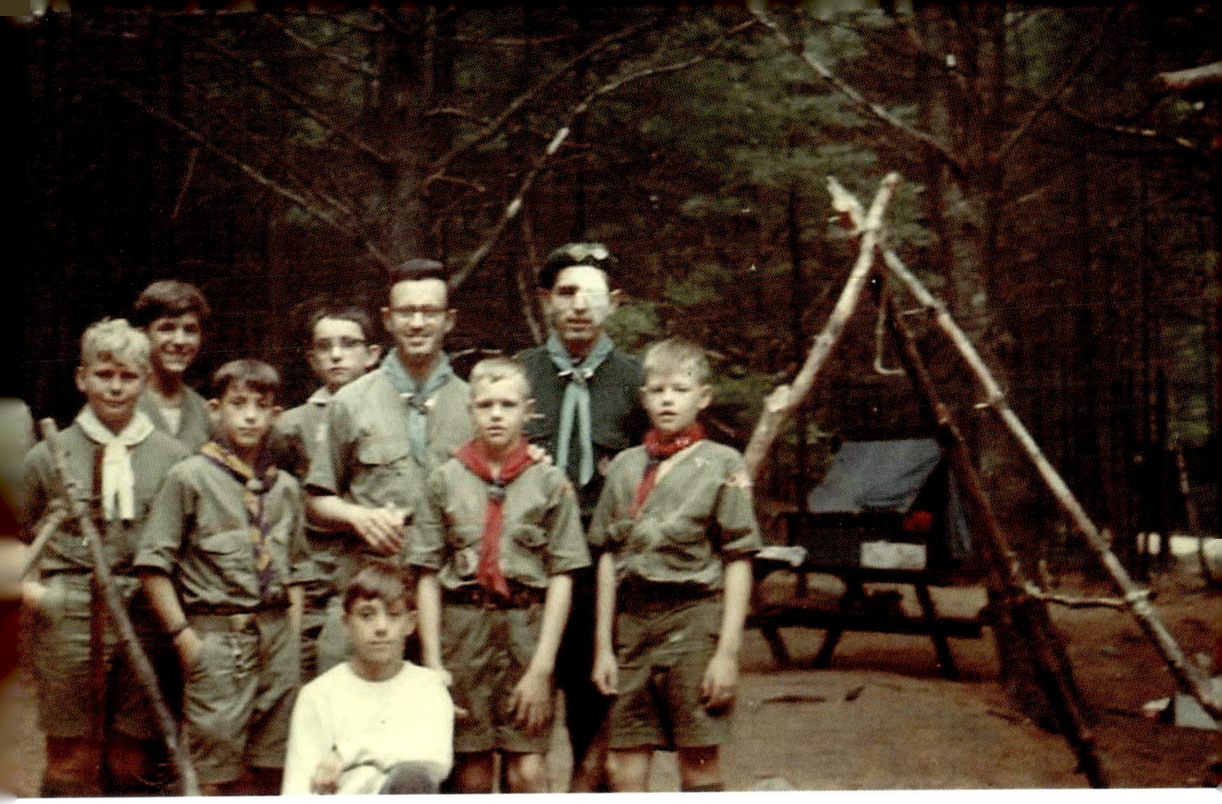

WILD GOOSE: In the post-war 50s and 60s families began moving to the suburbs. The Boston Council, BSA's desire to grow Adams Pond Camp was impacted by declining inner-city middle-class Scouts. Through a series of mergers and acquisitions, the council built a second camp on the property with an independent staff and program. They called it Wild Goose Camp, as it was located on the shores of the pond with the same name.

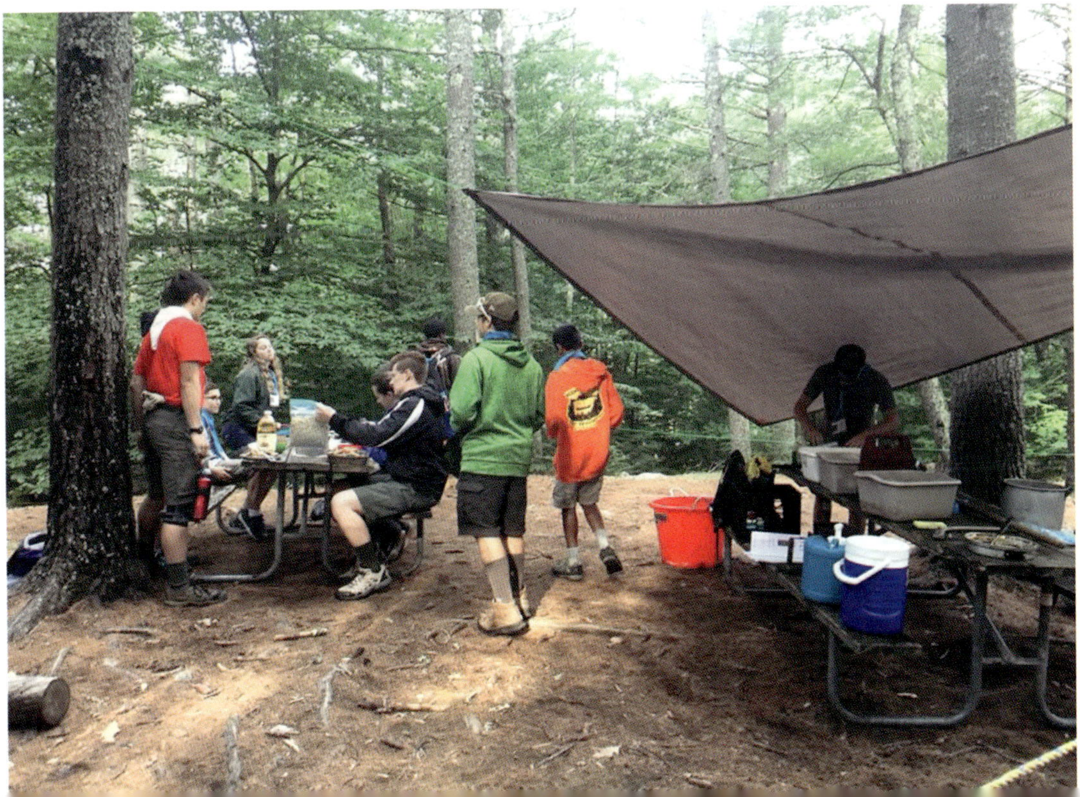

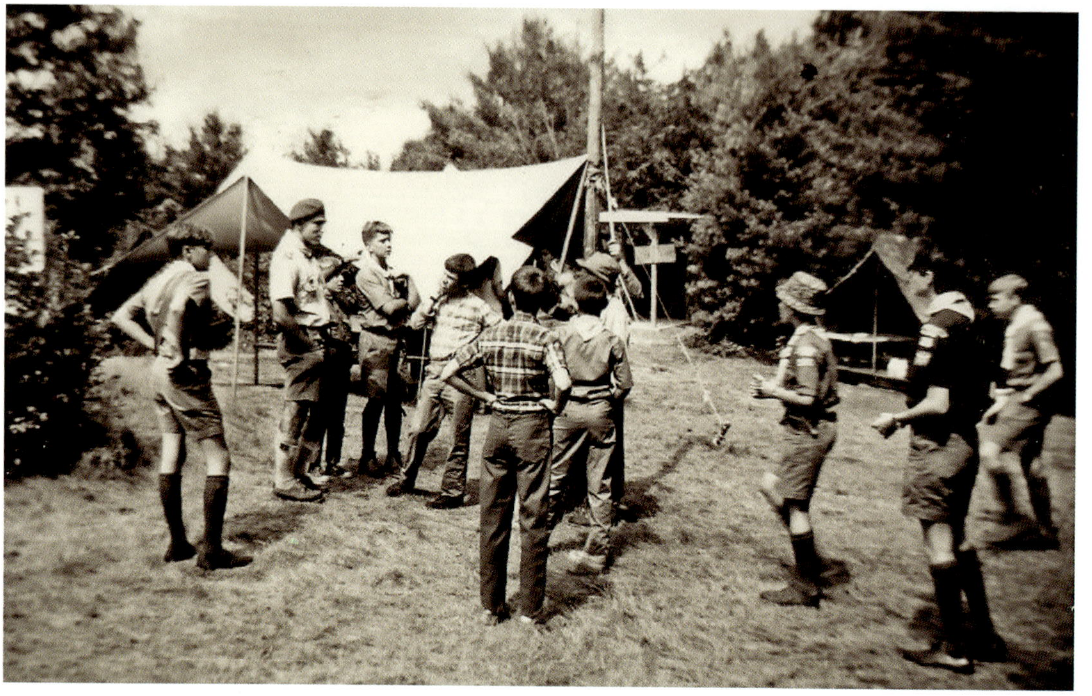

THE MEN FROM THE HILL: As a separate camp with its own unique culture Wild Goose was designed to develop unit leadership. The campers and staff of Wild Goose were known as "Goosemen" and "Men from The Hill." Most Goose troops did not use the Dining Hall. The Scouts cooked their own meals in their campsites which became an opportunity to develop their patrols. The two camps would hold separate Camp fires and both camps were told to sing loud to let the other camp know they were there. Today Wild Goose is used primarily for council-wide youth development courses such as Brownsea II and the National Youth Leader Training Course (NYLT). In both these programs Scouts work and live together in patrols of six-eight youth cooking their own meals.

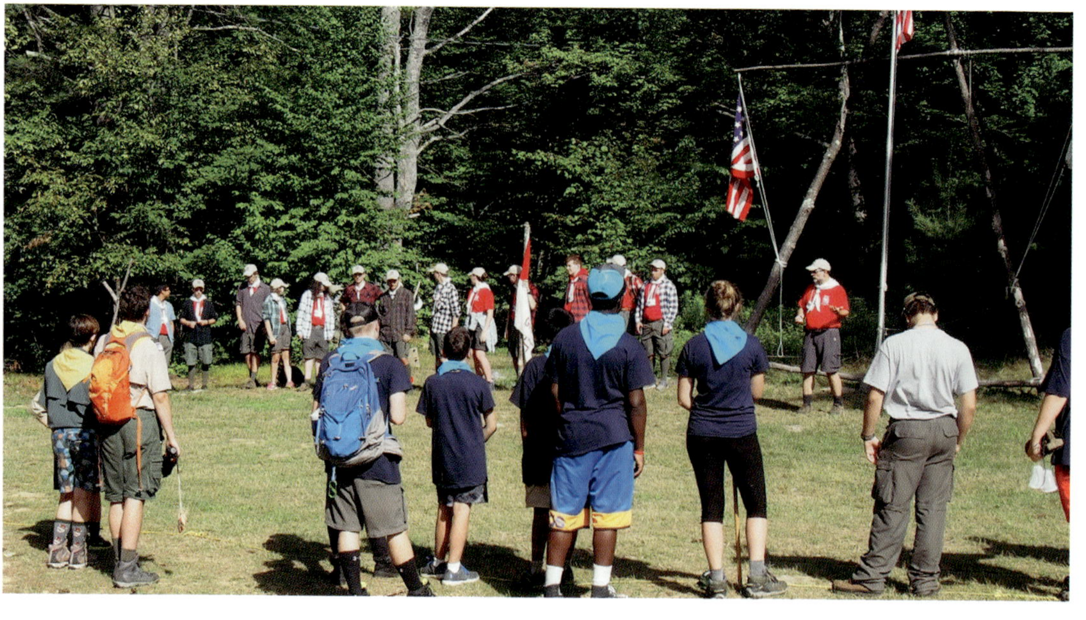

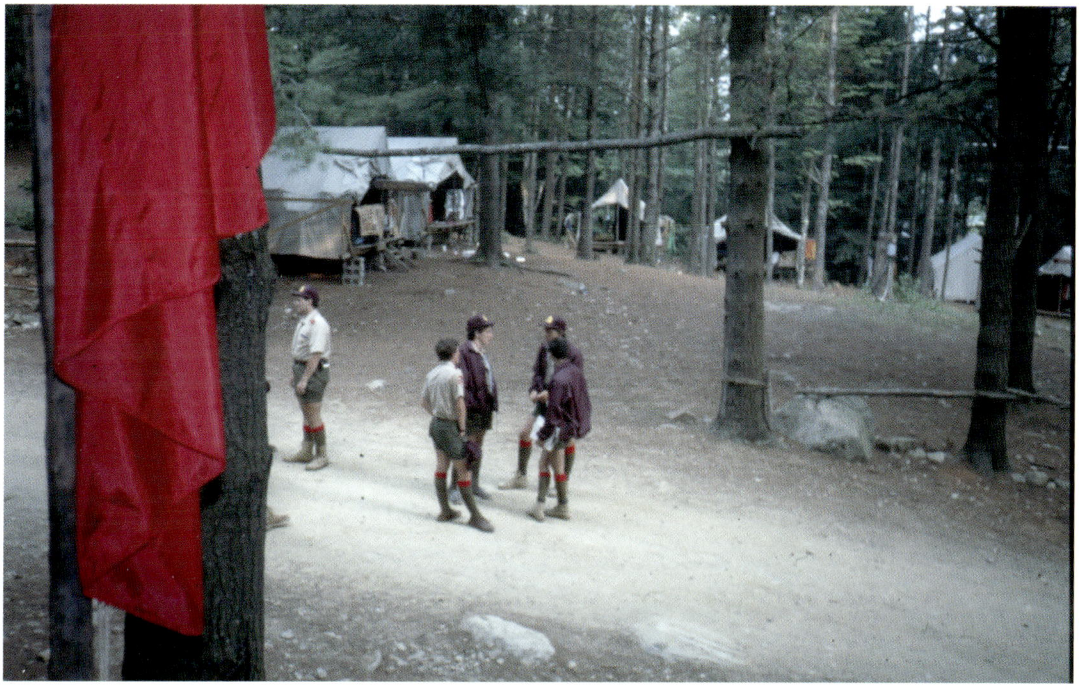

PARTNERSHIPS: To fill T. L. Storer to its capacity, a series of partnerships and shared camping agreements were established. For over a decade, Wild Goose became the camp for Scouts from the North Bay Council, BSA that had closed its own camps in favor of this partnership. In addition to Scouting partnerships, there have been several used by non-Scouting groups as well. In 2018, a new type of partnership was established for Troop and Crew 1787. ARKanum Summer Camp is the result of a joint effort between the Spirit of Adventure Council, BSA and the Islamic Society of Boston Cultural Center. This program combines regular BSA summer camp activities with faith-based instruction.

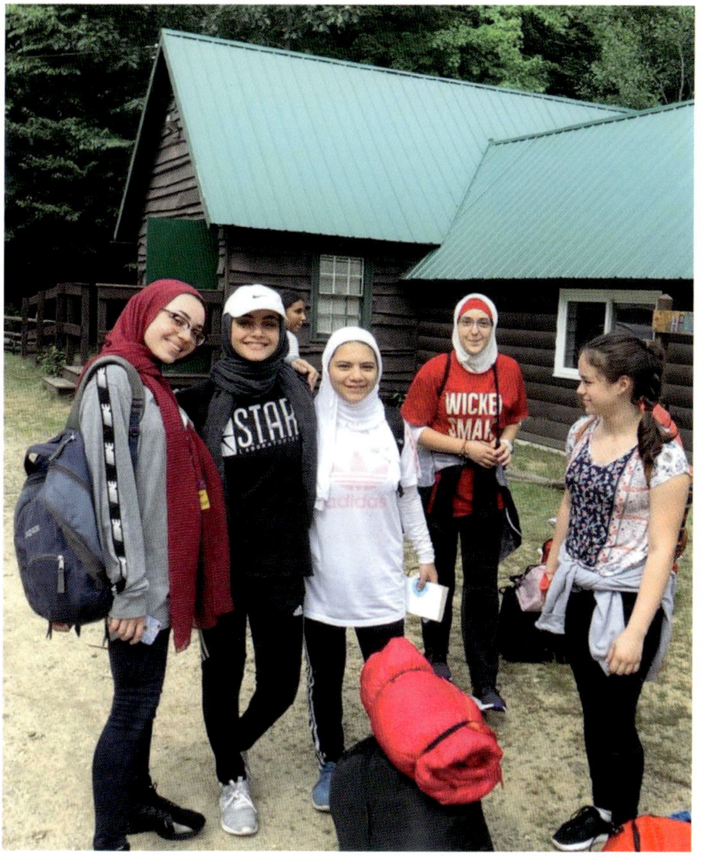

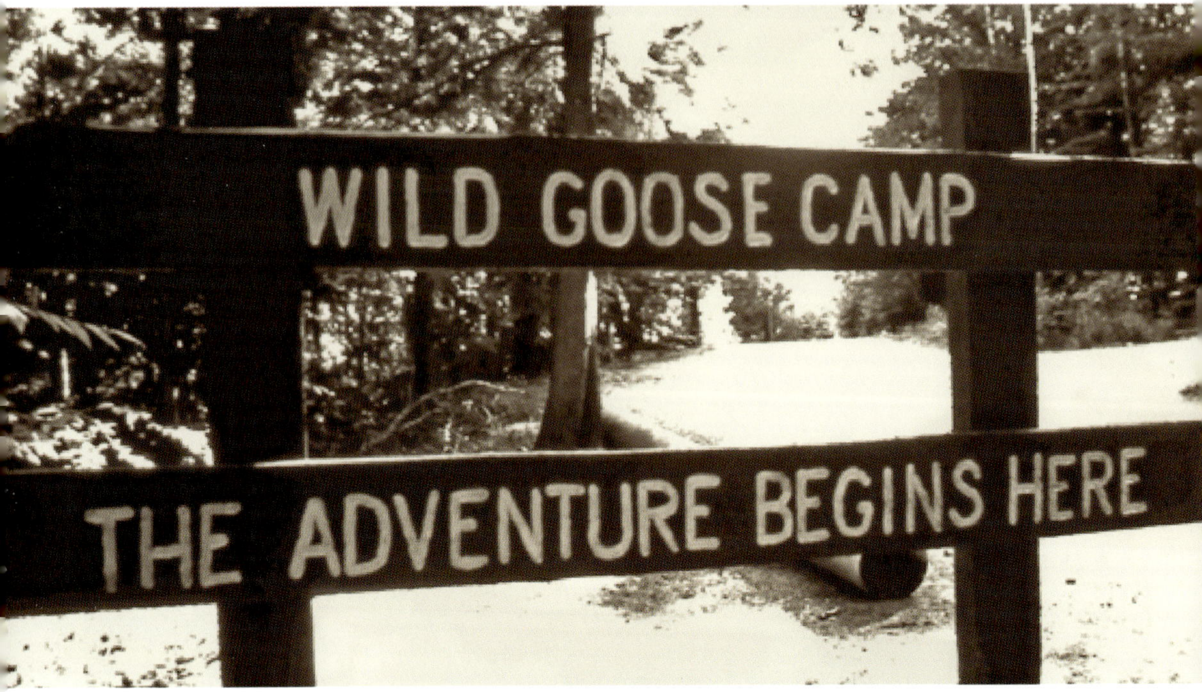

Adventure Begins: Many camps use the words, "The Adventure Begins Here," to designate the starting point that something big is ahead. At T. L. Storer Wild Goose was the "big adventure" program. Today that theme includes the climbing and ropes course areas.

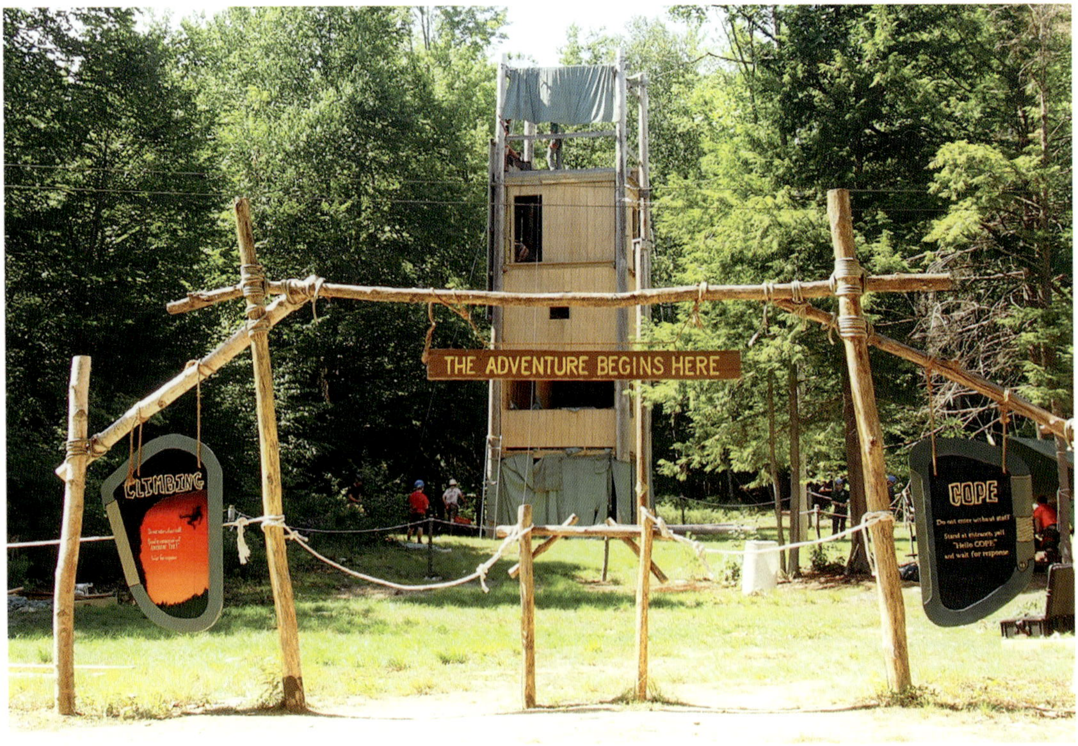

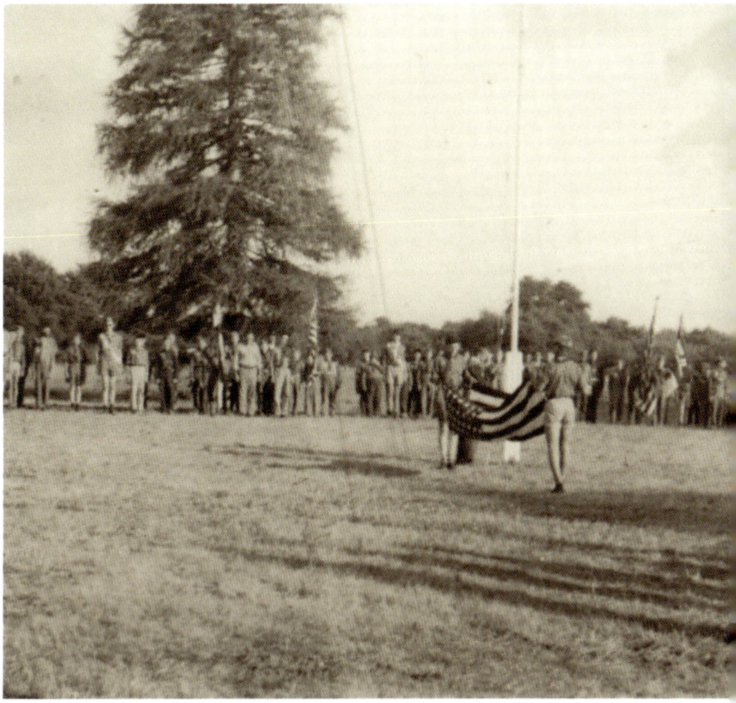

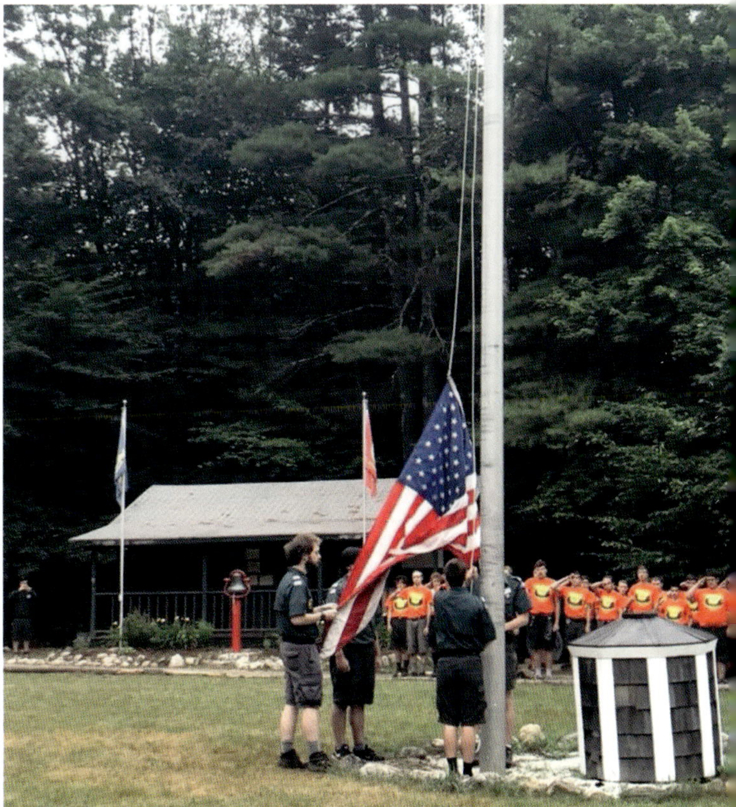

Evening Flag Lowering: At Loon Pond in the 1950s and continuing today at T. L. Storer, Scouts lower the flag before retiring for the evening meal. It remains a symbol of the Boy Scout's commitment of citizenship training. Scouting remains politically and ethnically diverse. At camp young people live in an environment that inspires active productive citizens.

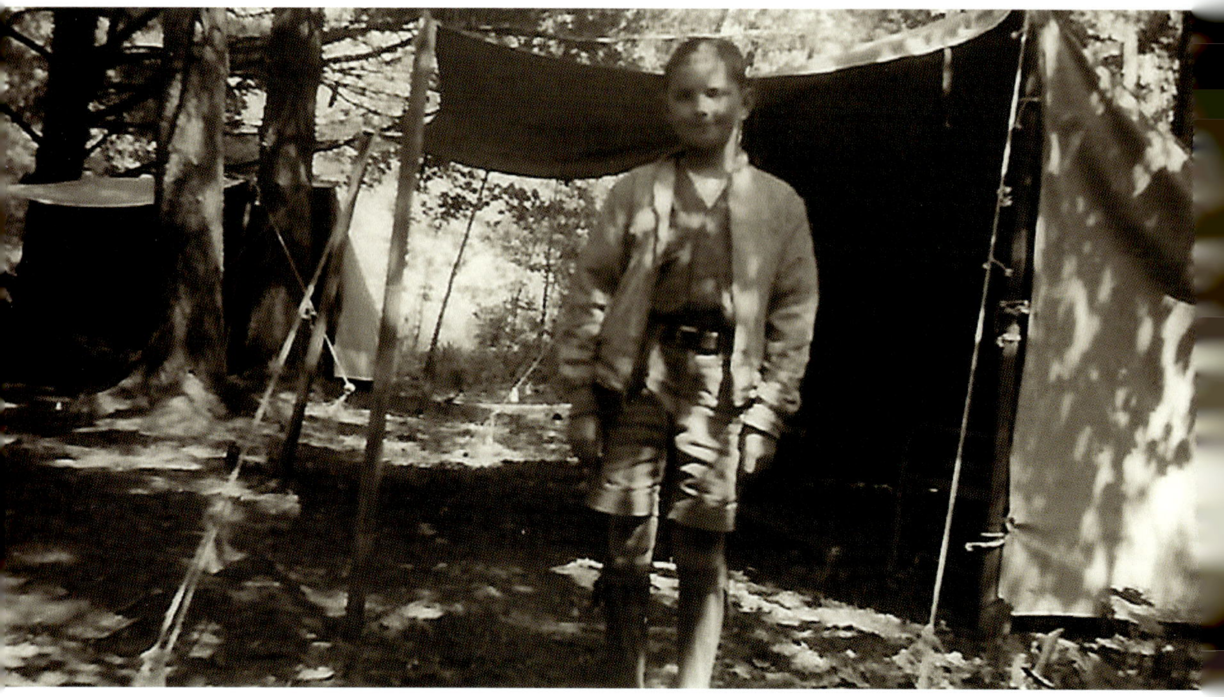

STORER CAMP LIFE: One of the most notable changes in camp life is family participation. In the 1960s most Scouts went off to camp on their own. In the last decade there has been a significant increase in Scouts attending camp with their parents. Adult leaders are predominantly the parents of the youth in the troop. The environment of Scout camp allows families to share the experience without digital and other distractions. In a time when families can be overwhelmed and rushed, the power of these simple experiences cannot be understated or undervalued.

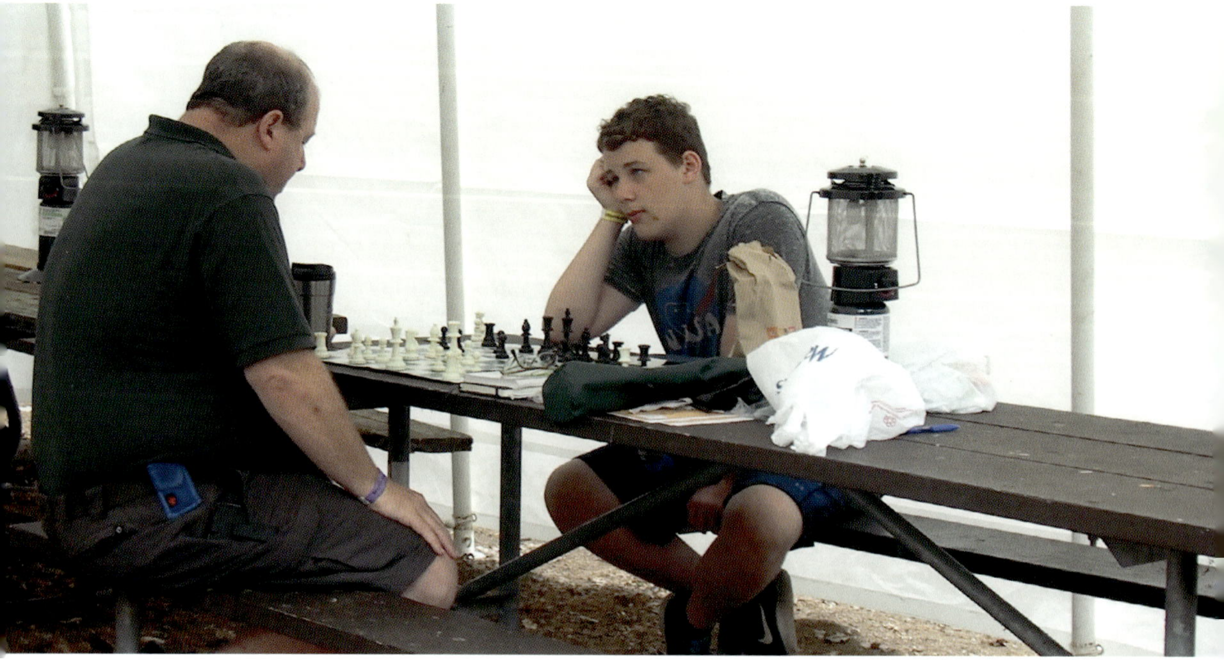

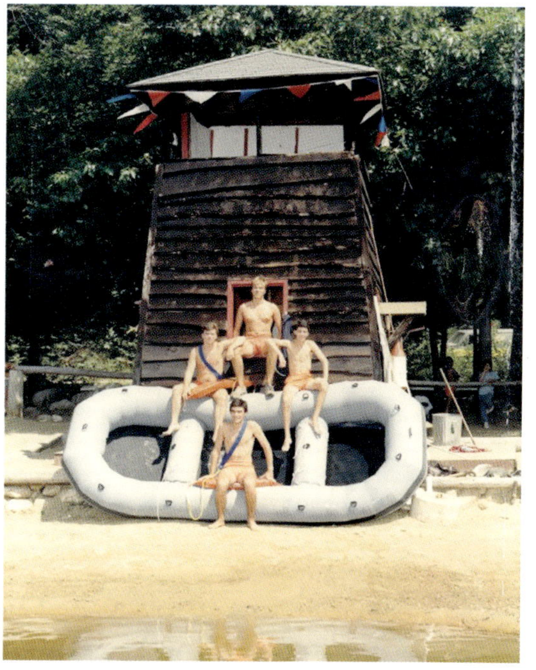

ADAMS POND WATERFRONT TOWER: On the shores of Adams Pond is a distinctive building, the Tower, that is the base for Aquatic Staff. Aquatics is the most popular summer camp activity. Scouts learn to swim, paddle and row. Water activities are a relief from a hot summer's day and an adventure unto themselves.

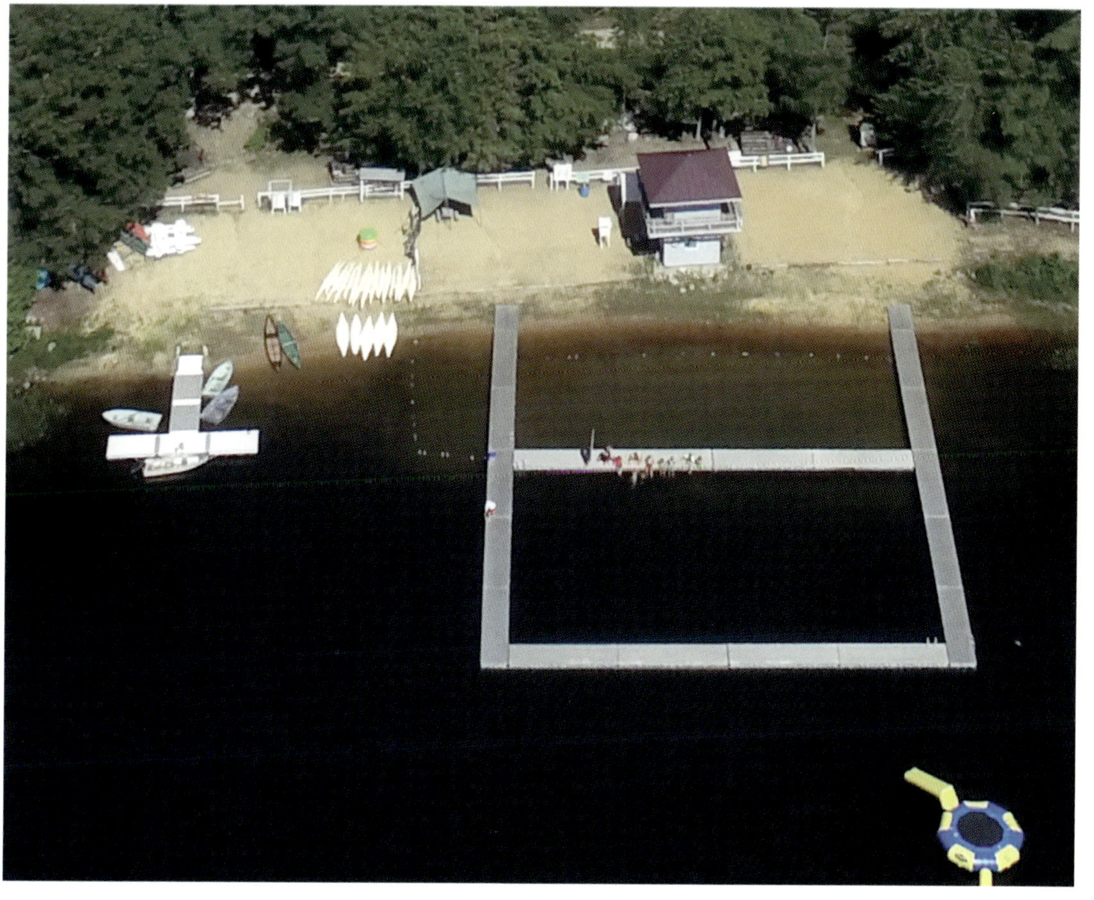

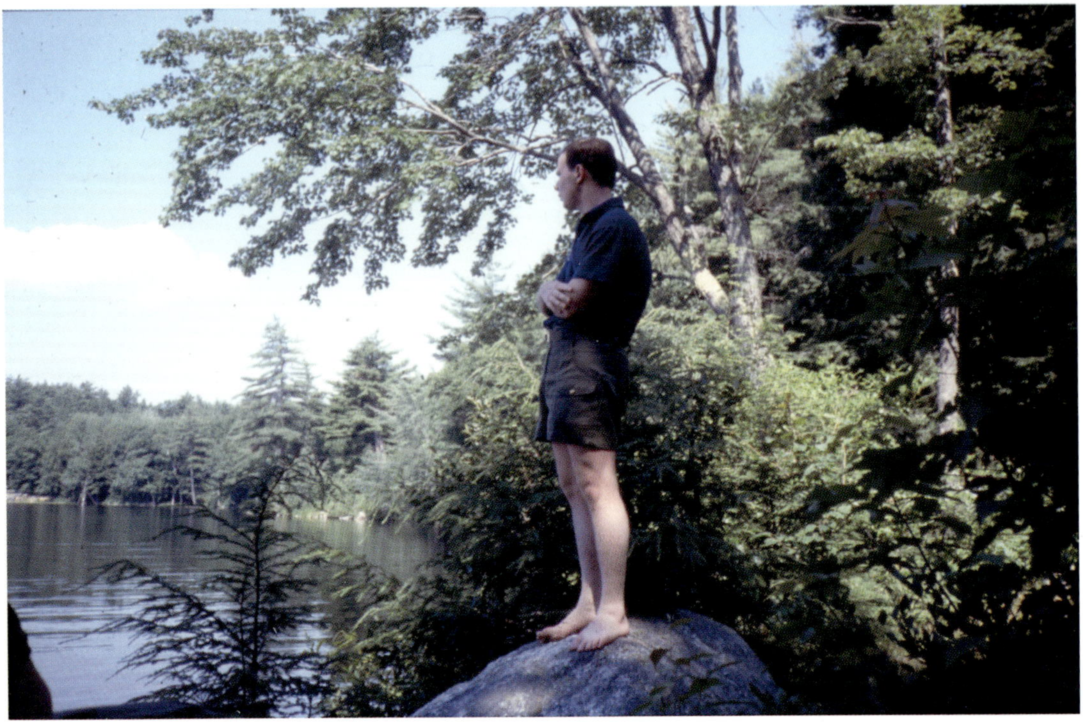

REFLECTIONS IN NATURE: The natural beauty of southern New Hampshire gives children and young adults the opportunity for introspection. One appeal of T. L. Storer is to escape the confines of urban and suburban life. Each year at T. L. Storer hundreds of Scouts slow down to take in the world around them.

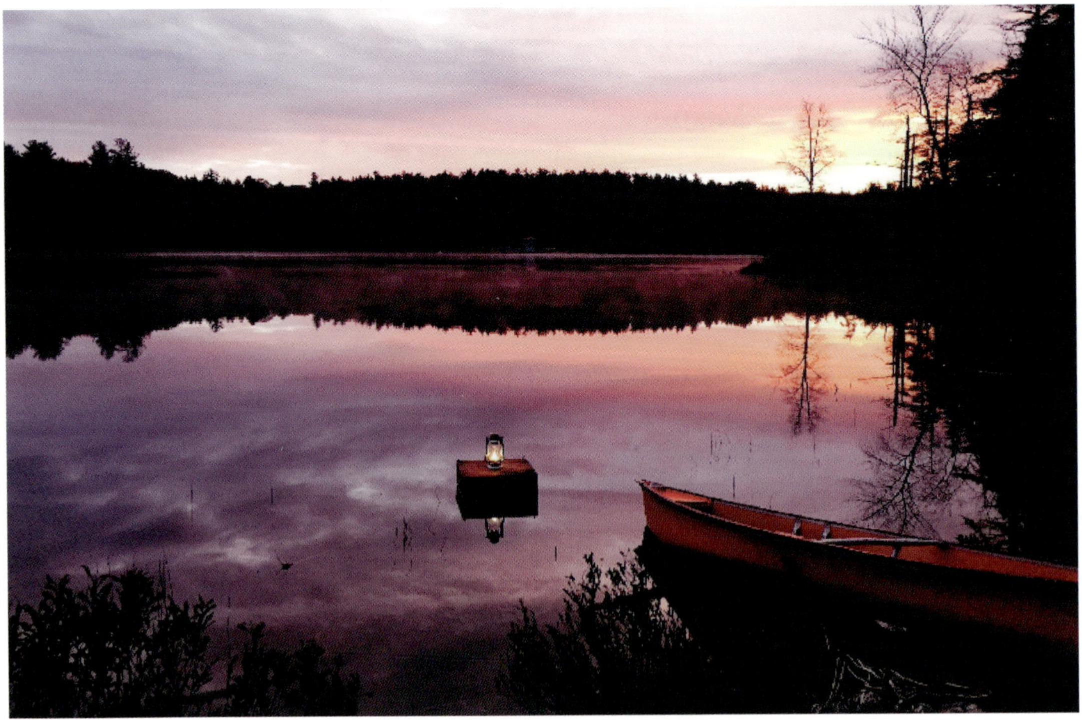

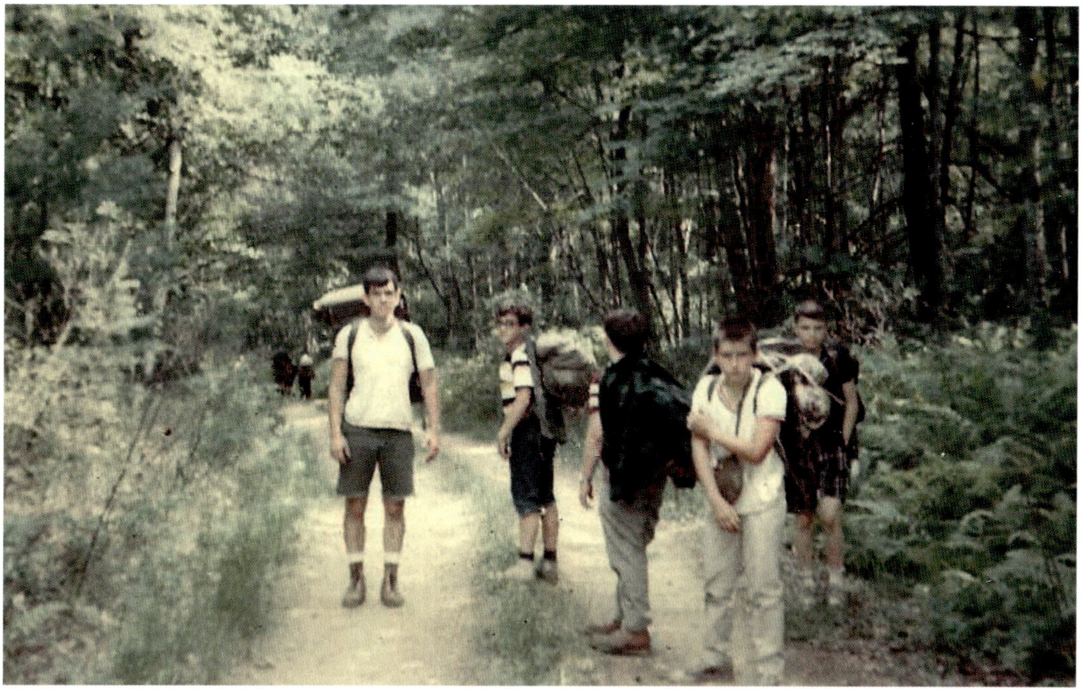

FOLLOWING THE TRAILS: Hiking is a staple of any summer camp experience. To a young person in a unique wooded environment, the idea of seeing were the trail leads has timeless appeal. Mark Twain wrote in *The Adventures of Tom Sawyer*, "There comes a time in every rightly constructed boy's life when he has a raging desire to go somewhere and dig for hidden treasure." This is still true today.

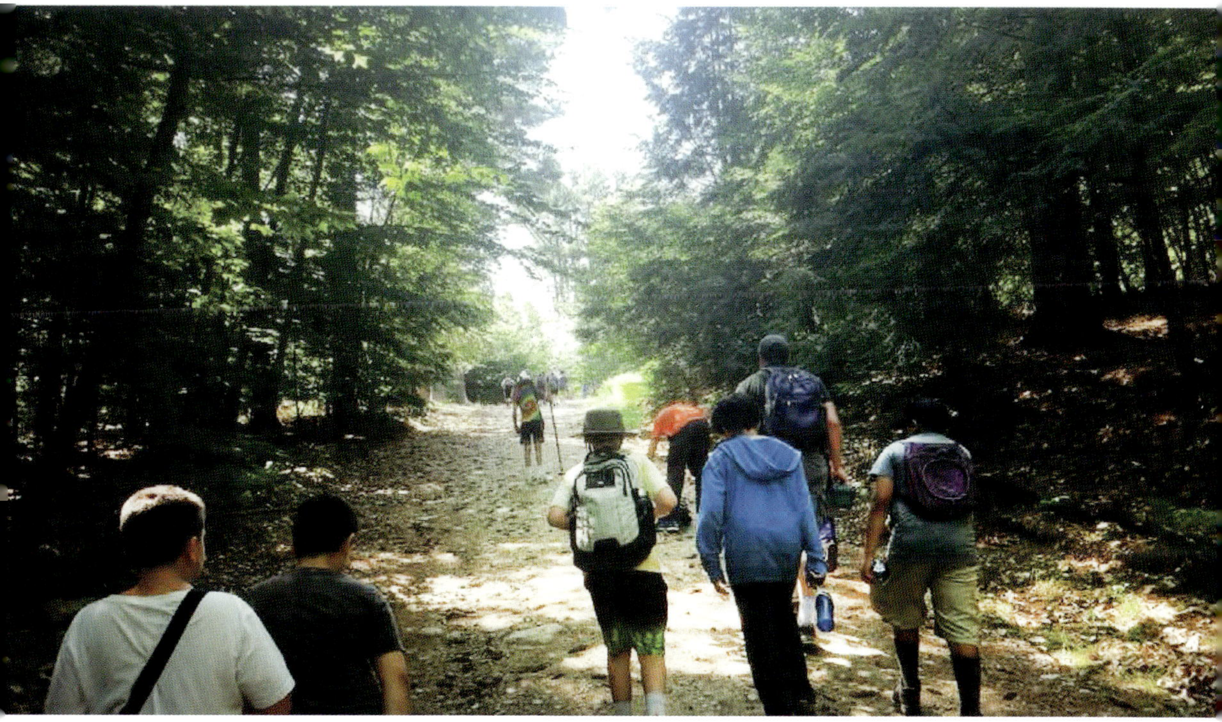

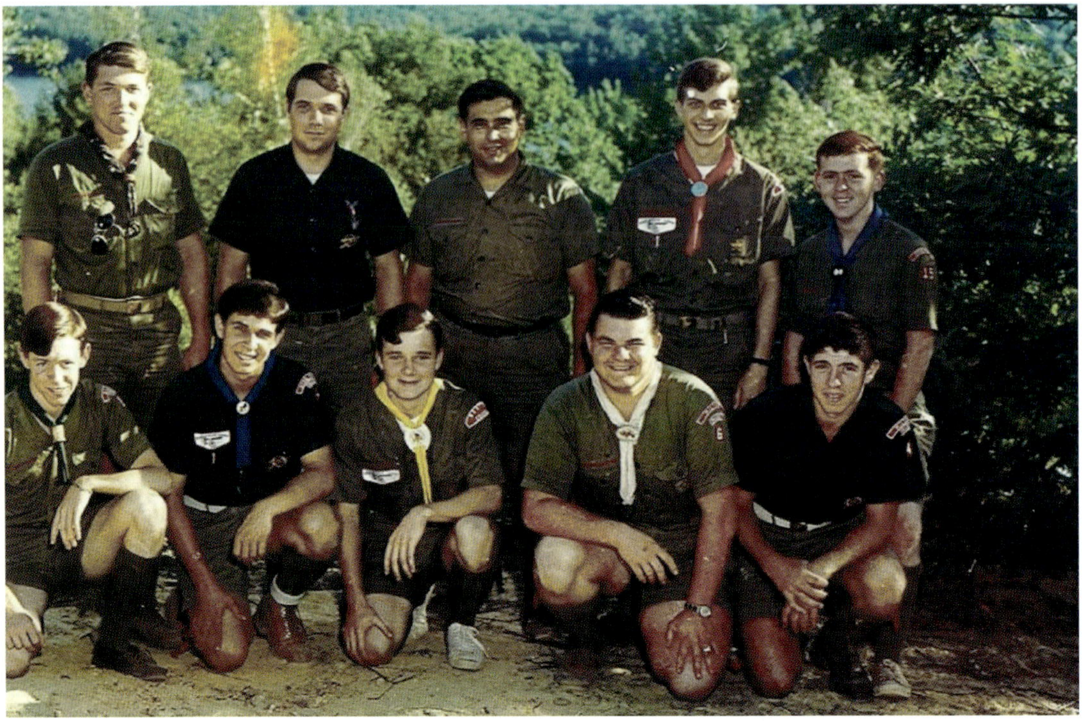

ADVENTURERS FOR OLDER YOUTH: Summer camp adventures come in all sizes and are directed to all age groups. T. L. Storer's proximity to several small mountains provide just such an adventure. The challenge of the high ropes course brings the adventure right onto the reservation.

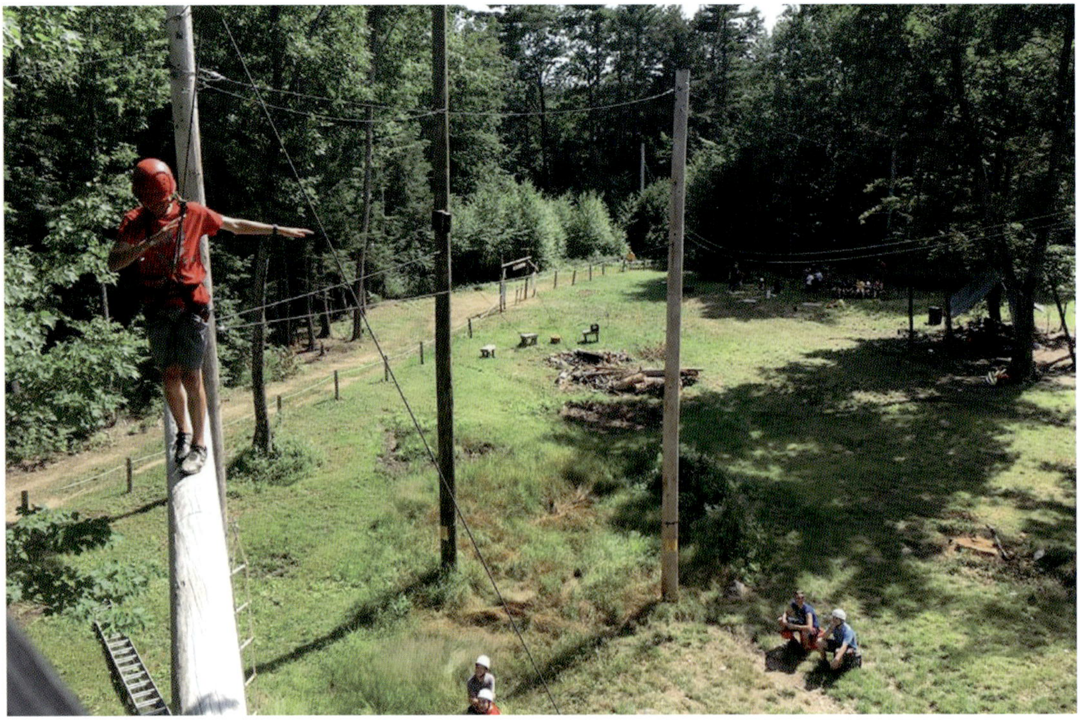

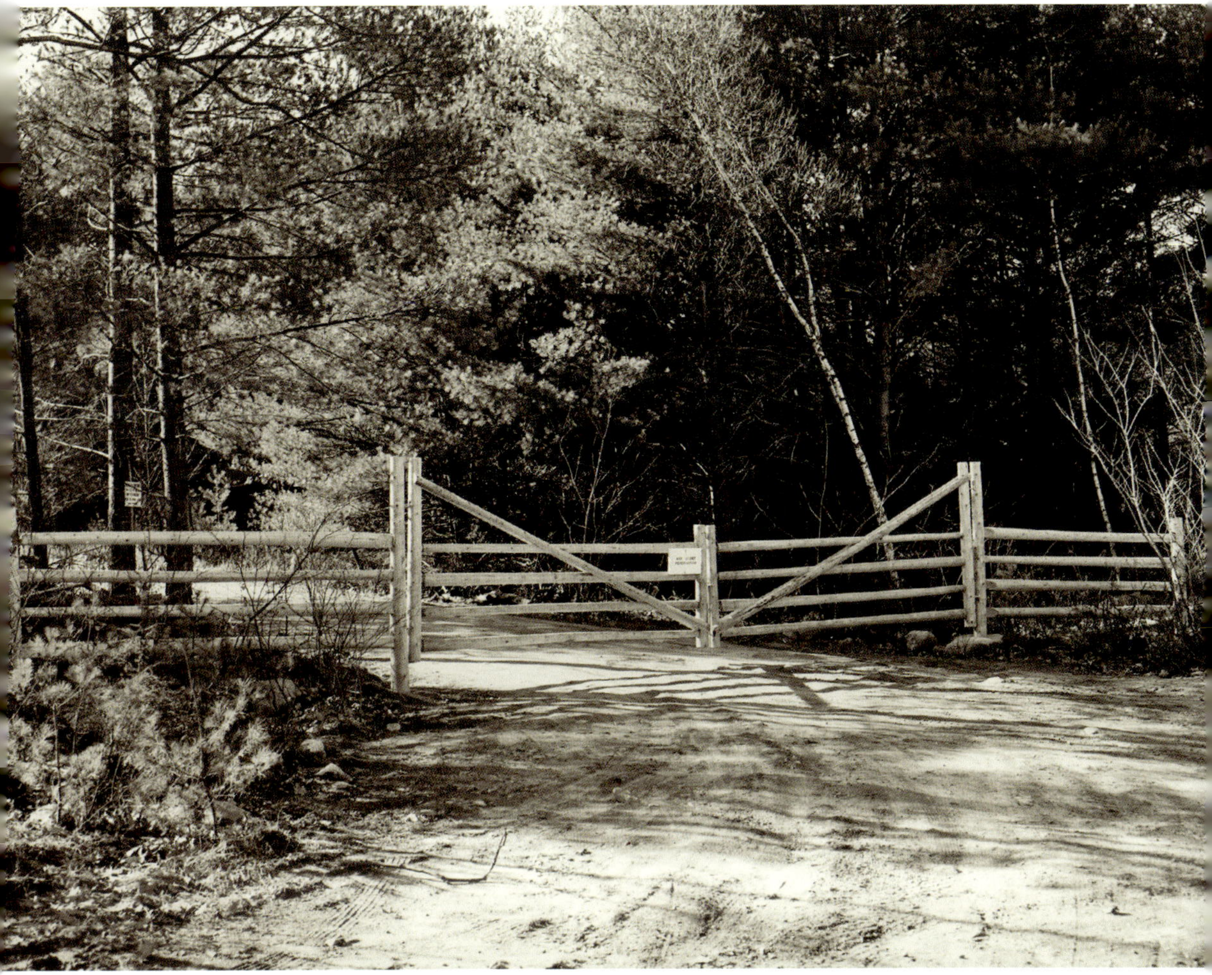

THROUGH THE GATE: The original gateway to Adams Pond Camp in 1958 is shown above. In the sixty years that have passed, thousands of young people have been deeply impacted by what lies beyond this fence. Each year hundreds of Alumni return to T. L. Storer to remember their time here and to make improvements for those who have yet to pass this way.

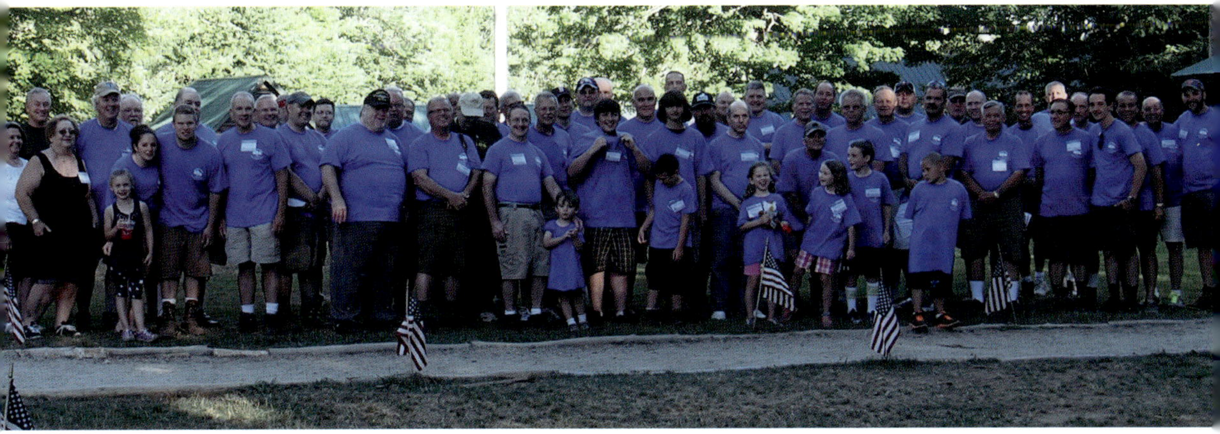

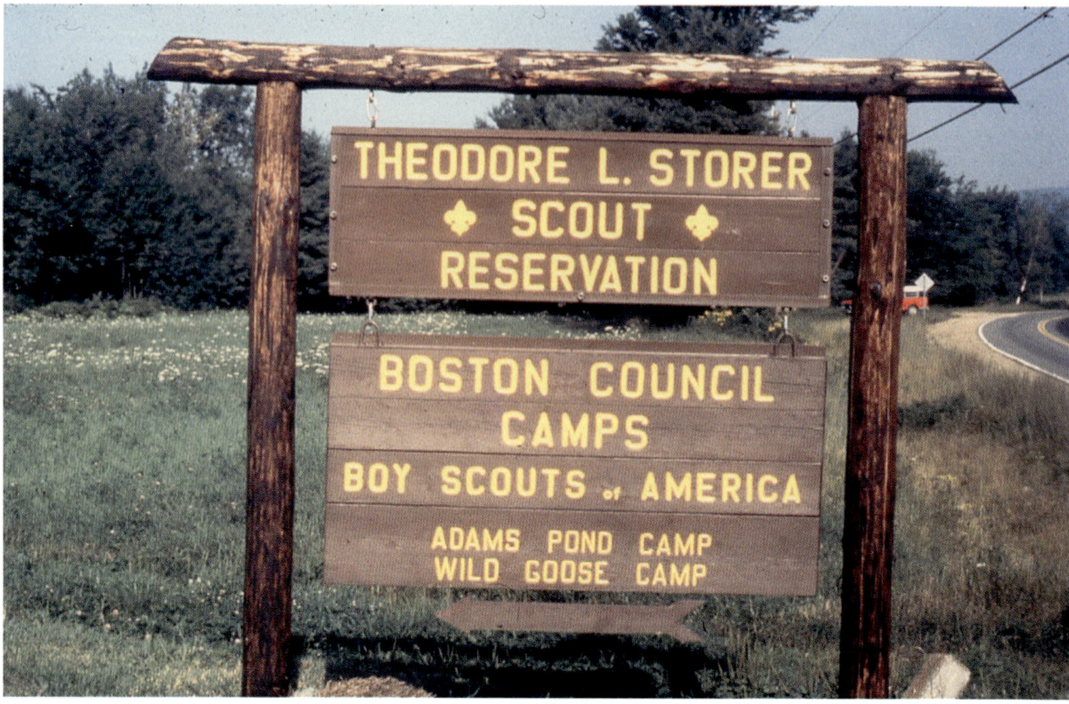

ADAPTING TO CHANGING TIMES: With the decrease in the number of troops and a decline in BSA membership, the goal of T. L. Storer to become a large-scale camp remains elusive. Efforts are underway to adapt the camp in a way that meets the needs and expectations of today's youth and families. Increasingly it will become a matter of quality vs. quantity. T. L. Storer's vast natural features and facilities can be adapted to create a sustainable growing program.

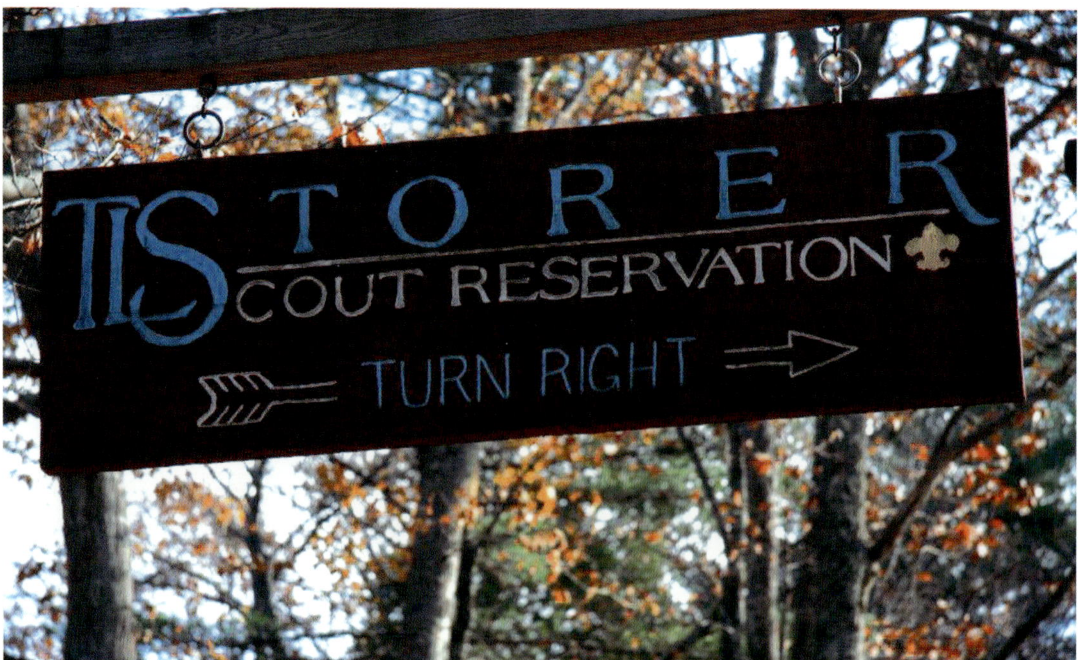

CHAPTER 7

WAH-TUT-CA SCOUT RESERVATION

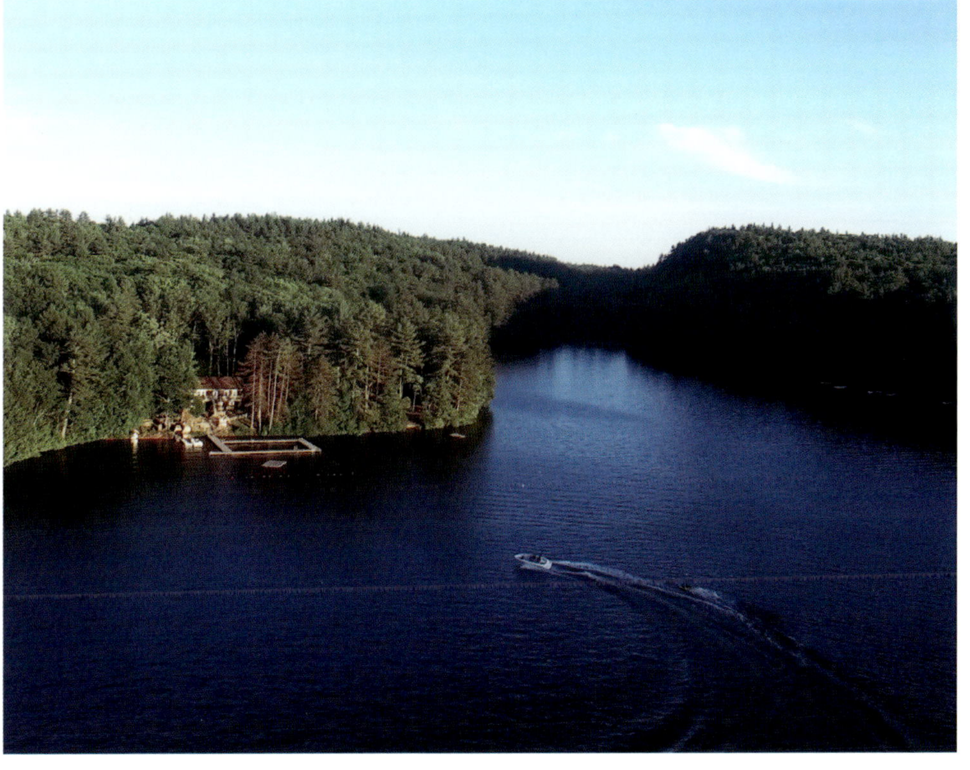

WAH-TUT-CA SCOUT RESERVATION—NORTHWOOD, NH: In 1936, members of the Greater Lowell Council, BSA were dissatisfied with their 11-acre trolley camp. Camp Chadwick was on rented land in Dunstable, MA. It had excellent attendance, but the simple parade field in the outskirts of Lowell, MA did not measure up to what these men thought a Boy Scout camp could be. They found that site in Northwood, NH. In the 1936 Greater Lowell Council BSA Annual Report, camping chairman Charles A. Hosmer described the Northwood site as a place for "voyages of discovery where young people can eagerly search for what is over there."

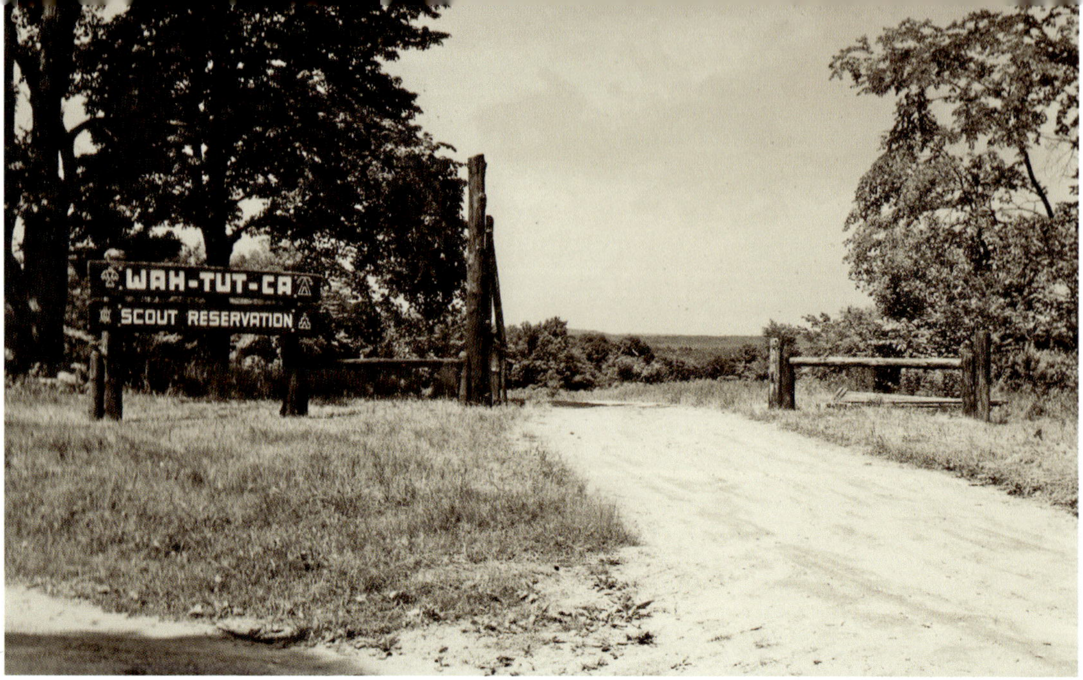

WELCOME HOME: Wah-Tut-Ca Scout Reservation was built to feel like you were home. This is expressed more clearly on the current entrance sign with the words "Welcome Home." It doesn't matter if it is someone's first time or if it is their fifth decade at Wah-Tut-Ca—everyone belongs and is invited to choose their own personal adventure.

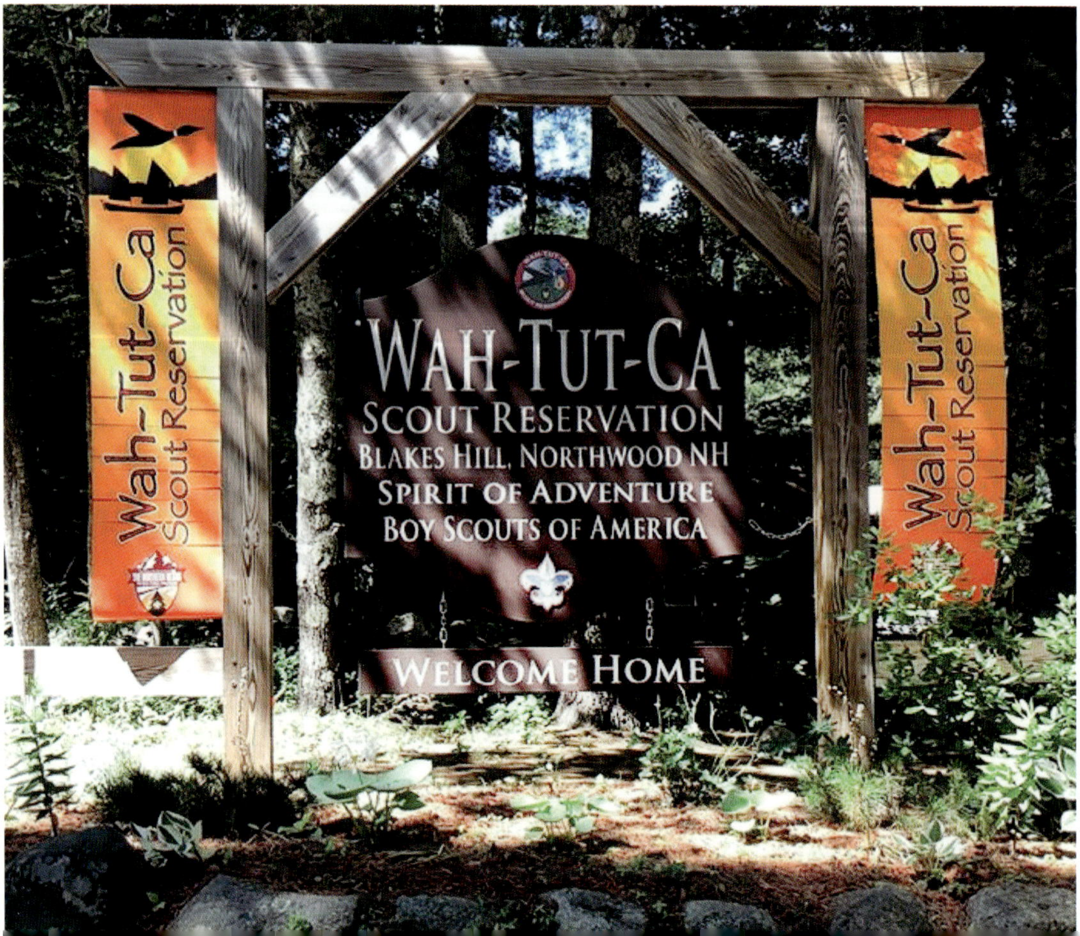

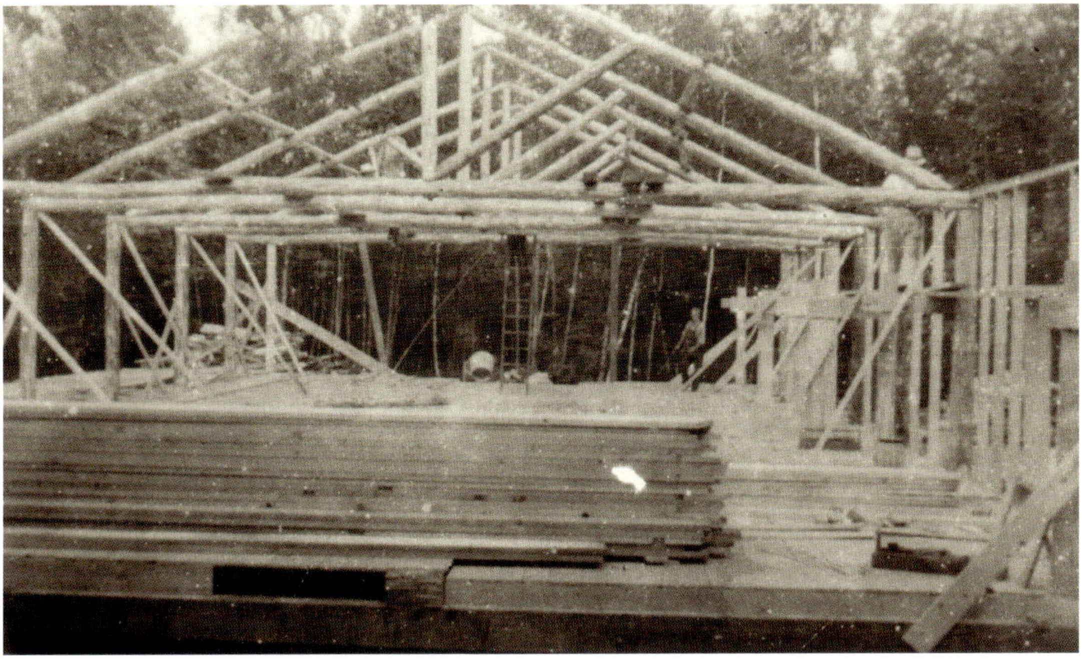

HANDMADE CAMP: During the height of the Great Depression, over 500 volunteers moved several of the buildings, board by board, from Camp Chadwick to the Northwood, NH site. A team of 500 volunteers from Lowell, MA undertook the daunting task of moving sixteen buildings sixty miles. They also built a new dining hall out of the red pines that stood on the Northwood site (pictured above). The handmade dining hall was built with top-notch craftsmanship that set the standard for hardworking, dedicated volunteers to come. The tradition continues today and in 2018 five new cabins for campers were built. These cabins are for campers who stay multiple weeks on the reservation.

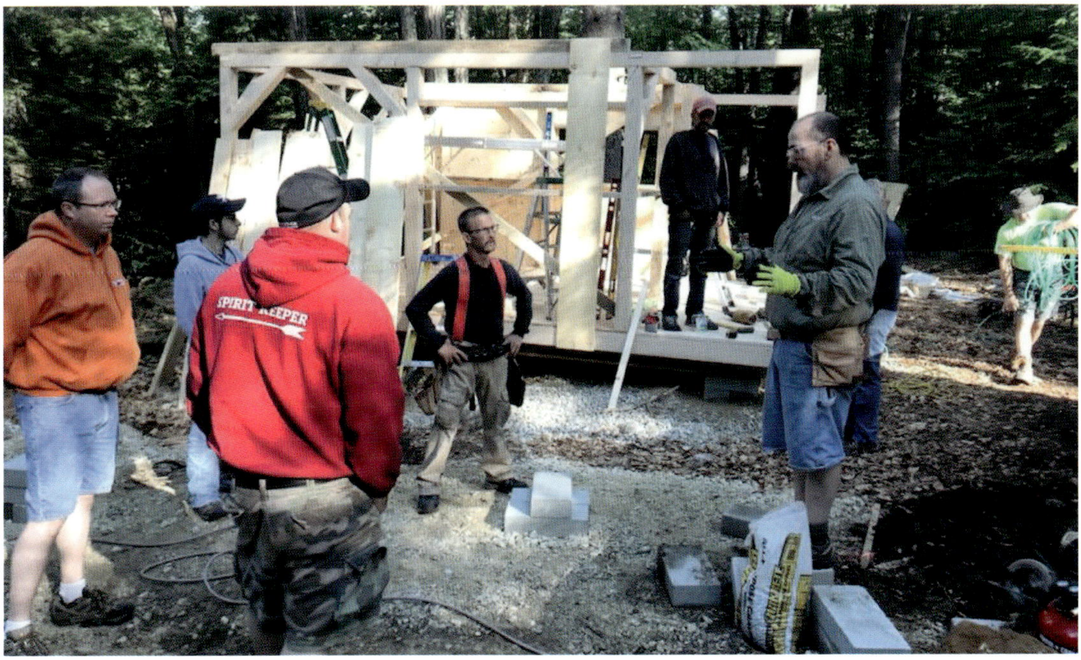

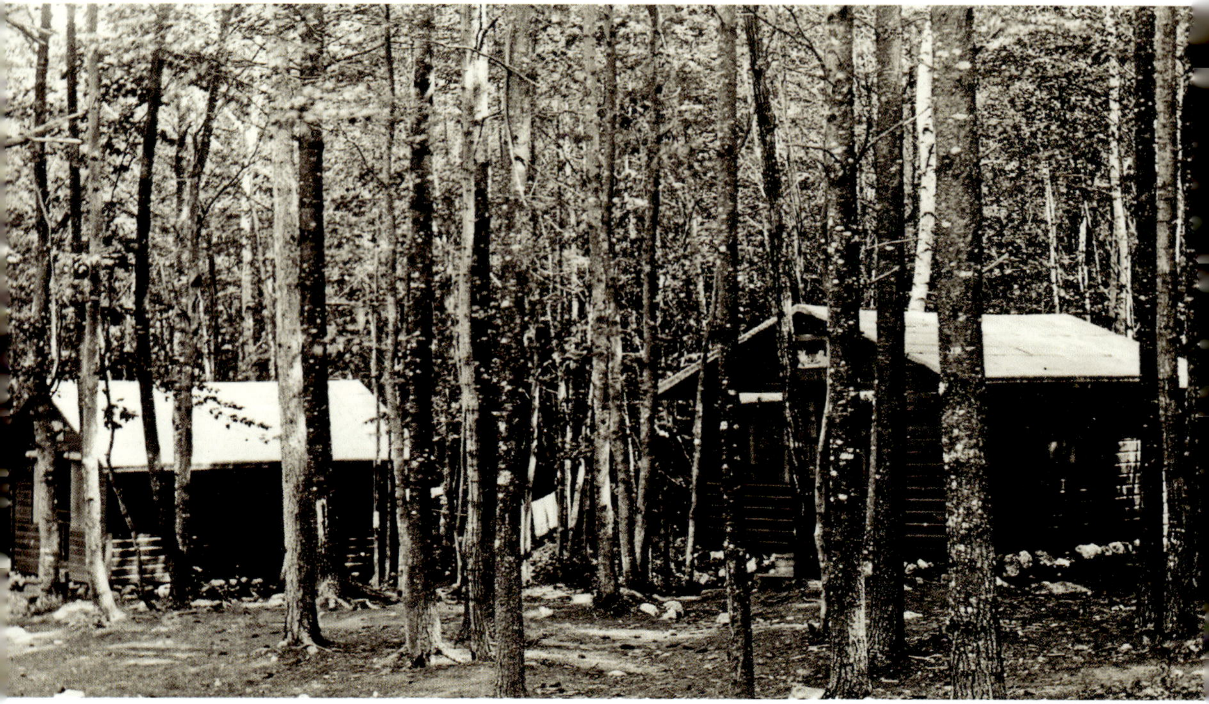

The Past Is Prologue: Pictured above is Wah-Tut-Ca's junior camp, So-Key-Tay. Scouts stayed in small four- to ten-person cabins. That type of housing was revived in 2018 with the building of the Shanawanda village. The new housing is directed to Scouts who go to camp without their troop and encourages them to stay for a whole or half summer during the camping season.

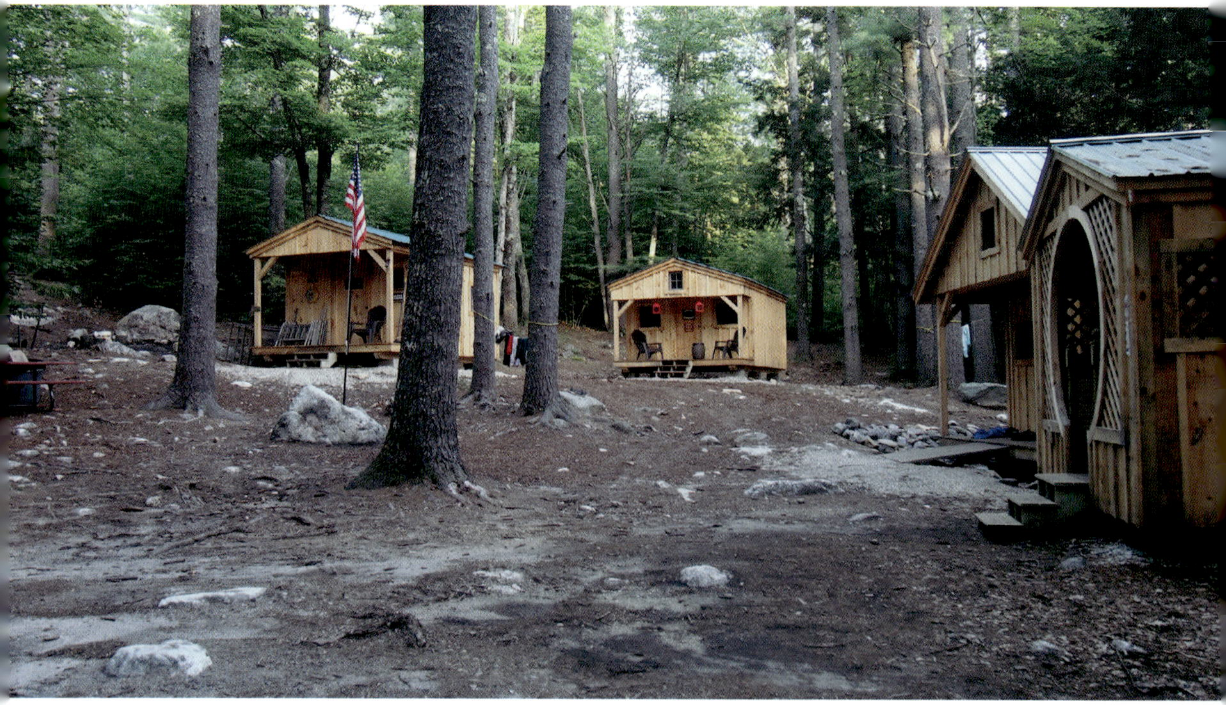

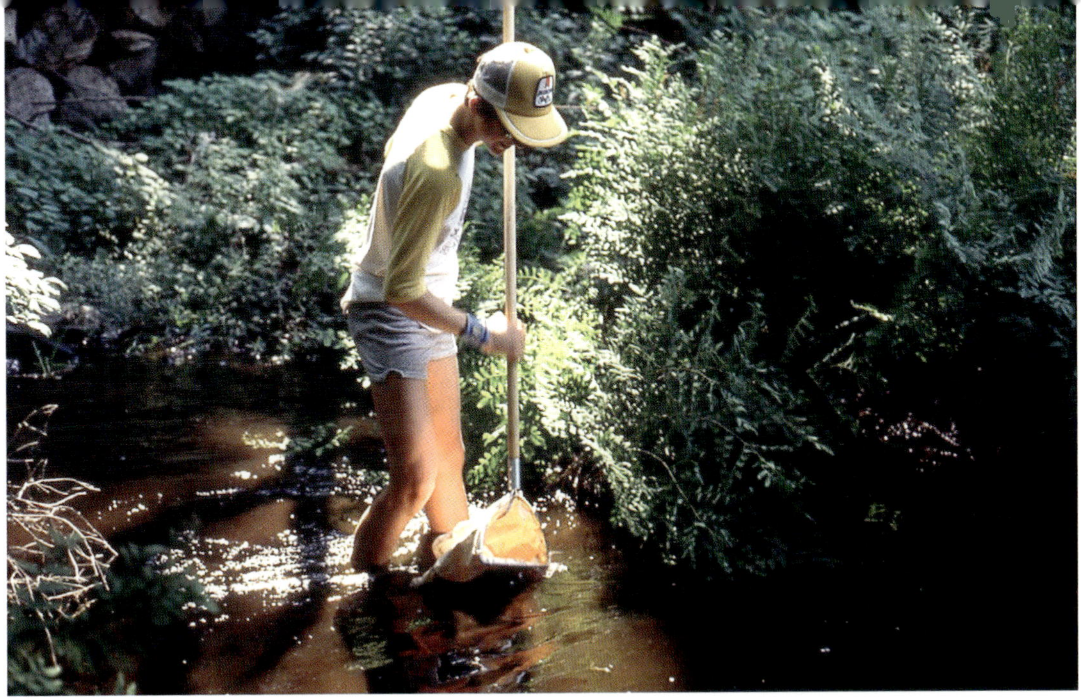

WATSON'S WEALD: Wah-Tut-Ca is a unique ecologically diverse property that has been studied for generations. Watson's Weald is 180 acres of wetlands within Wah-Tut-Ca Scout Reservation that is a thriving and undisturbed ecosystem. Four streams wind through cliffs and ancient trees while high-basin vernal pools accumulate in the expansive backwoods. The efforts of campers and staff to study and research this nature culminated with the USDA Wetlands Easement in 2011. The easement protects forever more than half of the Camp's property. The land is now used as a natural outdoor ecological laboratory.

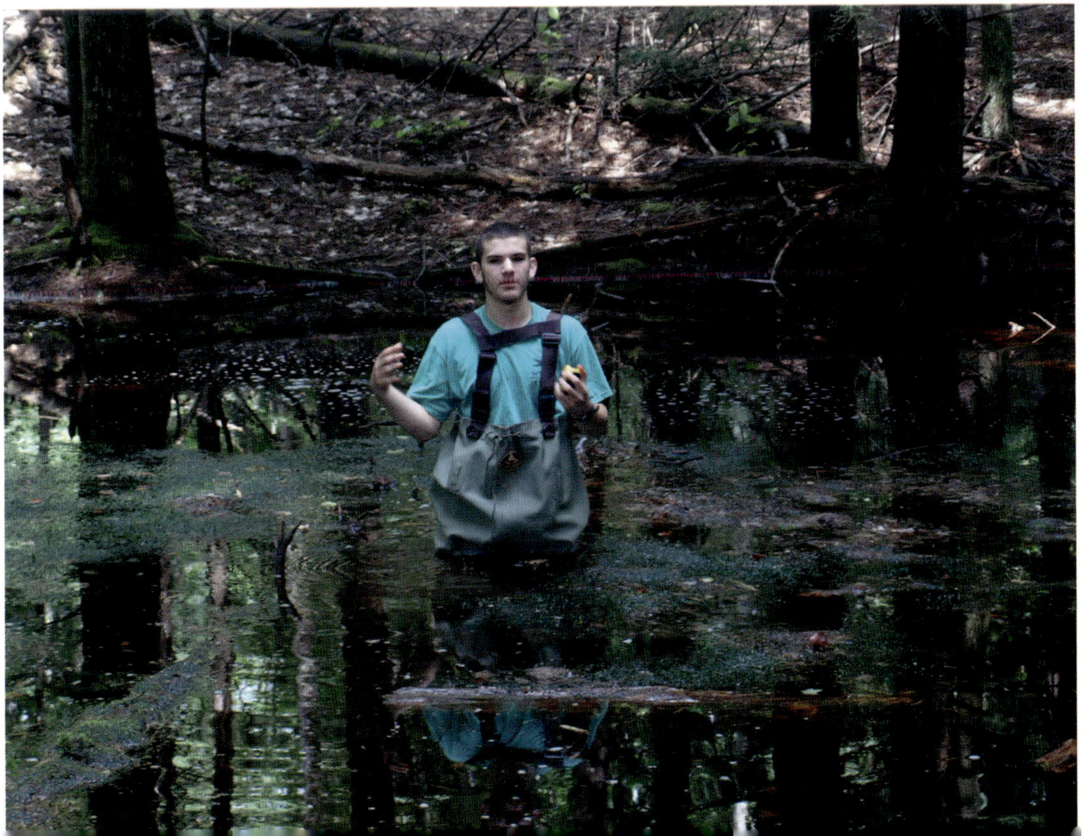

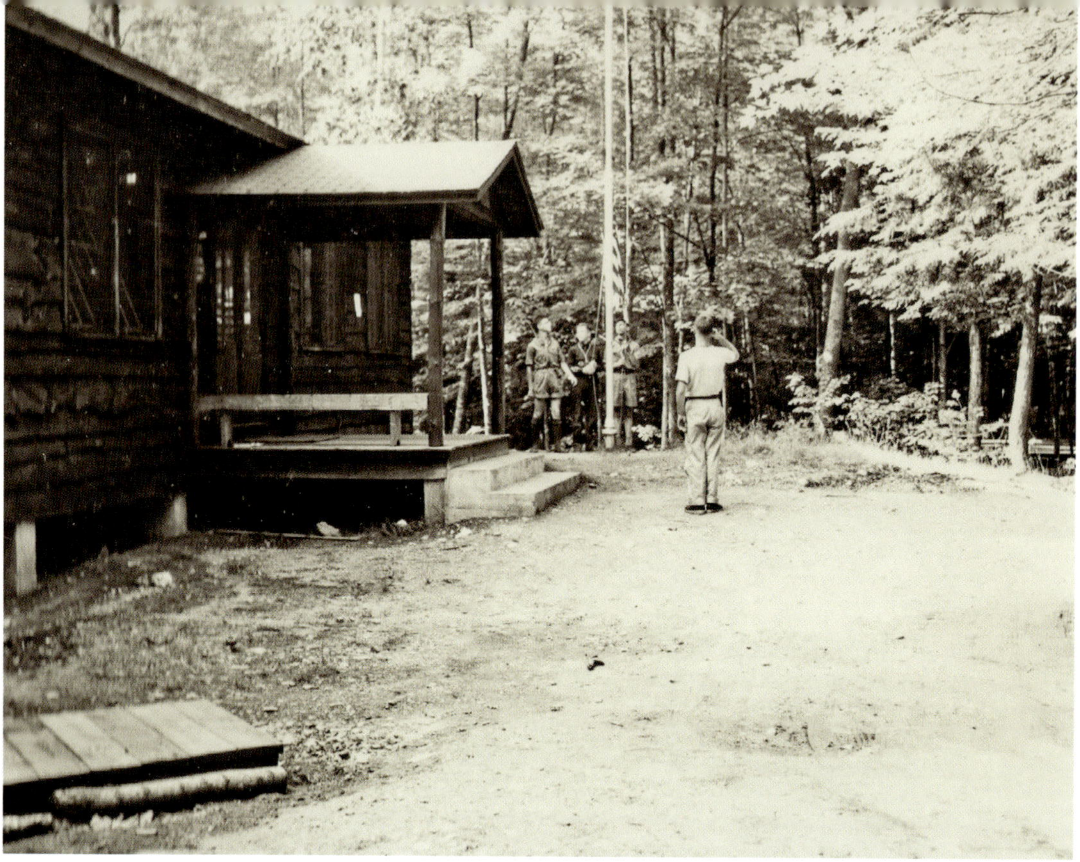

OATH & LAW: Understanding how to be a better citizen is at the core of the Scout Oath and Law. Boy Scout camps provide an opportunity to learn and demonstrate those values daily. It is a place where young people can become leaders, test their own abilities and strive to catch a higher vision.

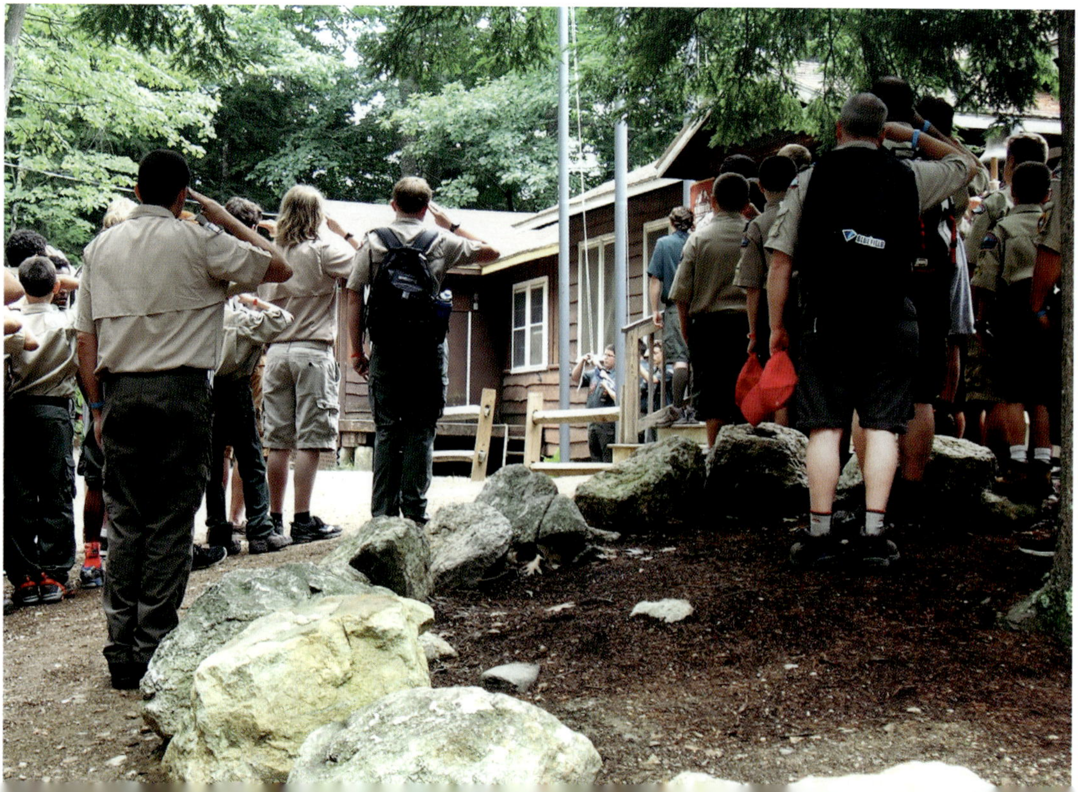

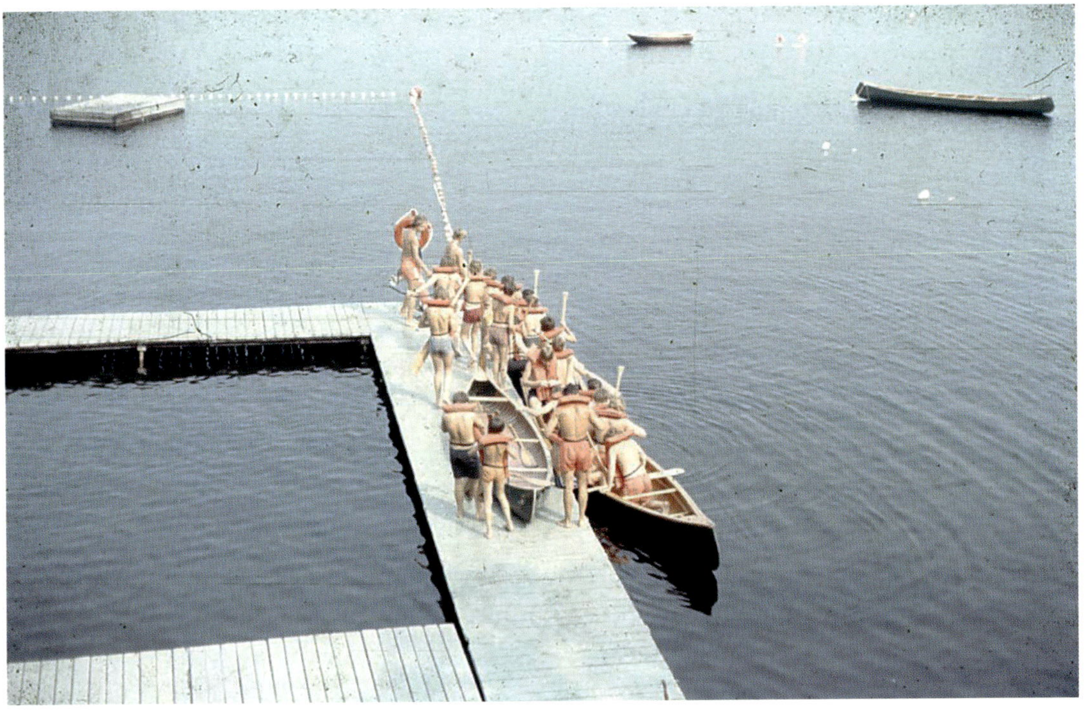

THE TEN-MANS: Three Chestnut ten-man canoes were brought to Wah-Tut-Ca in the late 1950s. Like the Craig Ryder Whaleboat, these canoes are one of the signature adventures experienced by three generations of campers and staff. After almost six decades of service, the canoes were rendered unusable from wear. In 2018 they were completely restored to their original manufactured condition and once again are ferrying Scouts along the length of Northwood Lake.

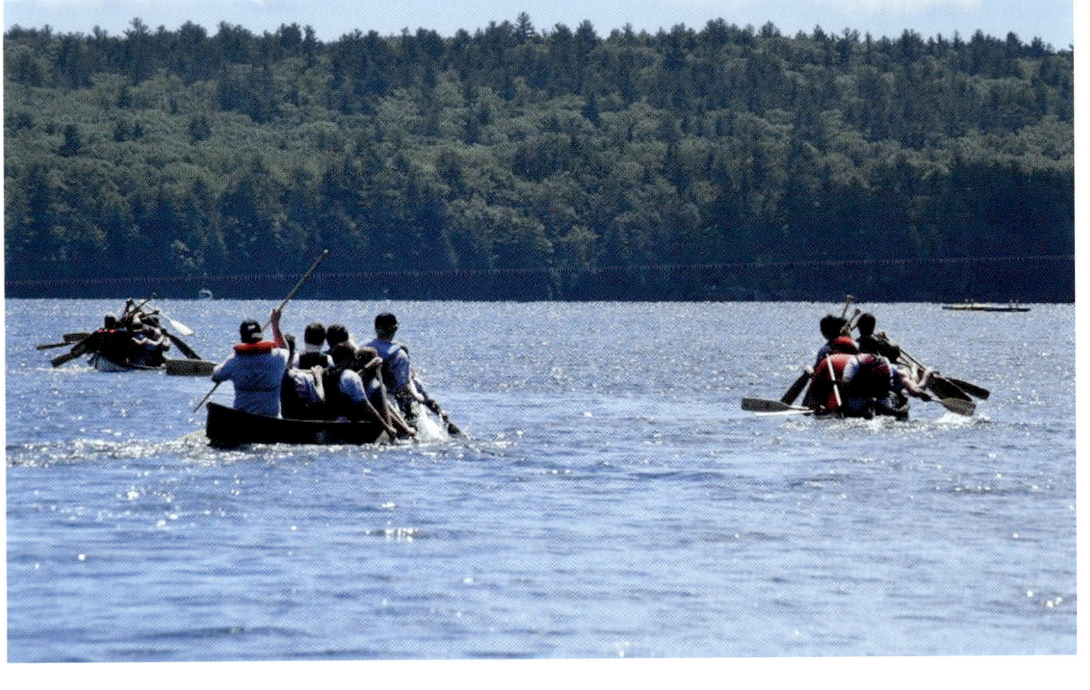

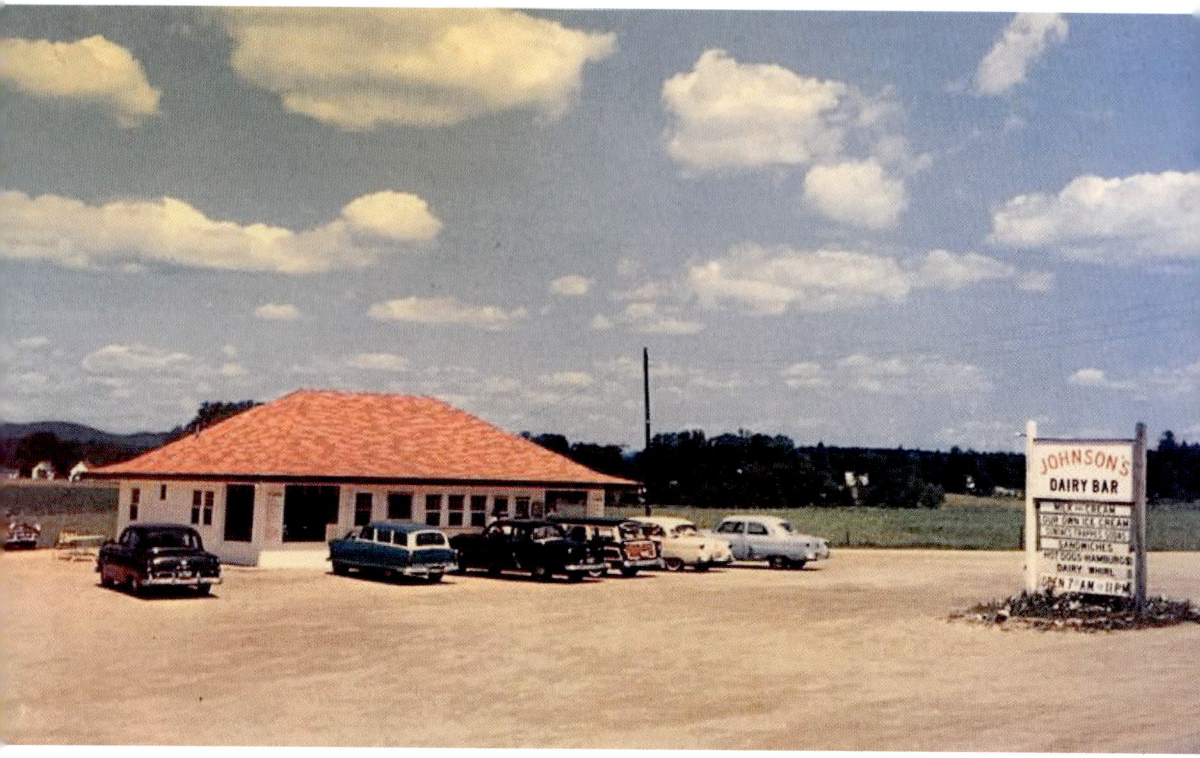

THE DESTINATION—JOHNSON'S DAIRY BAR: Located a mile and a half down Northwood Lake from camp Johnson's Dairy Bar has been the defined goal for water treks across the lake. While campers are always excited by the oversized ice cream portions the value of this experience is something greater. These trips are about the adventurous journey across the big lake. Generation after generation tell their stories about trips to Johnson's.

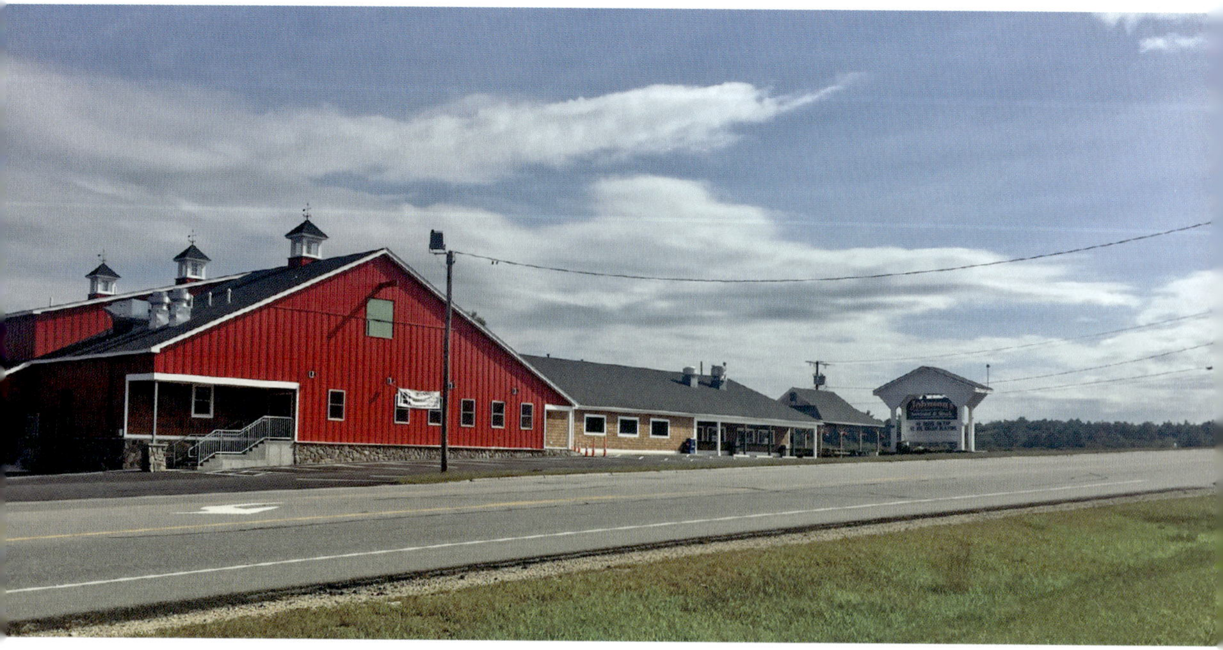

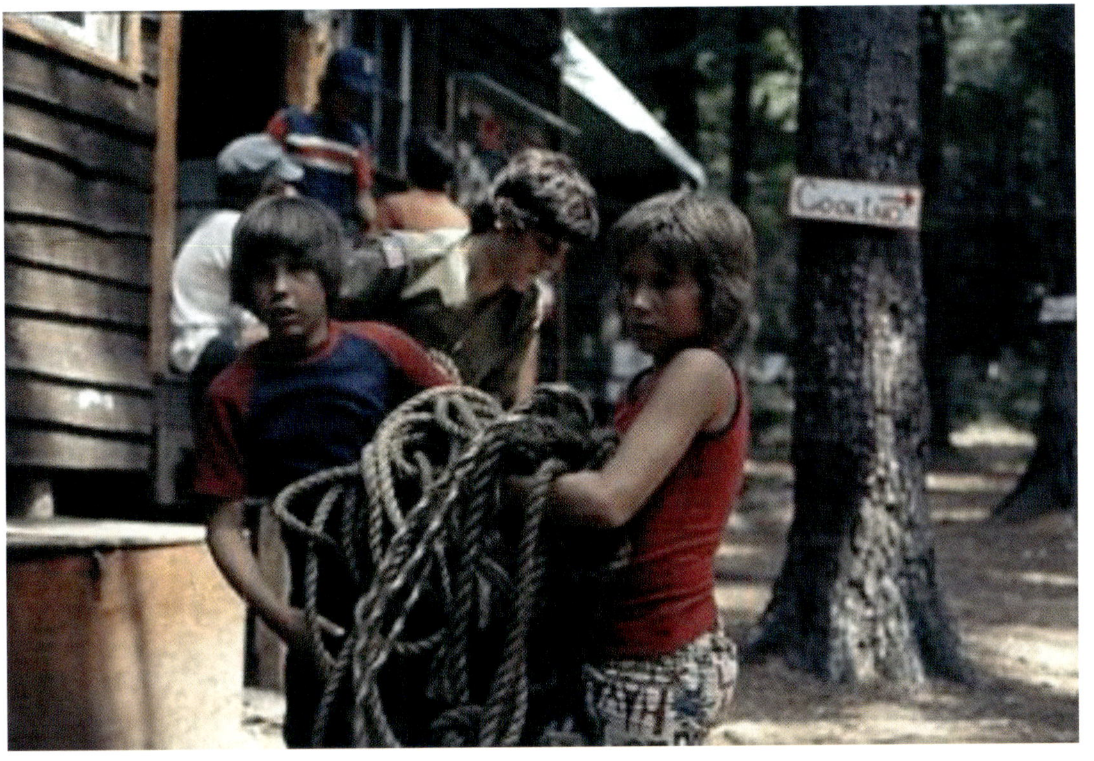

HANDS-ON PROGRAMING: In the 1970s Wah-Tut-Ca developed an open program format that allowed campers to choose their own adventure. The rigid structure of classes with kids sitting at picnic tables gave way so that campers could work at their own pace. Scouts can demonstrate the skills they already know and receive guidance and support on the things they need to learn. For almost half a century the quality of the Wah-Tut-Ca Program has been a hands-on experience for Scouts.

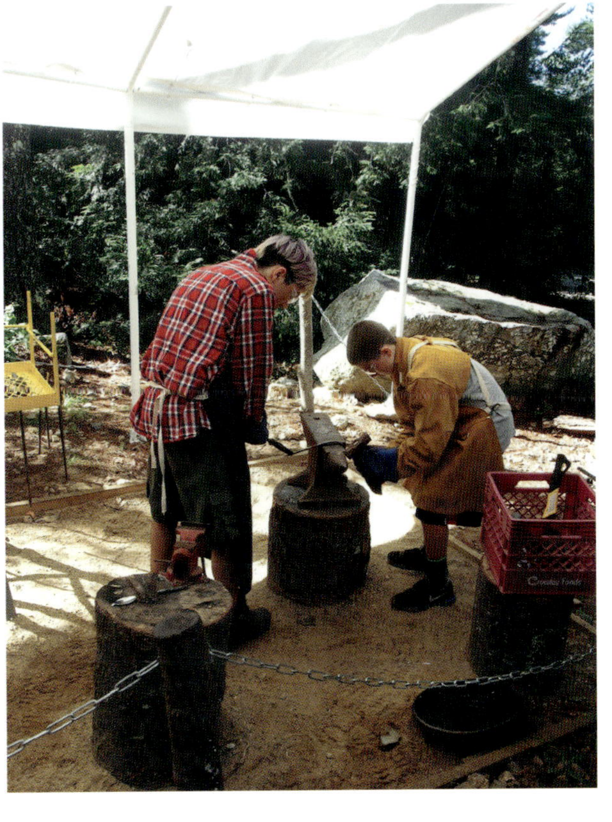

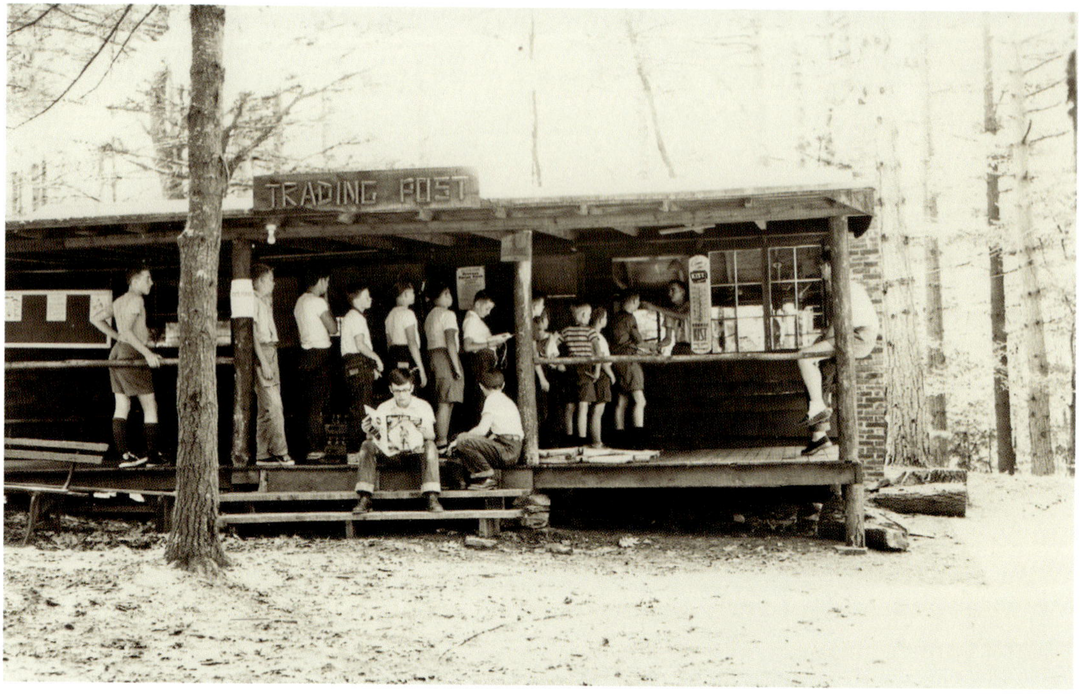

WIRELESS SOCIAL NETWORKING: Wah-Tut-Ca has a central meeting space that serves as a town square. It is a place to gather and trade stories, ideas and plan out special activities. Shown above and below are the two Williams Lodges that were named after the camp's first director, Gordon Williams. These cabins have served dual purposes as both Trading Post and camp Office. This is where people gather to share stories about their day and make plans for the next adventures. Having a central place such as this allows for relationships and life-long friendships to be built. Whether by playing a game of chess, gathering around with a few acoustic guitars, or simply joking around, it plays a major role in team and spirit building at the camp.

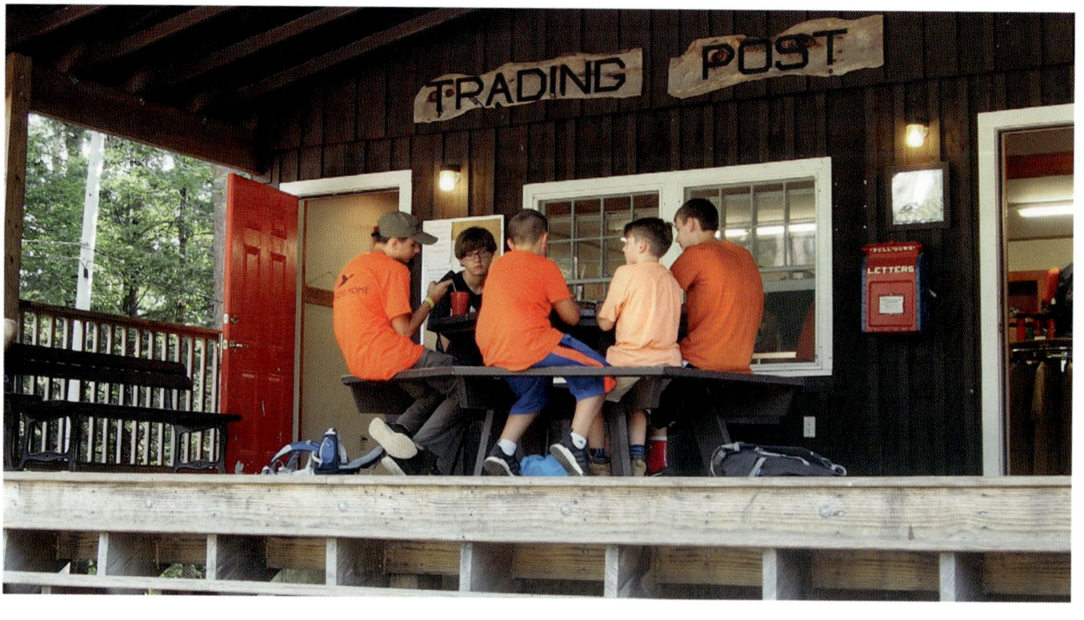

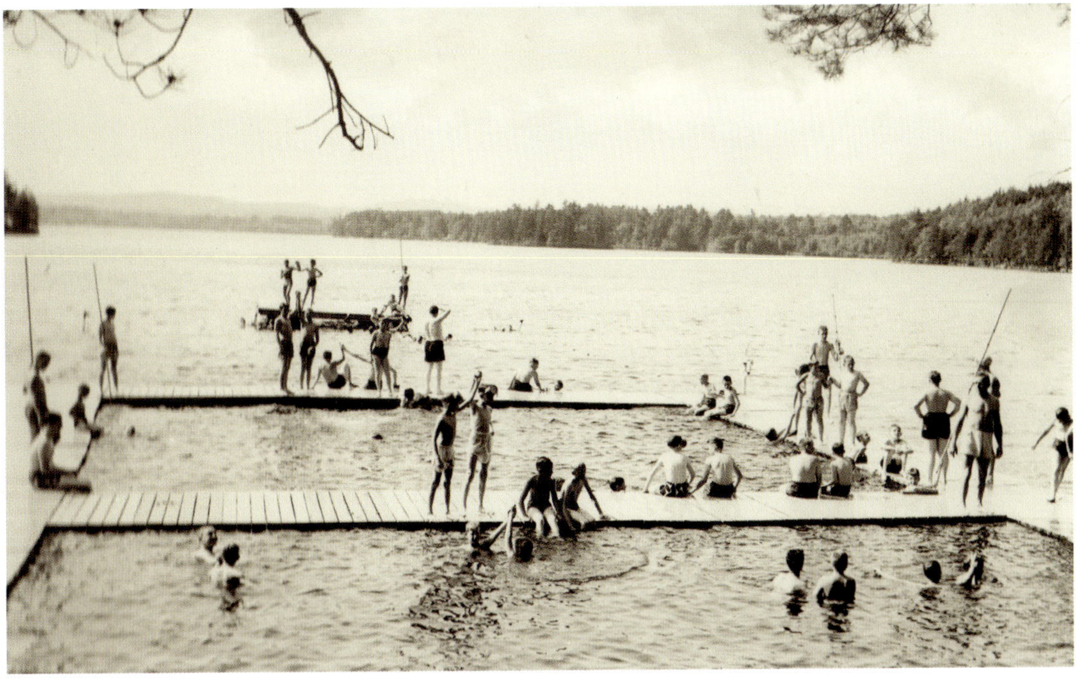

FREE TO SWIM: One of the most defining moments of growing up is learning how to swim. Summer camp has always provided great opportunities to learn just that. Passing the BSA swim test that provides access to the aquatics program is the first challenge that awaits a camper arriving at Wah-Tut-Ca. Those that don't pass on the first try are offered patient attention by a dedicated staff member to help them learn. Countless numbers of people have conquered their fears and learned to swim in the refreshing waters of Northwood Lake.

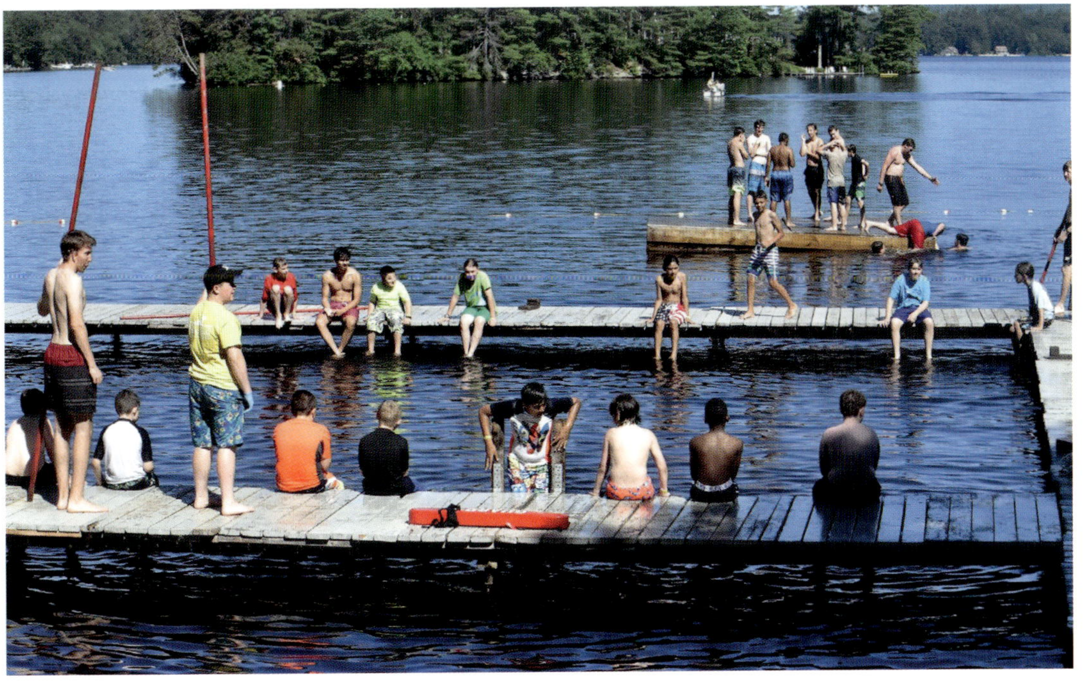

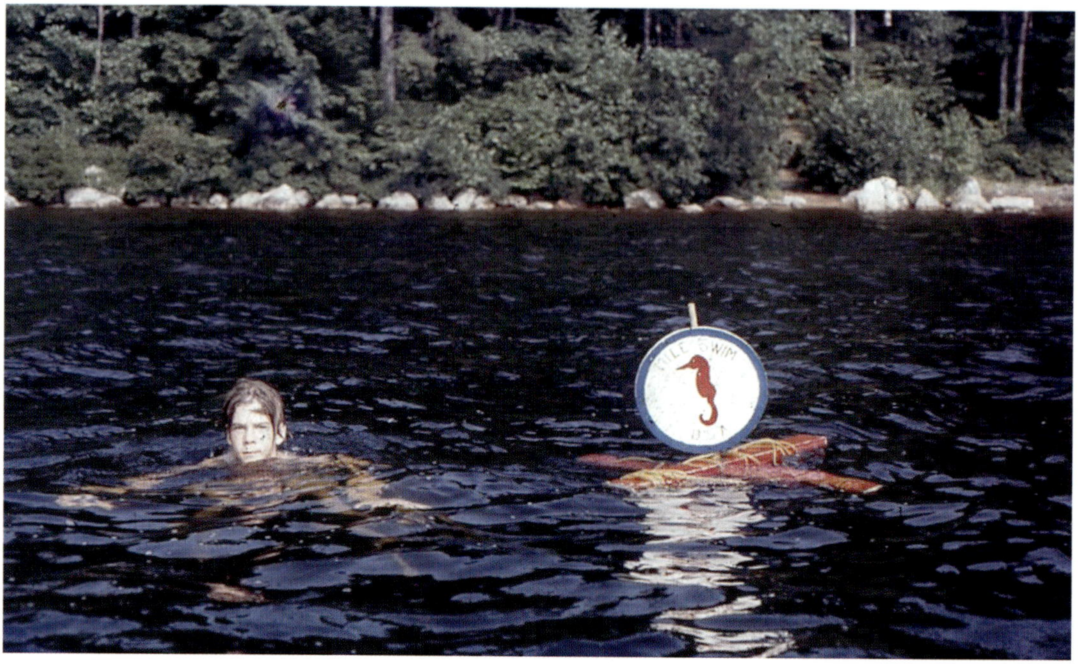

GOING THE DISTANCE: The BSA mile swim badge has long been a test of a swimmer's strength and endurance. Today, it has been surpassed by Scouts who swim the entire three mile stretch of Northwood Lake at the annual Andrew Curry-Green Lake Swim. This swim honors and remembers a former staff member who died while aboard American Airlines Flight 11 on September 11, 2001.

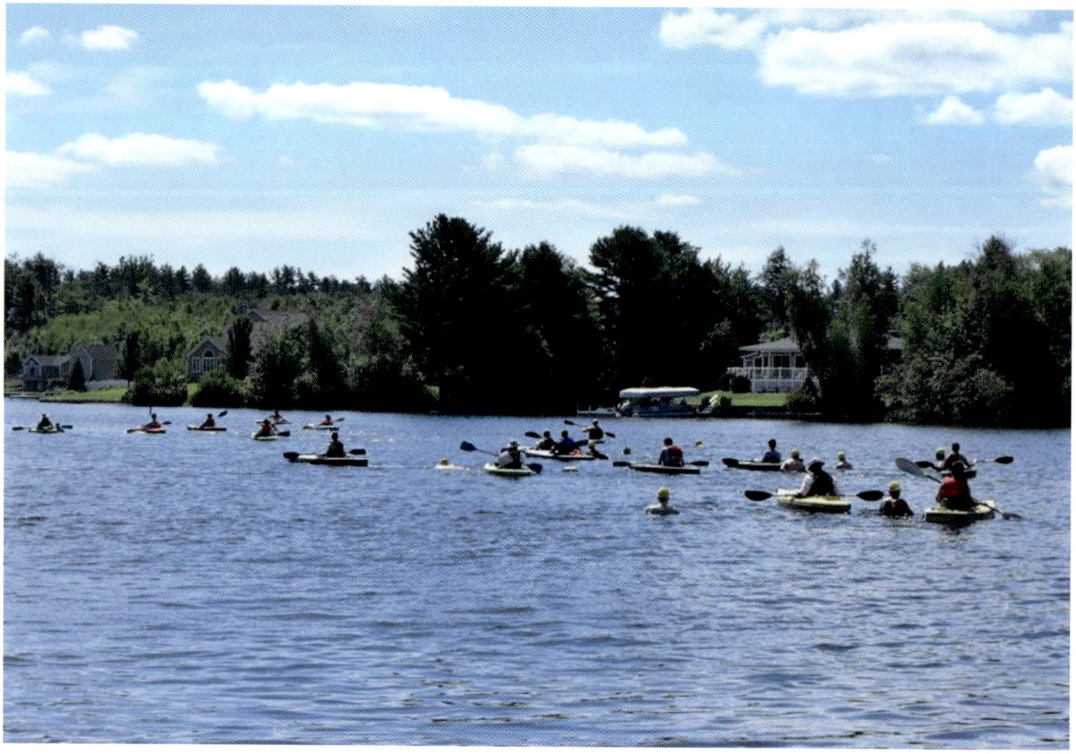

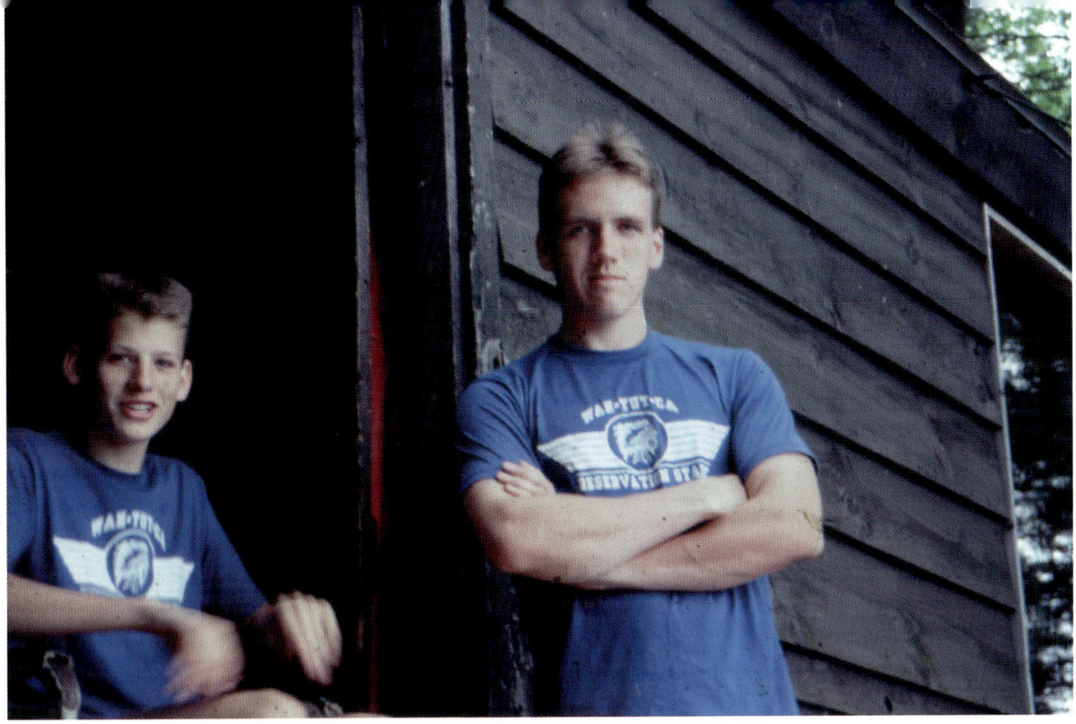

GENERATIONS: The Wah-Tut-Ca experience is powerful, and legacies contribute to keeping its spirit thriving. Many campers grow up to become Scout leaders who eventually return to camp with their sons and daughters. Brothers and cousins start out as campers then join staff together. Through its 80-year history Wah-Tut-Ca has a shared experience within and between families. Pictured above in the 1990s is aquatic staff member Curtis Eckelkamp (seated), and next to him (standing) is the late Craig Ryder. Craig served as aquatics director and in later years camp director. Below in 2018 is Curtis's son, Casey (seated) and standing next to him is aquatic staff member Allison Ryder, who is Craig's daughter.

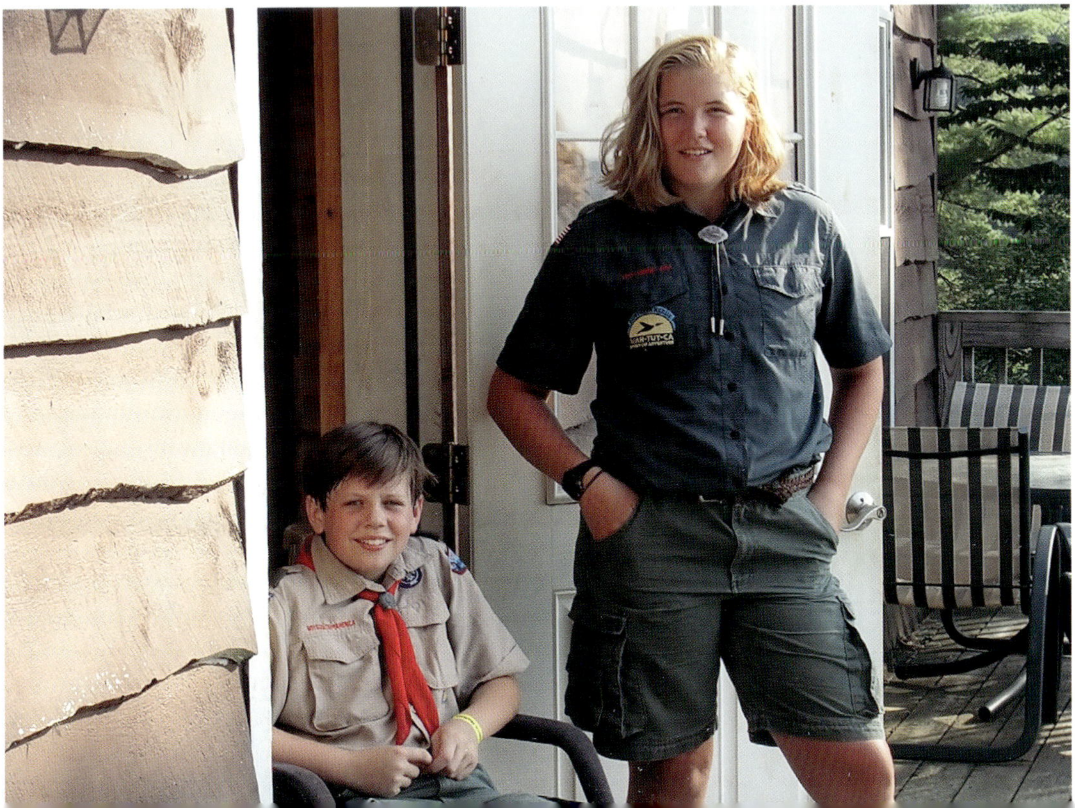

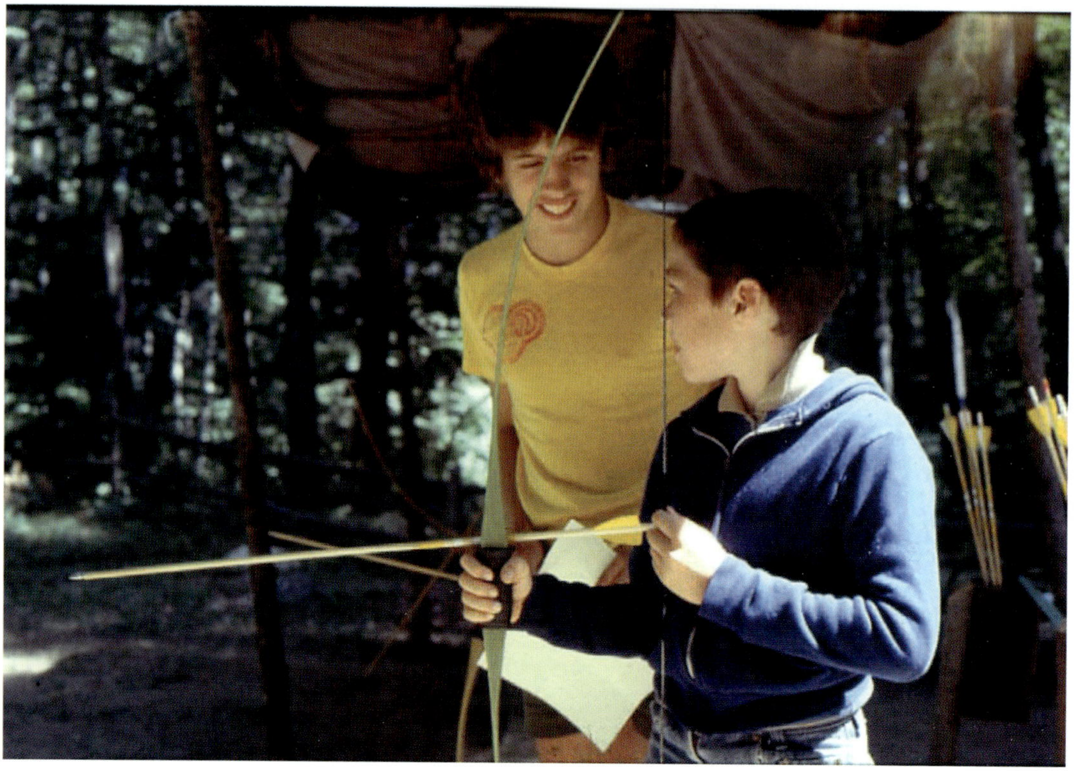

THE FAMILY BUSINESS: Pictured above is archery director Jeff Eckelkamp teaching a young camper in the 1980s. Pictured below is his niece, archery director Elizabeth Eckelkamp, in 2018. The culture of camping at WTCSR spans multiple generations. Now more than ever with the changes in BSA policy and its inclusion of young women in Scouting.

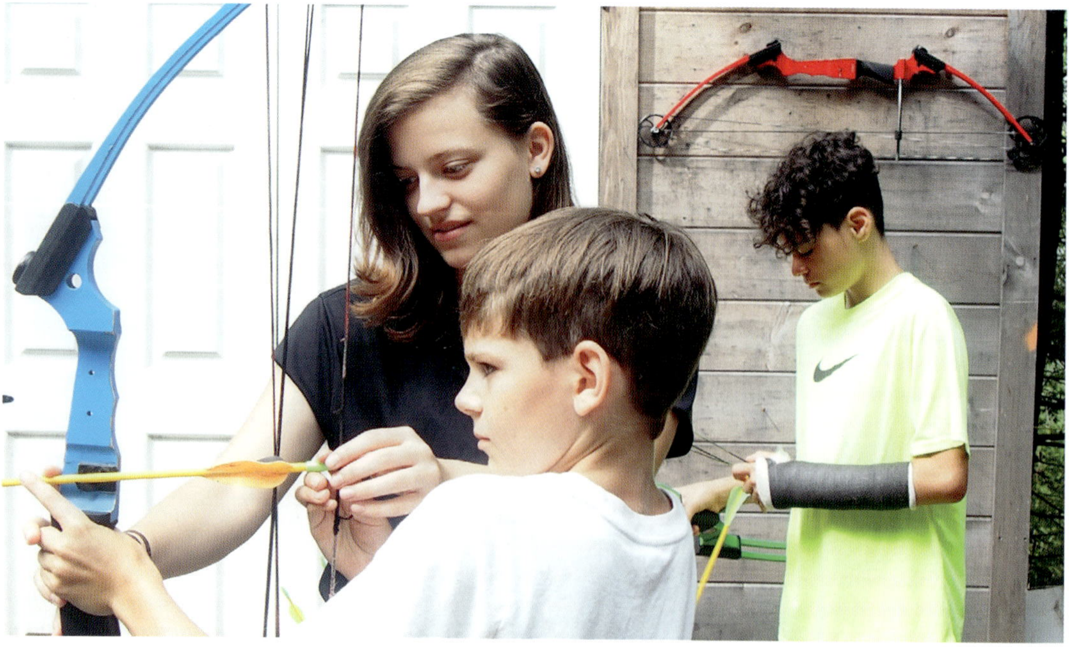

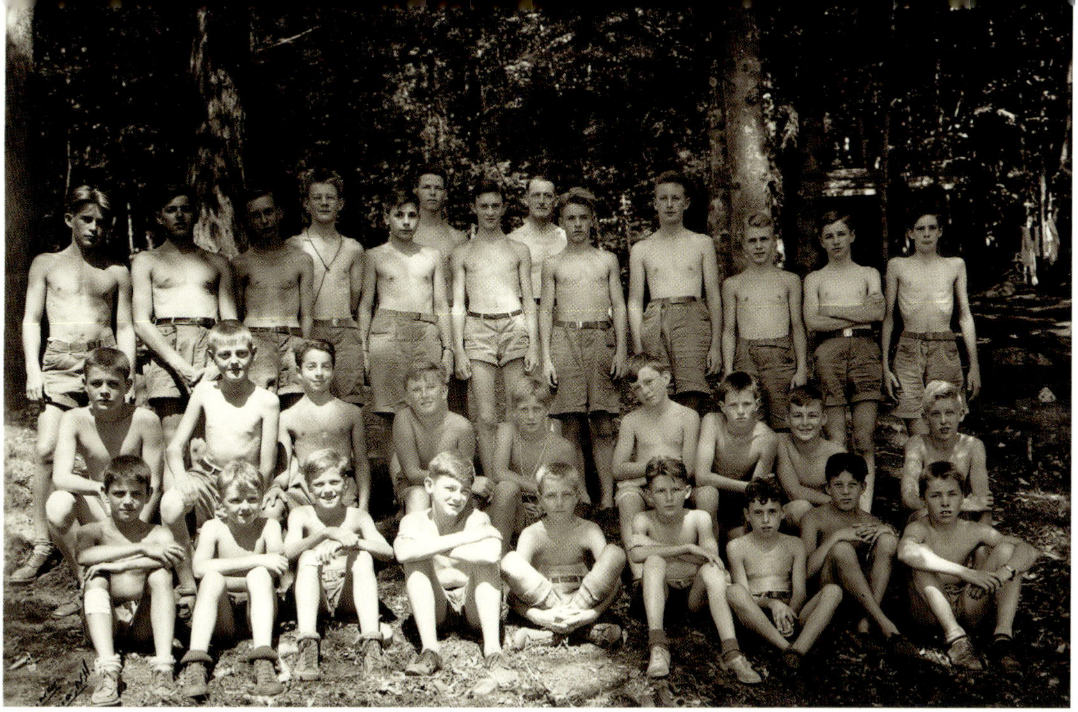

A Thing of the Spirit: The power of the Wah-Tut-Ca experience is a feeling of ownership and belonging. It is more than just a place you go, it is a place you become a part of. Pictured above are campers from week one of the opening of Wah-Tut-Ca Scout Reservation in 1937. John Goodwin, the camp clerk, was a part of that founding group. Almost seventy-five years later, he is pictured with camp director Kevin R. Dion at his final visit to Wah-Tut-Ca Scout Reservation. John Goodwin was a member of the last staff of Camp Chadwick and a founding staff member of Wah-Tut-Ca. The last of his generation, he passed a few years later at the age of ninety-one. He left this world knowing that Wah-Tut-Ca was in good and capable hands. He had confidence that determined and worthy successors would keep the spirit alive.

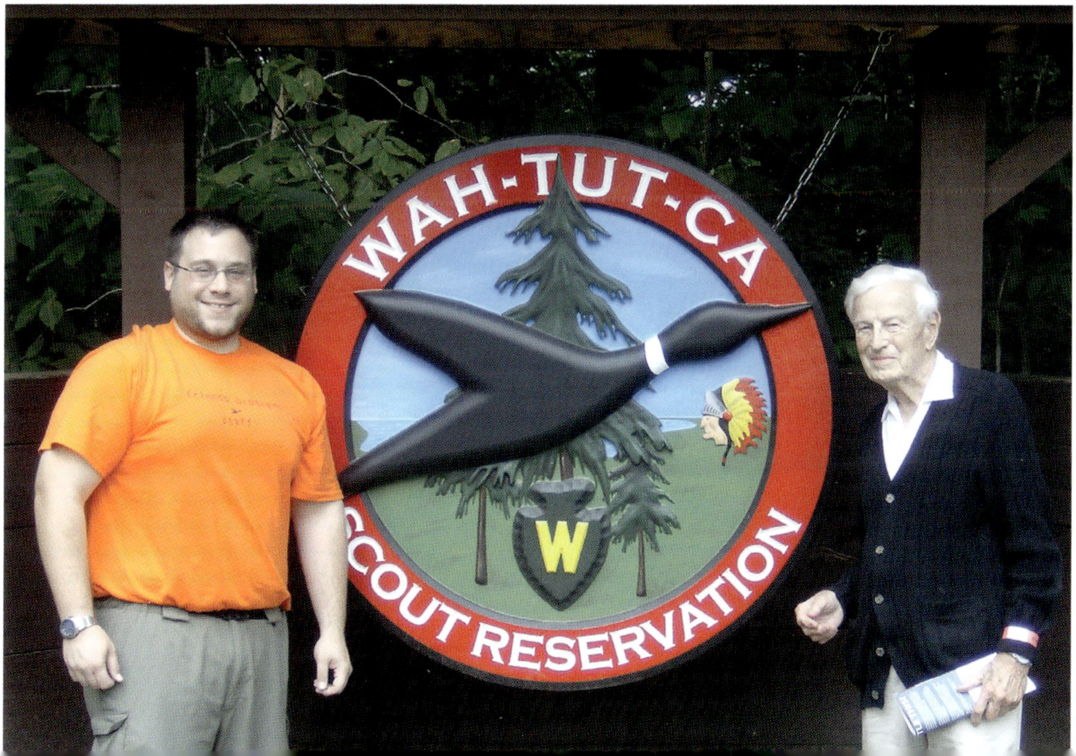

CHAPTER 8

NEW ENGLAND BASE CAMP AND CAMP SAYRE

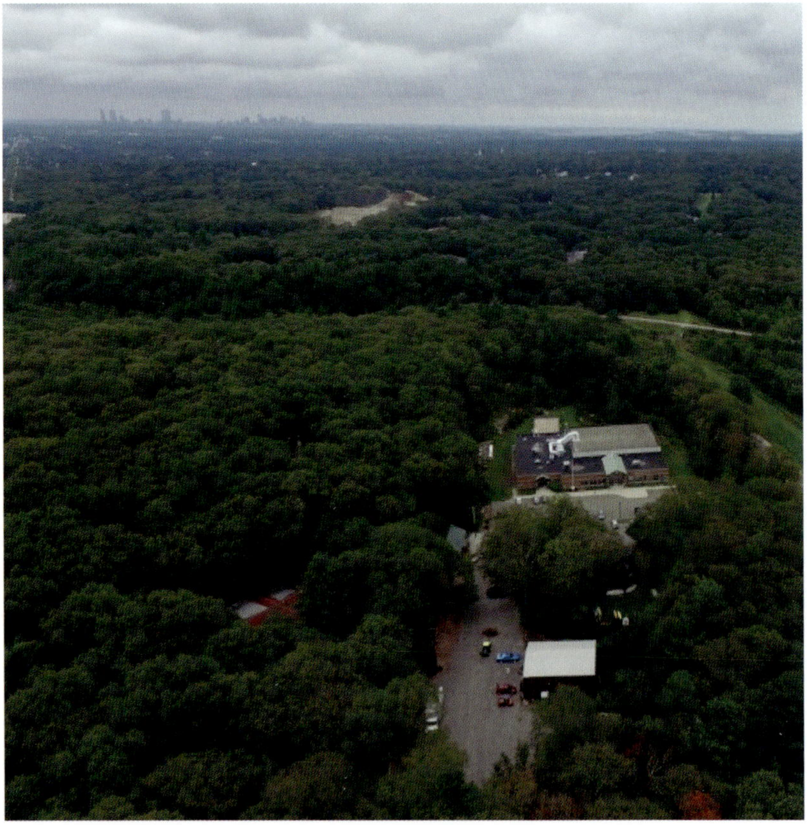

NEW ENGLAND BASE CAMP AND CAMP SAYRE—MILTON, MA: The Boston Council, BSA received a donated section of land less than ten miles southwest of Boston in 1951. The 110-acre plot was donated by Mr. and Mrs. Elliot Henderson in memory of their son David Sayer Henderson. The land was dedicated to the training of youth and adults and offers short-term and weekend camping experiences.

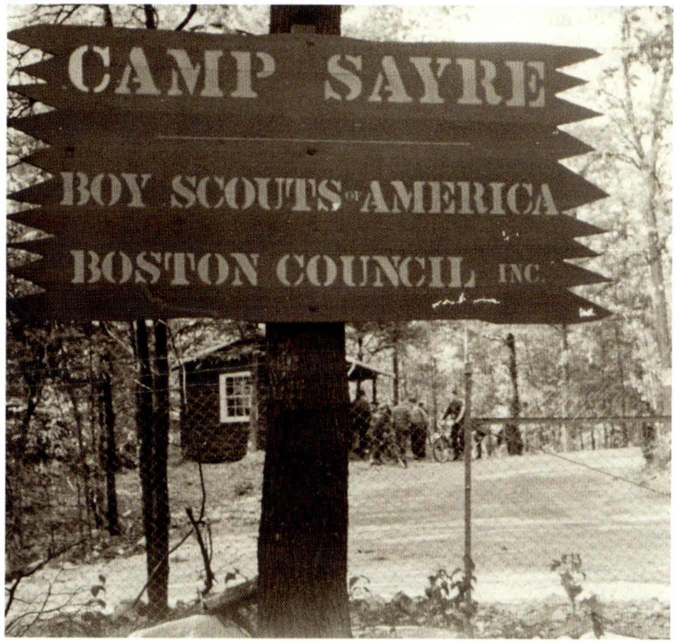

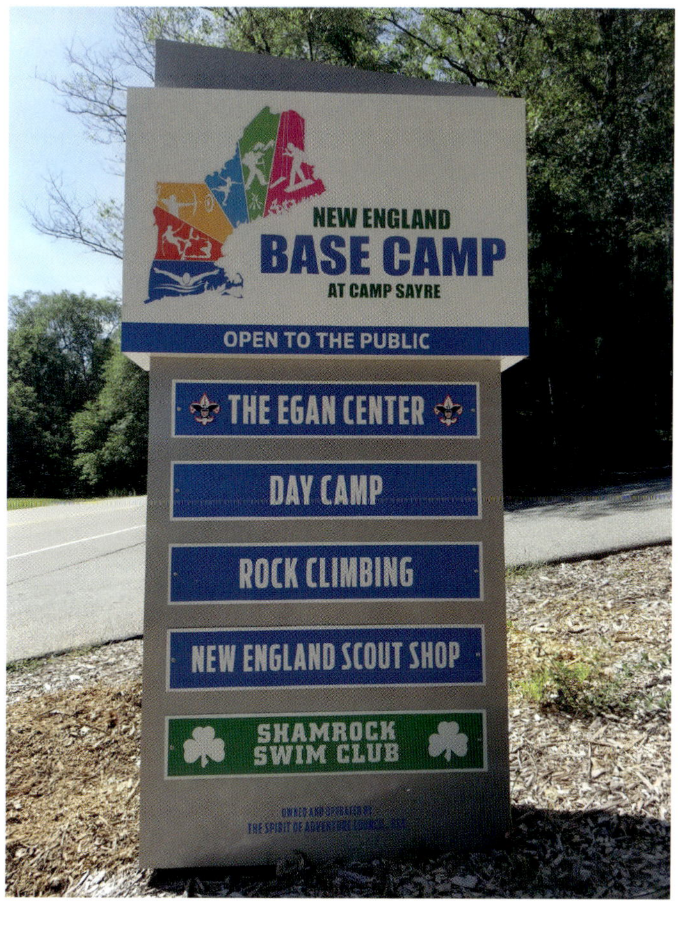

NEW ENGLAND BASE CAMP & CAMP SAYRE: For over sixty years, there has been an evolution in the life of young people. Today children and young adults live primarily indoors. The opportunity to play outside is restricted. A camp, just eight miles from the city of Boston, tucked into the Blue Hills Reservation, is a wonderful outdoor opportunity. In 2015, Camp Sayre was dually named New England Base Camp. It is a highly innovative program that consolidates multiple outdoor activities into one location. It is an outdoor adventure center, not just for Scouts, but is also open to the public, serving thousands of youth and families.

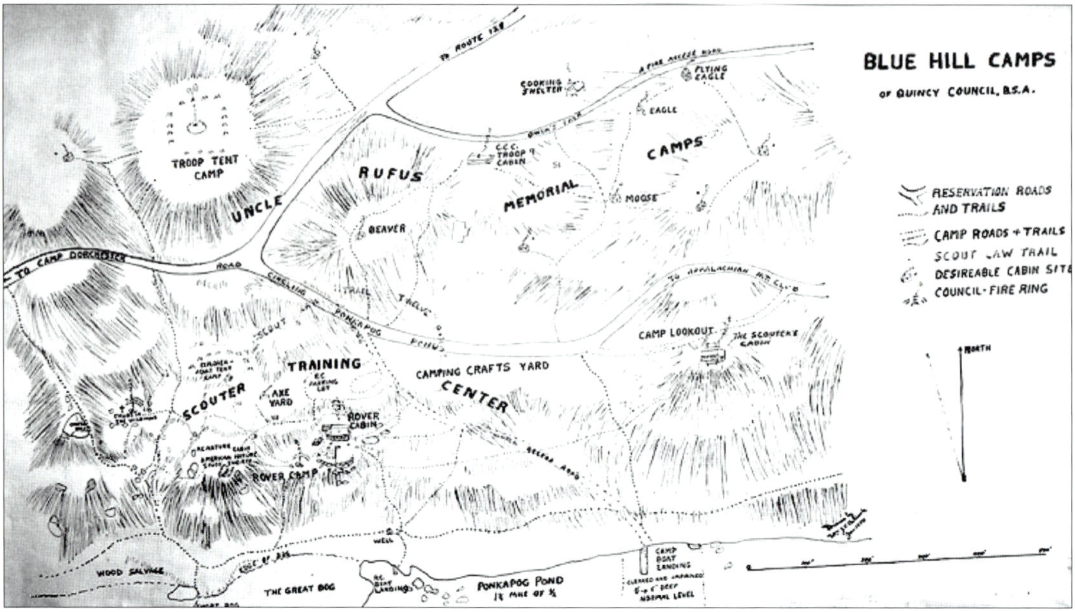

MINUTES FROM BOSTON: The Blue Hills is a convenient location for adventure in the Greater Boston Area. In the early years of Boy Scouting the location was named The Blue Hills Camp. It was the site of early trolley camps of the Boston Council, BSA. The advantage of a wilderness area being close to an urban center is still an advantage today because New England Base Camp and traditional Scout outdoor activities are accessible. Scout programs include a ropes course, rock and ice climbing, shooting sports, outdoor cooking, woodcraft, orienteering, swimming, knot tying, and first aid training. These basic Scout programs have been expanded to include a STEM lab and music room.

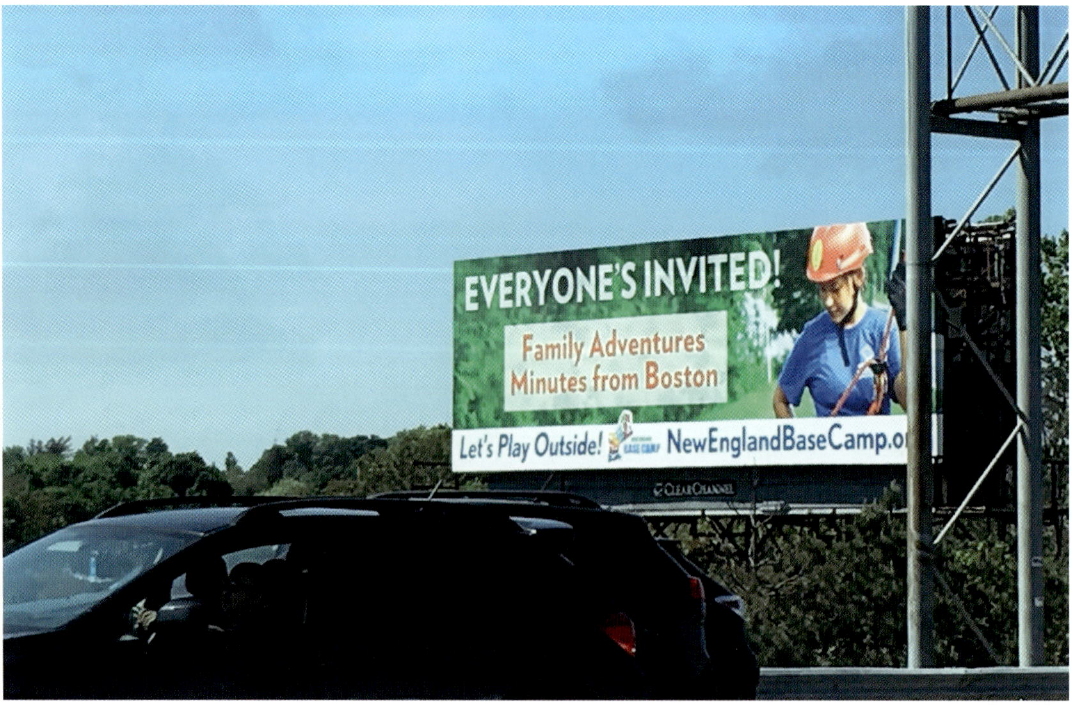

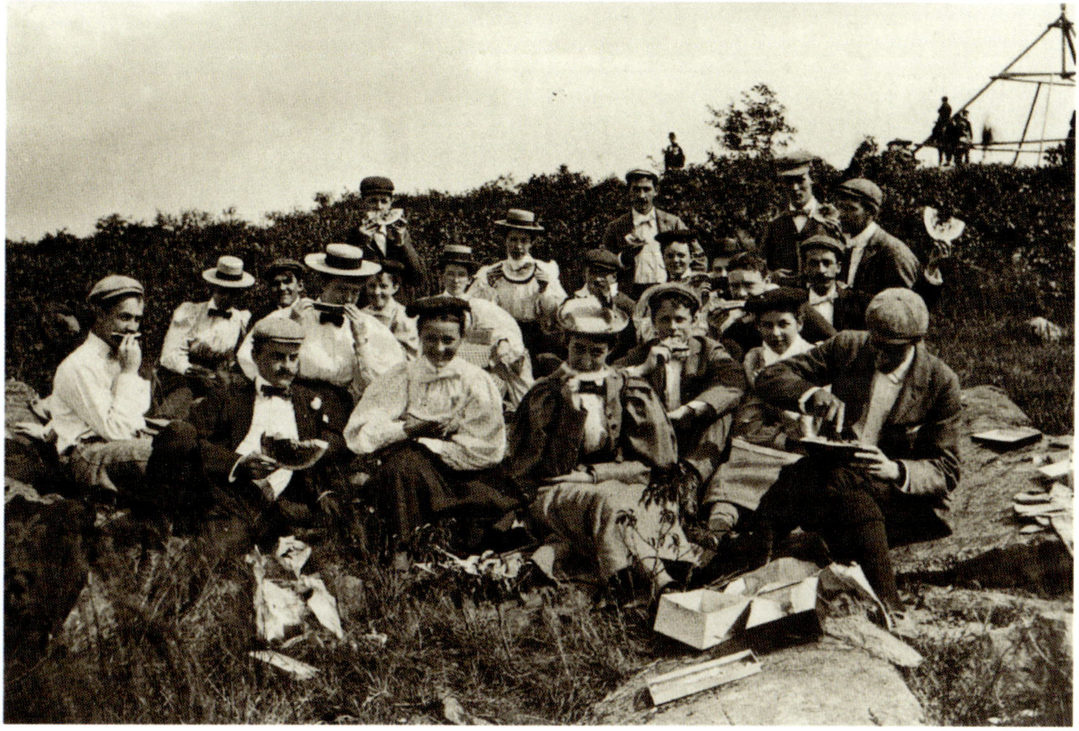

THE BLUE HILLS RESERVATION: Camp Sayre is a few miles from the Blue Hill Reservation in Milton, MA. For more than a century groups would climb to the summit of The Great Blue Hill. In January of 1885, fireworks were set off for the opening of a weather observatory that remains to the present day. Now a National Historic Landmark, Scouts continue to climb the Great Blue Hill today.

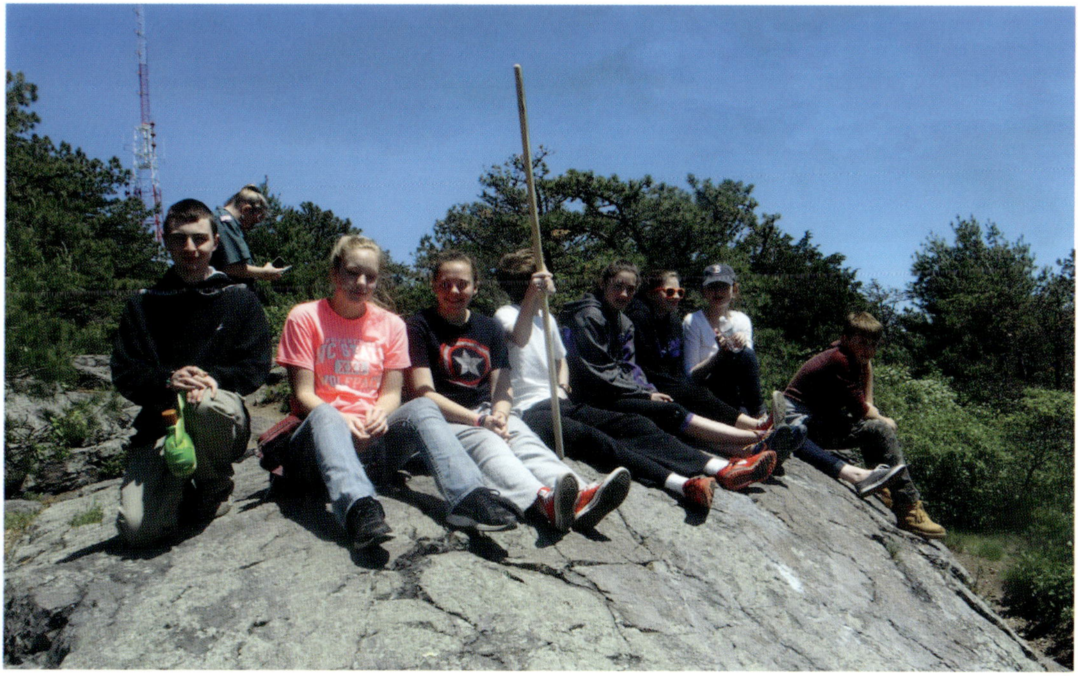

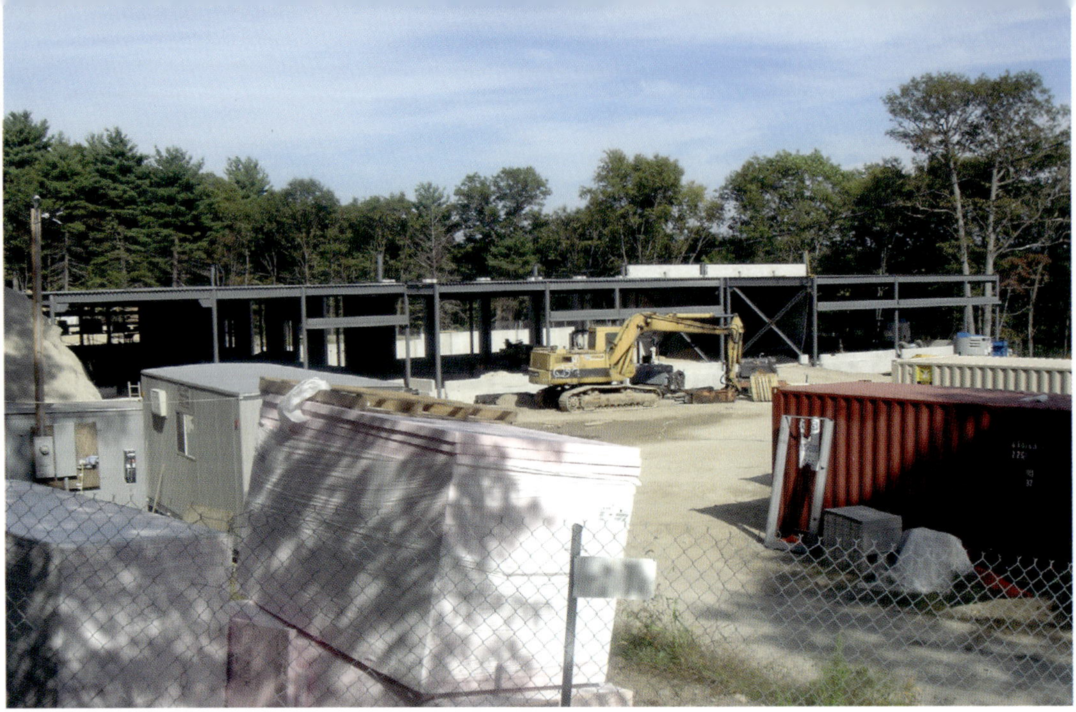

THE EGAN CENTER: To better serve the youth, the Boston Minuteman Council, BSA constructed the Egan Center in 2007. The building houses an indoor pool, office area, and classrooms for training. The lack of an aquatic program was a limitation that hampered Sayre from the beginning in 1951. Building a swimming pool solved that problem. Unfortunately, the project nearly bankrupted the Council. For several years the pool was incomplete and left empty. The operational costs of maintaining an indoor Olympic sized pool were overwhelming. In 2012, a partnership between the Boston Minuteman Council, BSA and the Shamrock Swim Club was established. The Swim Club took over the operations and maintenance of the pool while making it available to Scouts on weekends.

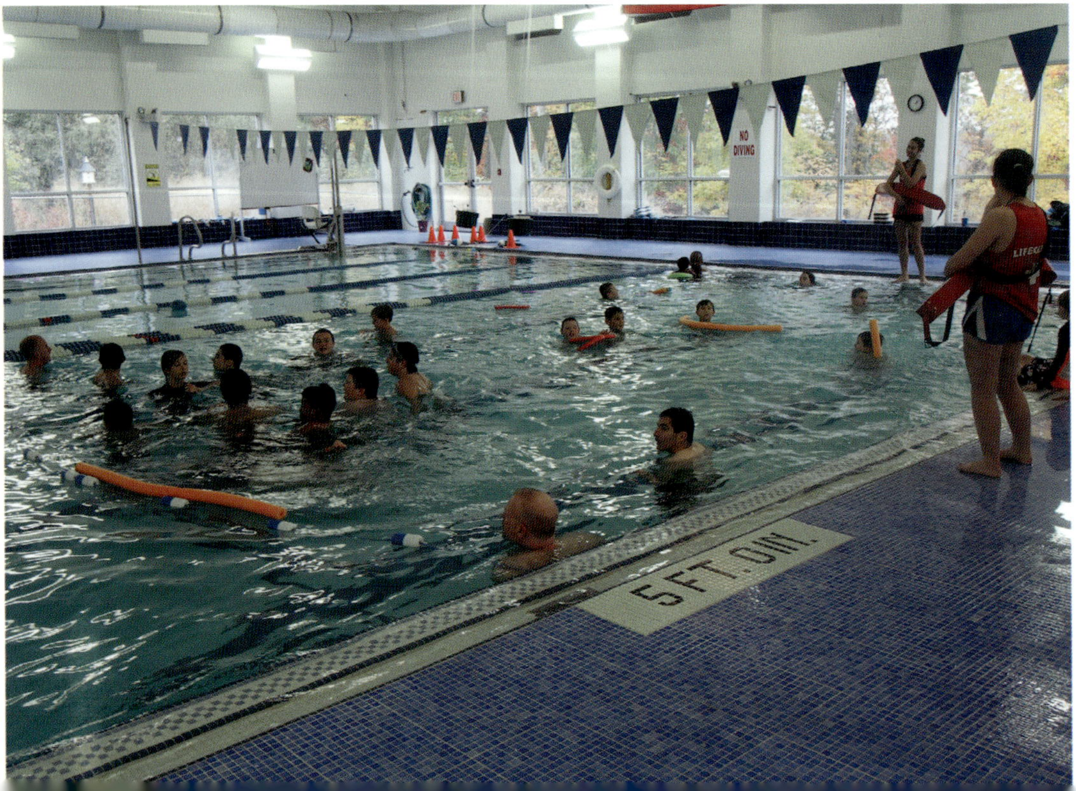

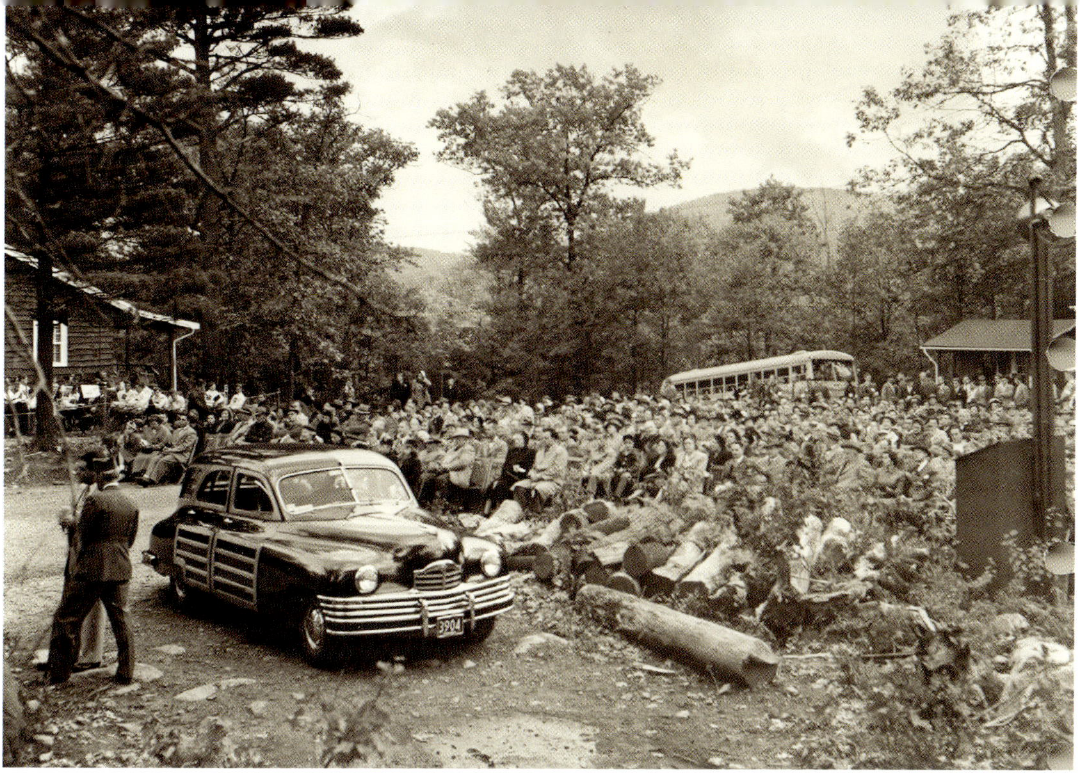

HERITAGE: New England Base Camp, in the Spirit of Adventure Council, BSA, is often the place where the individuals and events that have shaped the Boy Scouts of America for over 100 years are recognized. The first gathering is pictured above. Camp Sayre was dedicated on October 20, 1952. Below, in March 15, 2016, is the Thomas A. Kershaw Scouting Heritage Atrium. This space recognizes community members, sports figures, artists, and other notable individuals that have participated as youth in the Scouting Program.

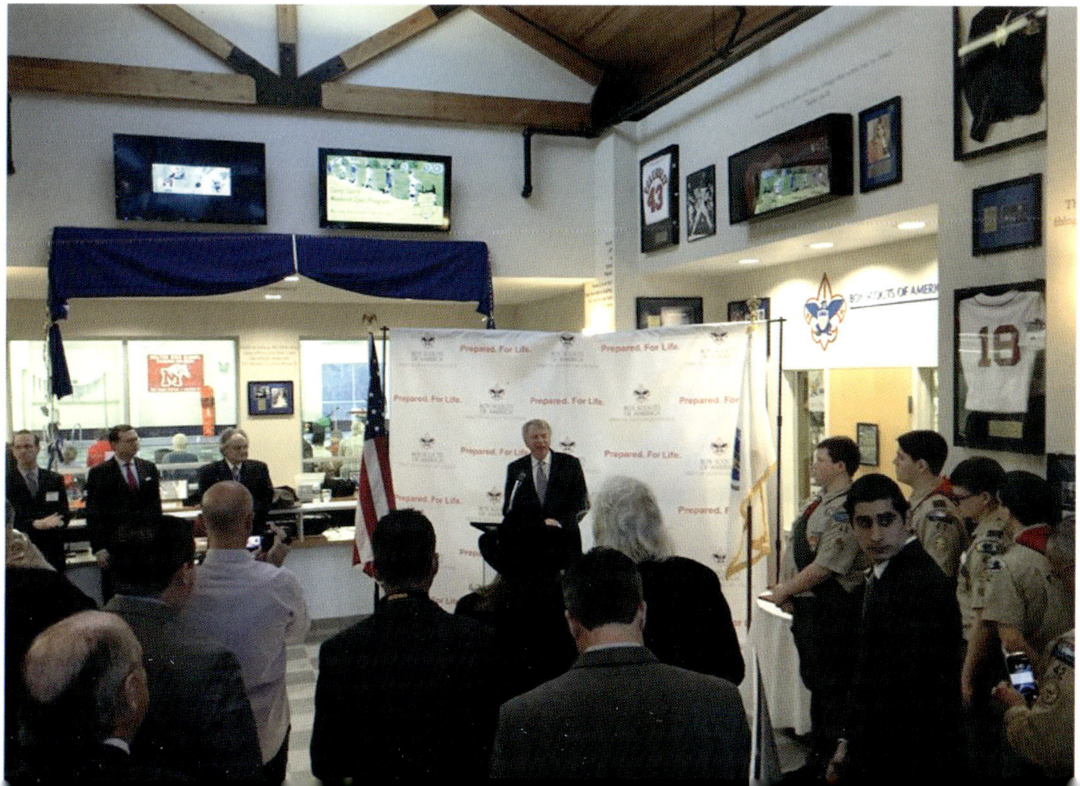

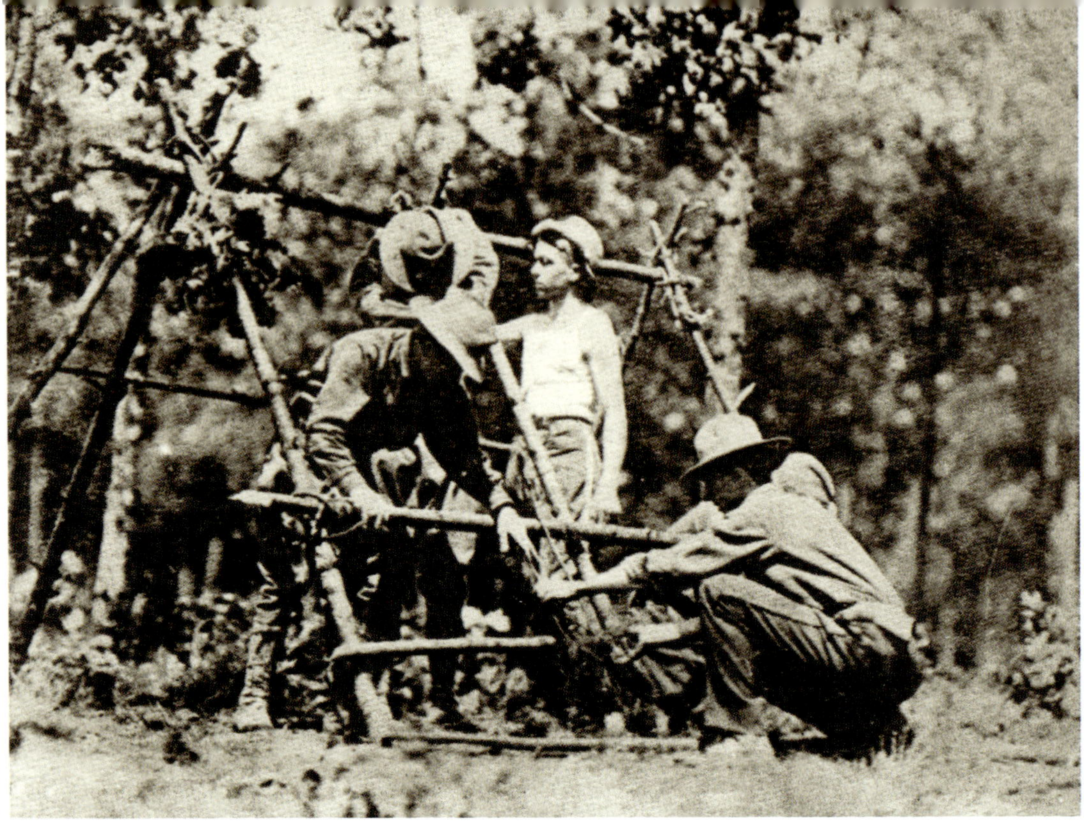

BUILDING SHELTERS: The construction of a shelter is a fun activity that is natural play for young people. In a time when kids are locked into a digital world building a shelter in the outdoors is a healthy alterative to sitting behind a computer screen.

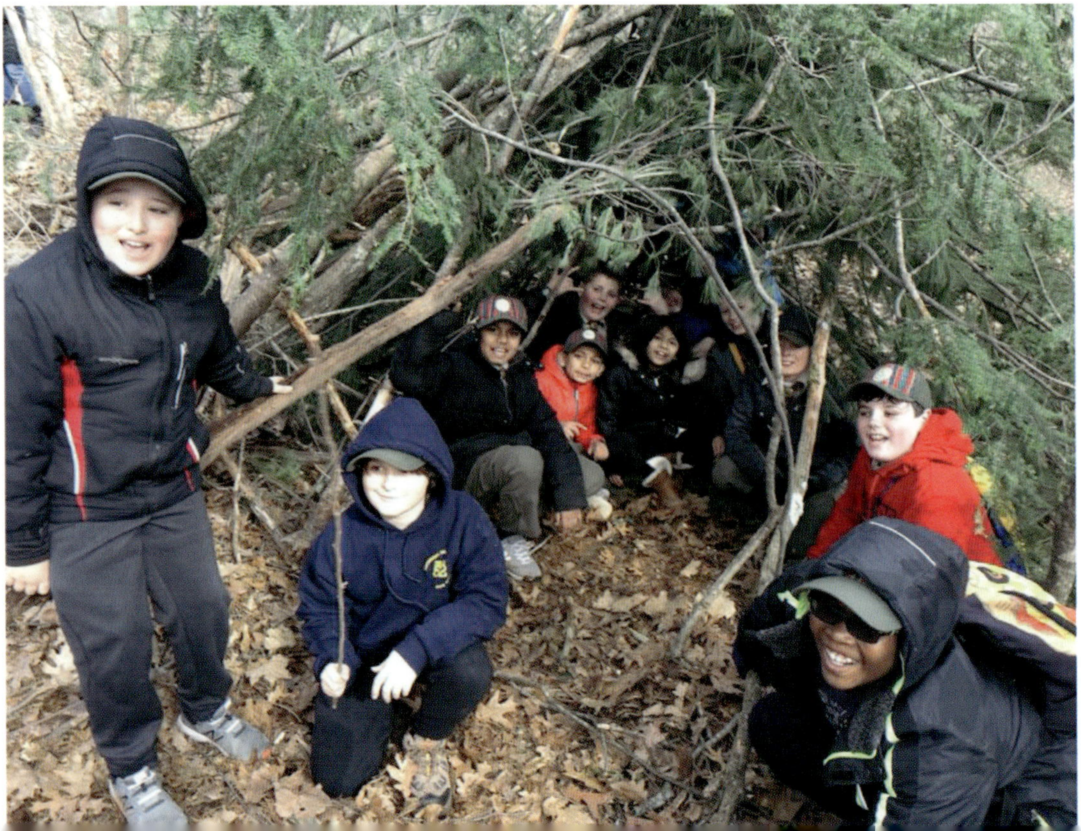

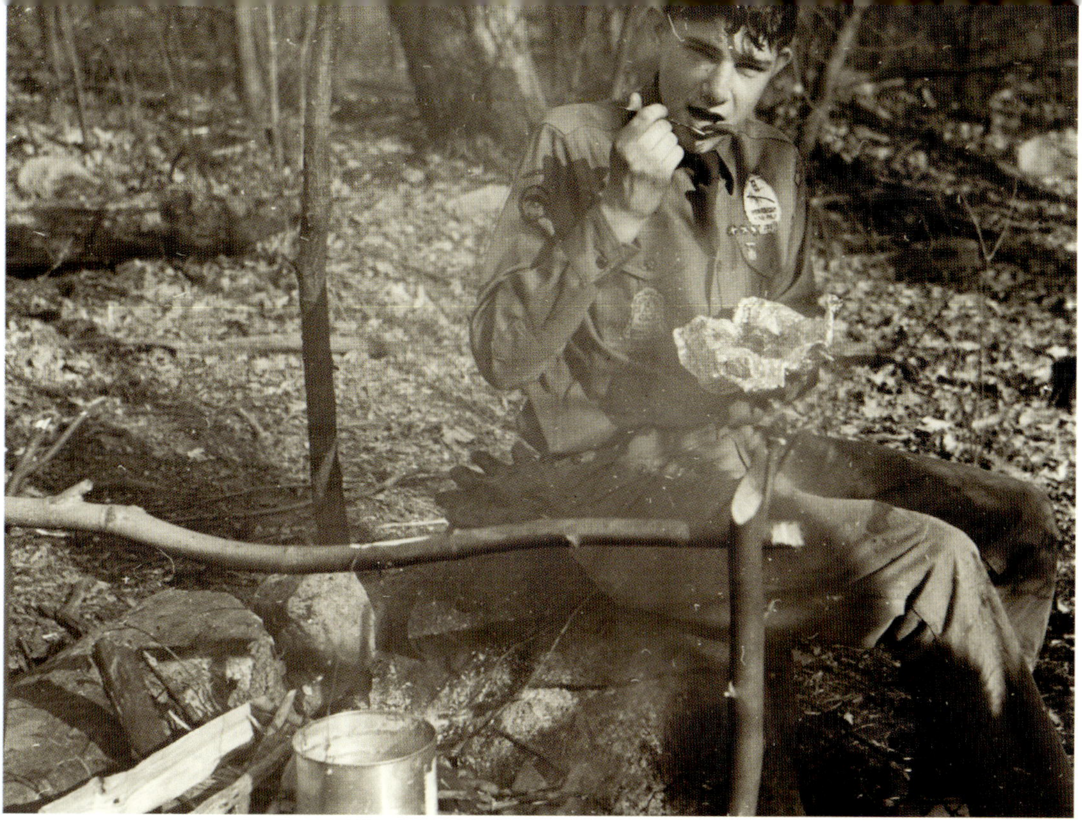

OUTDOOR COOKING: Scouting's advocates say that they have acquired important life skills by being a member of the Boy Scouts of America. In 1919, in his book *Aids to Scoutmastership*, Scouting Founder Lord Baden Powell once said, "A week of camp life is worth six months of theoretical teaching in the meeting room." Learning how to cook is an essential life skill. In the twenty-first century the cooking program has changed to accommodate allergies, religious and other dietary restrictions while more emphasis and instruction is given to assure food safety protocols are followed.

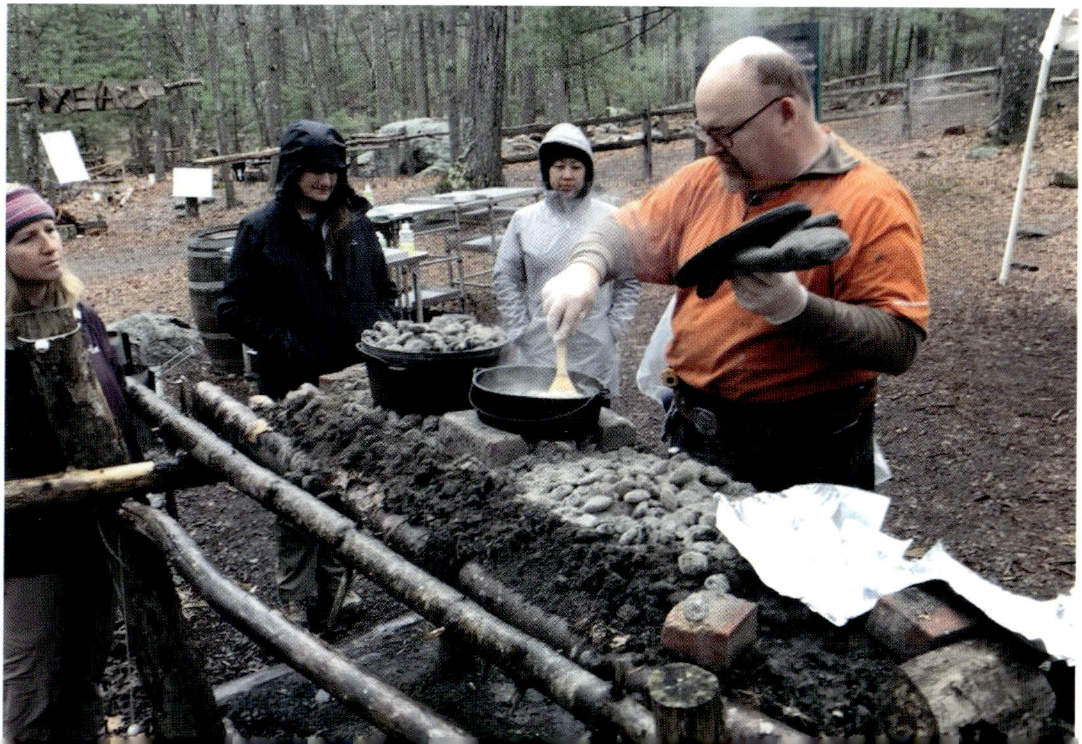

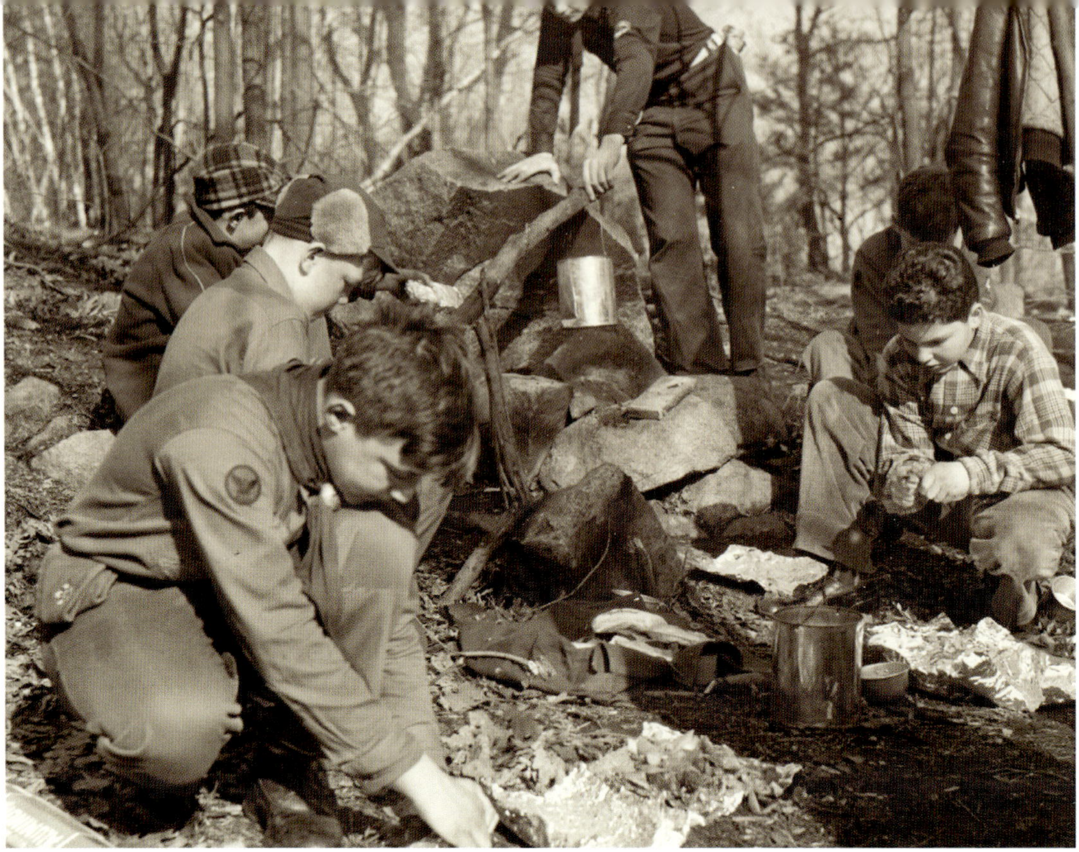

FOILED AGAIN: Aluminum foil was first commercially produced in 1910, the same year as the founding of the Boy Scouts of America. Serendipitously it became the most popular outdoor cooking utensil for Scouts. Aluminum foil is used to line pots for quick clean up or to create tasty combinations of hamburger, potatoes, and vegetables that simmer in a pouch over an open fire.

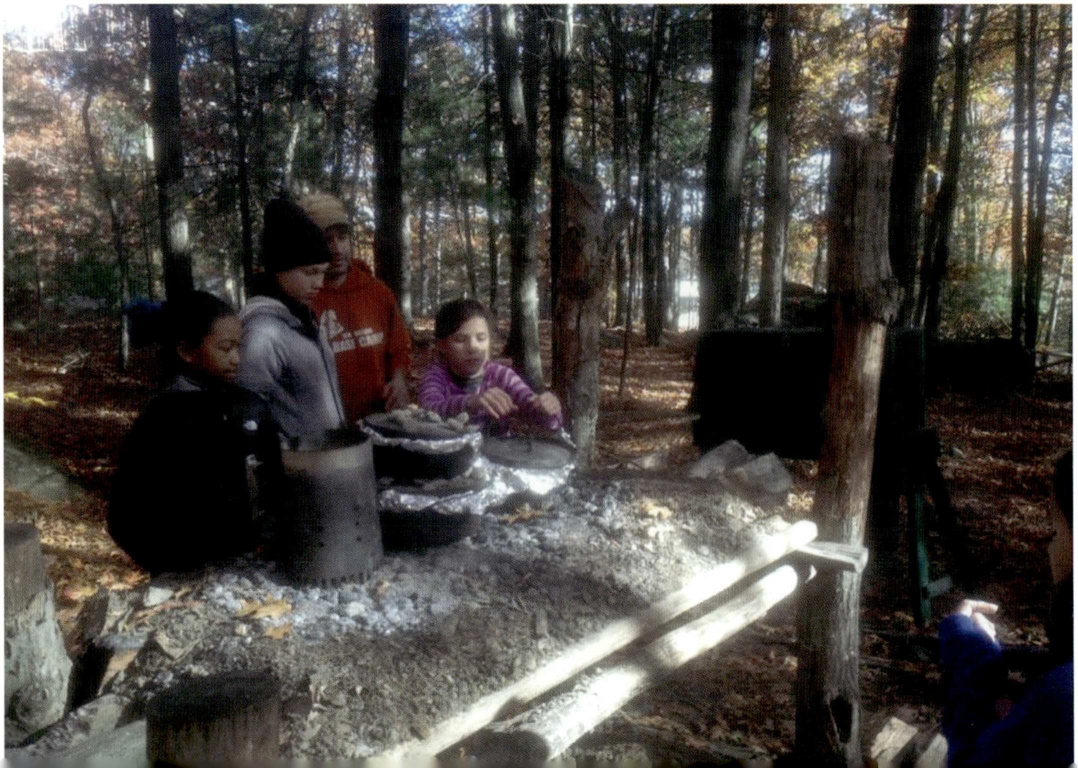

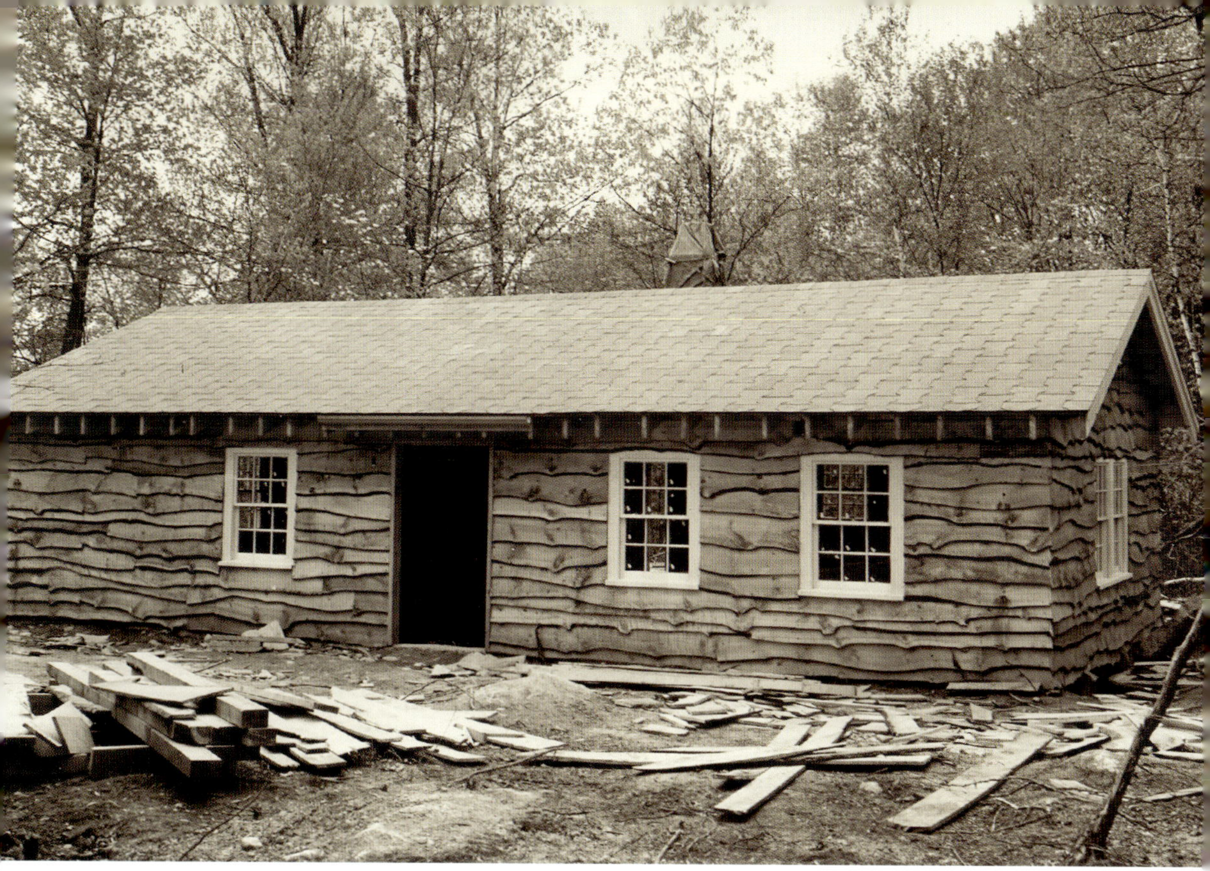

SAYRE CABINS: The cabins at Camp Sayre, originally constructed in 1951-1952, have been renovated several times over the years. These cabins are used extensively throughout the year by Scouts and other youth groups across the Northeast for weekend stays at New England Base Camp.

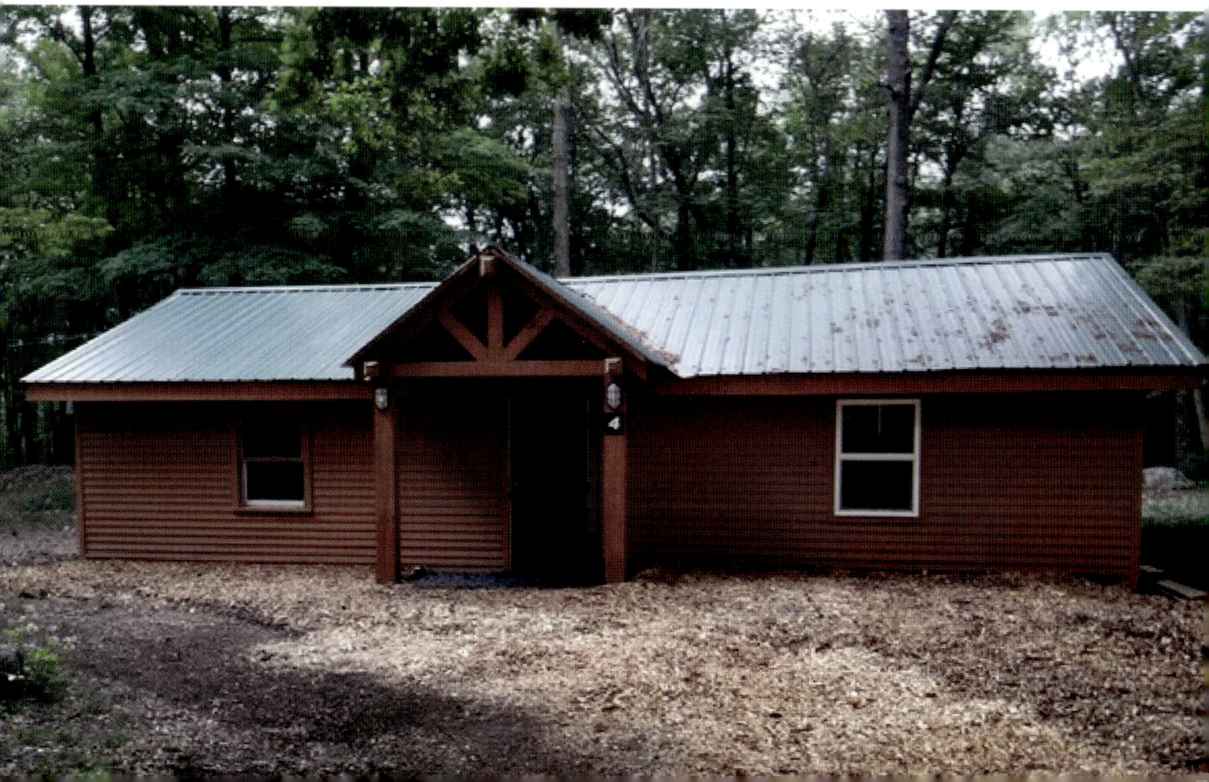

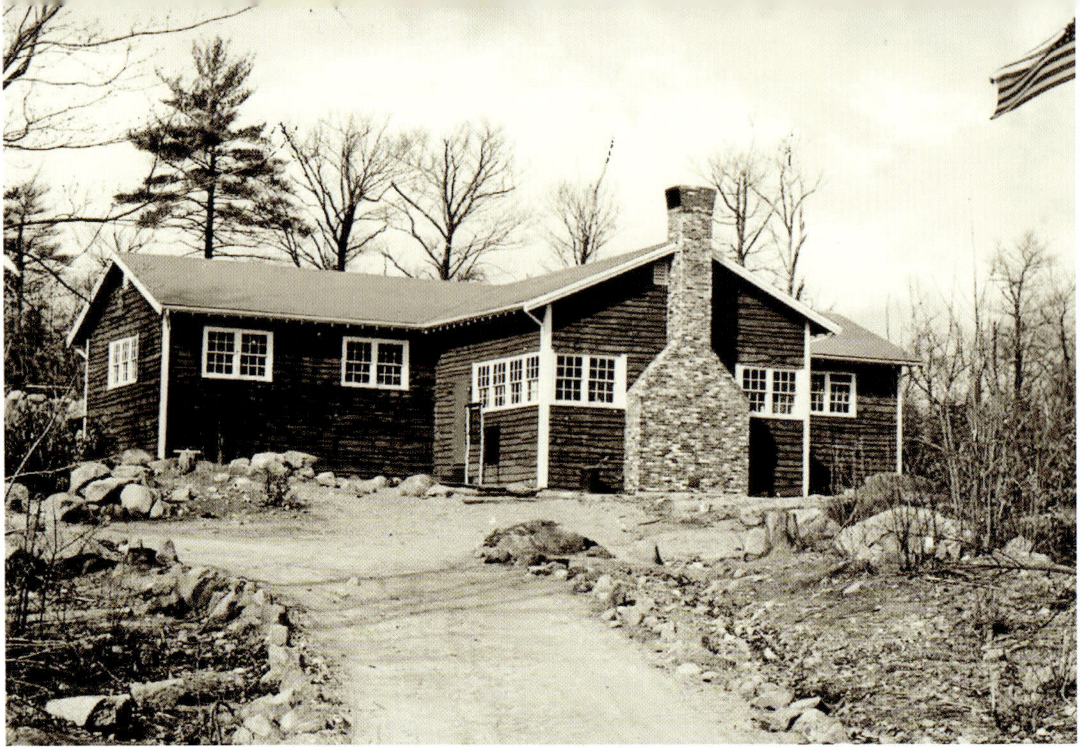

Hayden Lodge: Used for youth and adult training Hayden Lodge includes a full-service dining hall and kitchen. Out of state troops and other visitors often choose to get their meals from the menu of the lodge's kitchen.

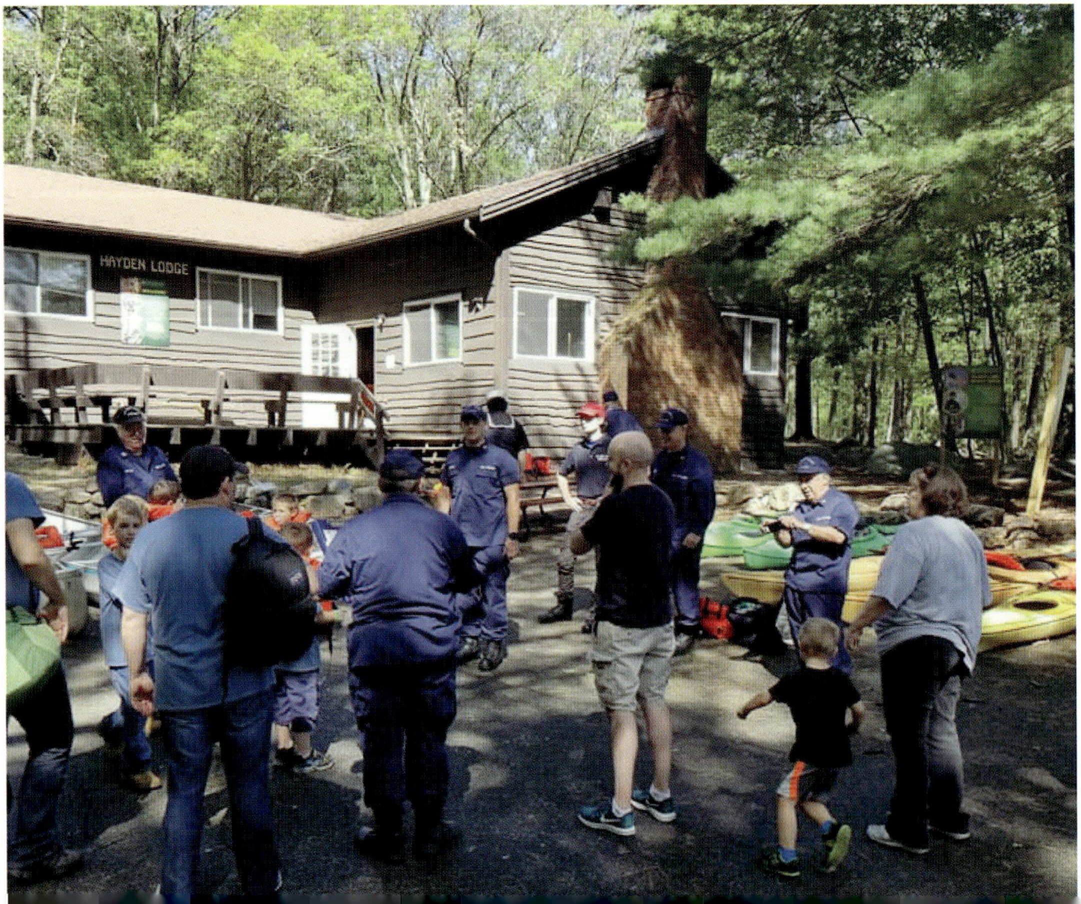

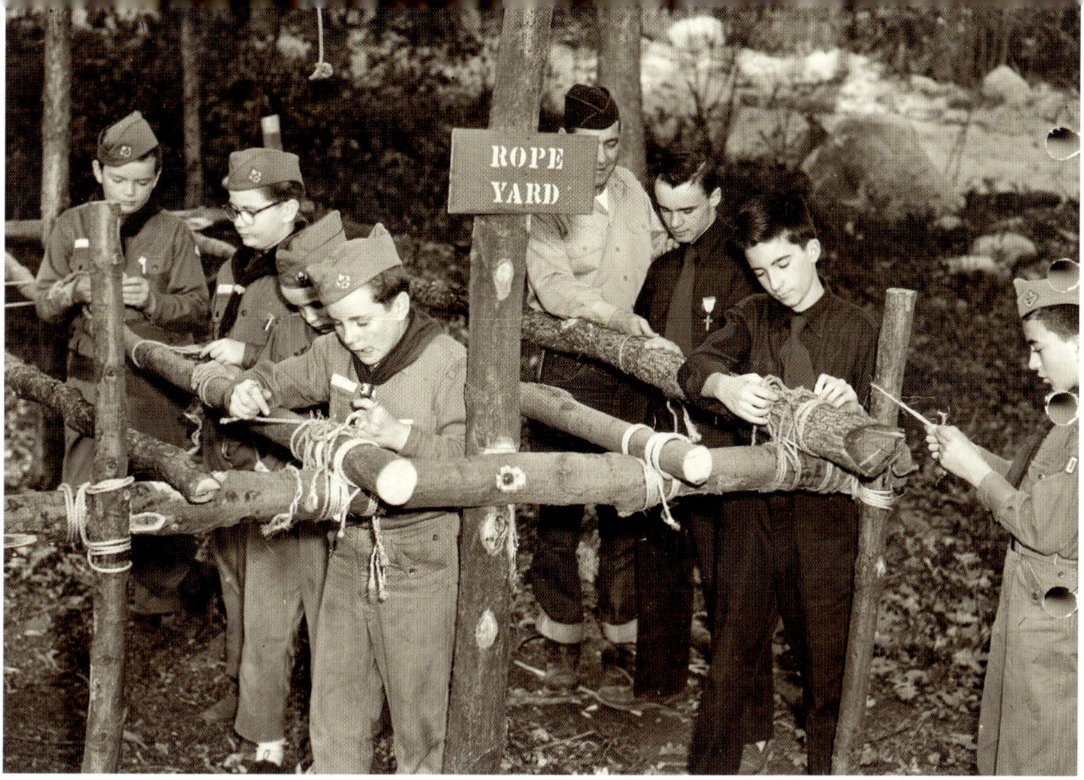

BINDING TIES: Scouts tying knots is an image that is almost a cliché. It is a simple skill that one Scout can teach another. When this happens, both kids are learning. Learning to teach and give instruction is a useful life skill. Knot tying skills are useful in the outdoor programs of the BSA. Combining these skills gives an opportunity for adventure. Building a fort is a childhood activity that has become all but lost in the twenty-first century. At New England Base Camp, the idea of friends getting together to build something is encouraged and celebrated.

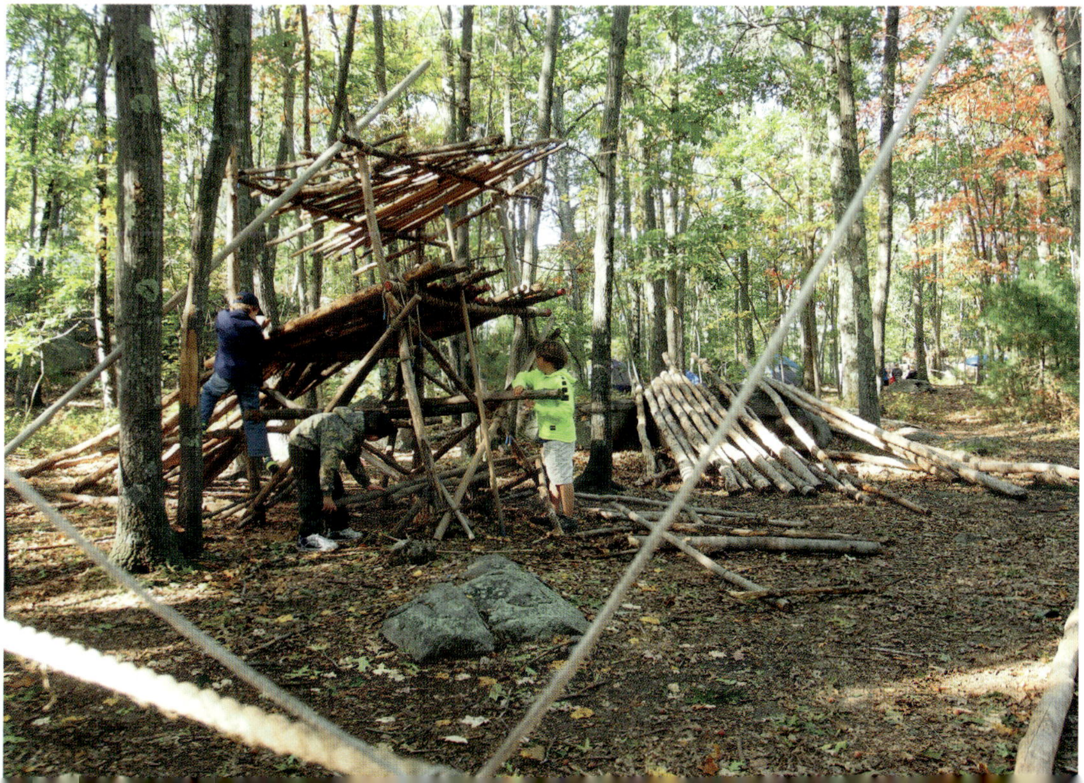

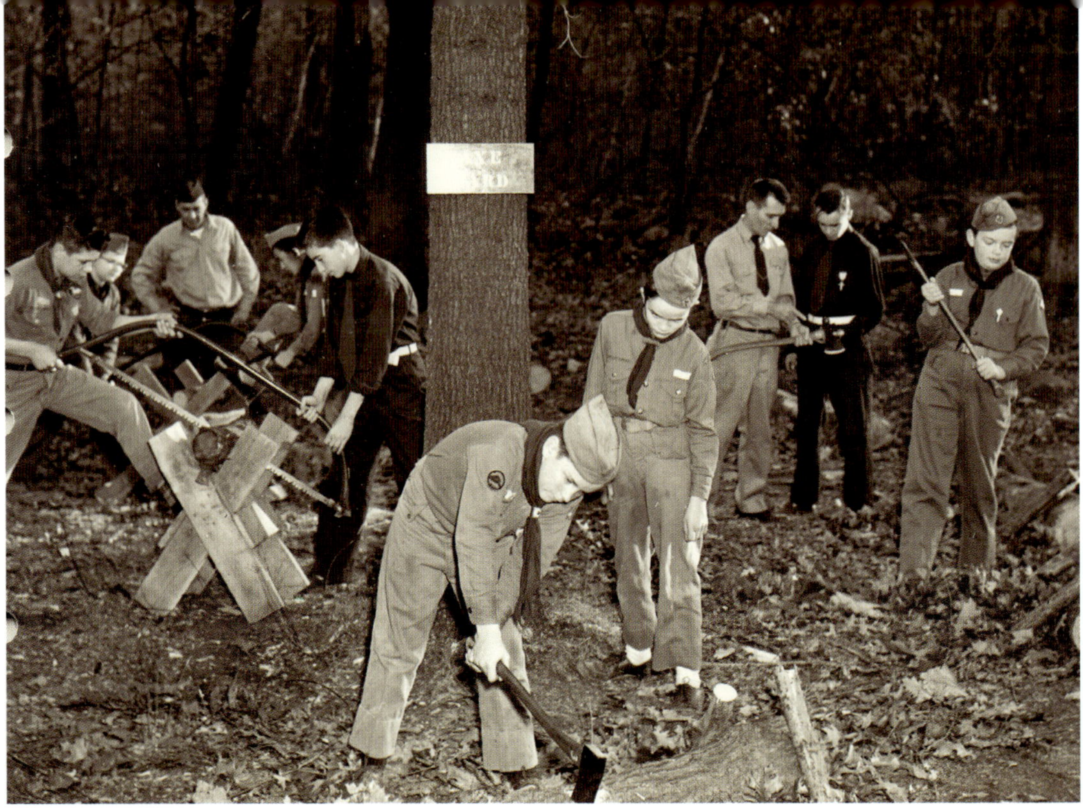

HAND TOOLS: Using wood tools is another activity that few kids in the twenty-first century have access to. At New England Base Camp, young people get to use their hands in a safe and controlled environment. It is a very low tech and ancient experience. Splitting a log or sawing a beam provides a sense of real accomplishment that no computer application can provide.

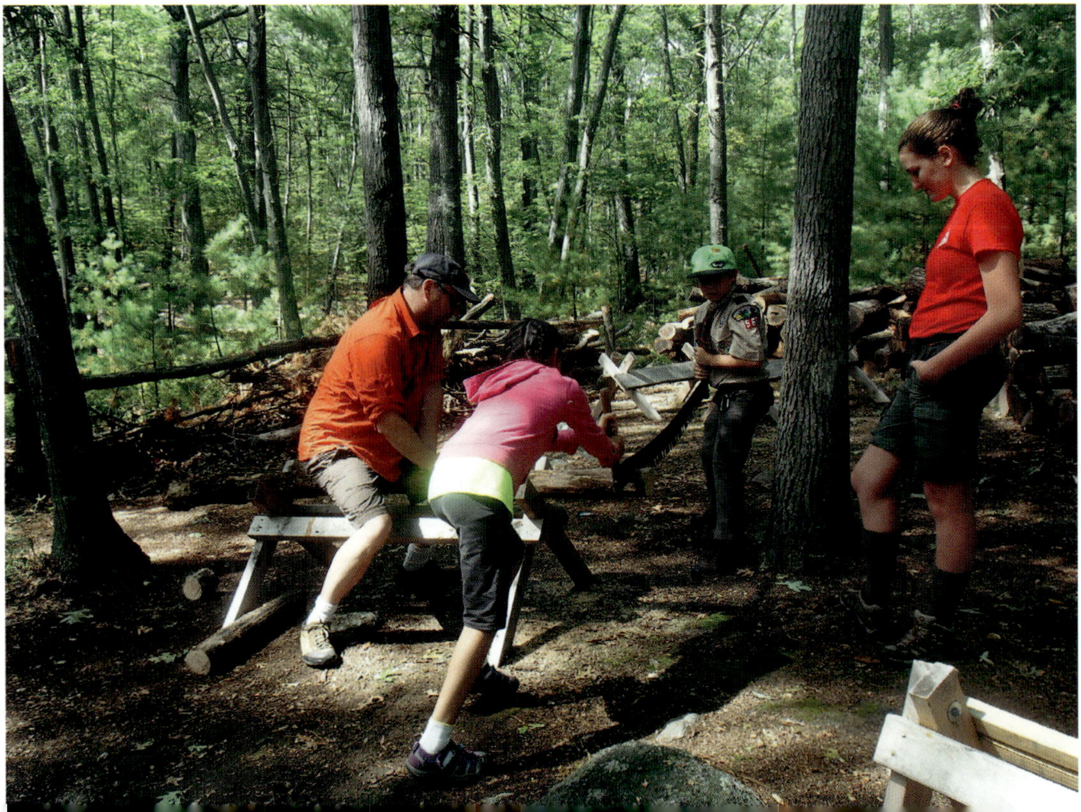

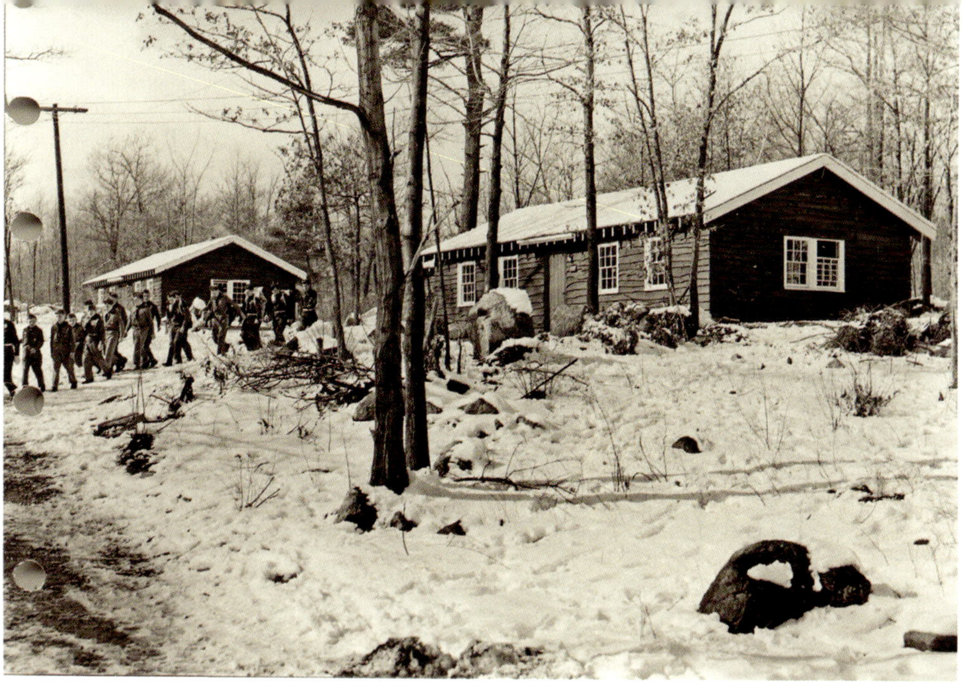

A CAMP FOR ALL SEASONS: The Scouting program is offered year-round and even during the months of a New England winter groups stay in the cabins and explore the winter scenery of The Blue Hills. There is hiking, sledding and snowshoeing. Ice climbing has been an added popular attraction. Scaling the ice to reach the top of the 42-foot "Look-Out Rock" is a real challenge. It is an adventure the brings both physical and mental benefits.

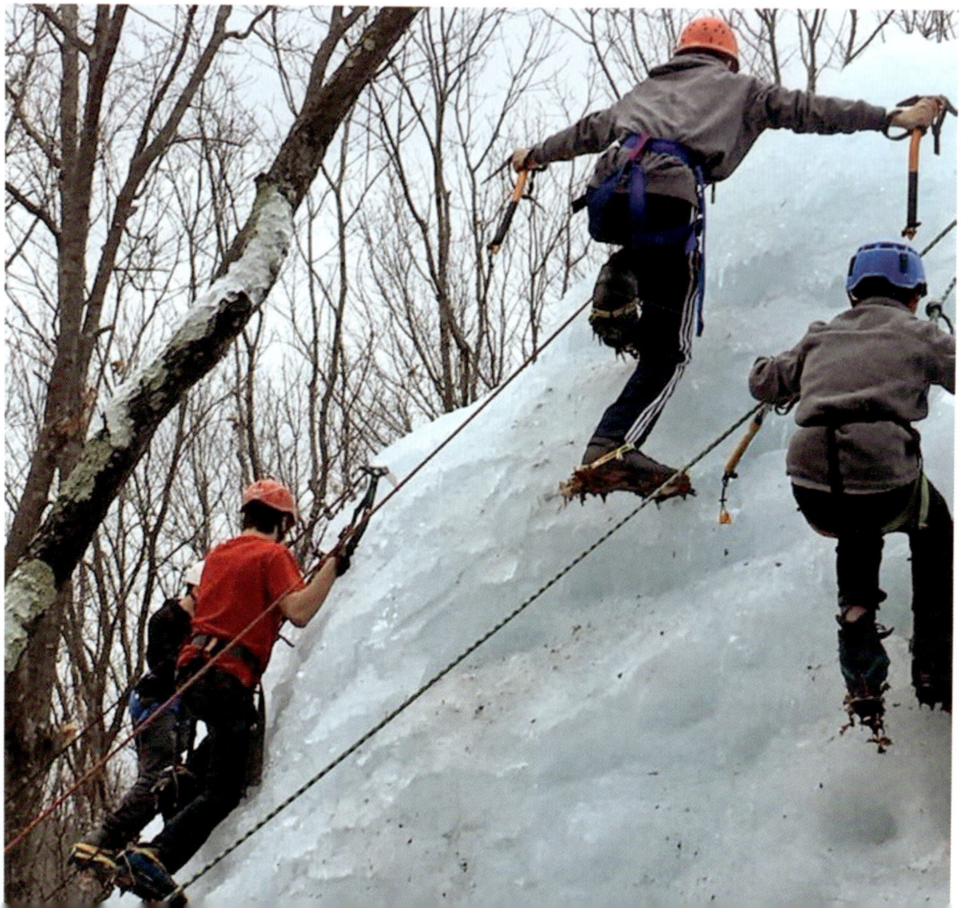

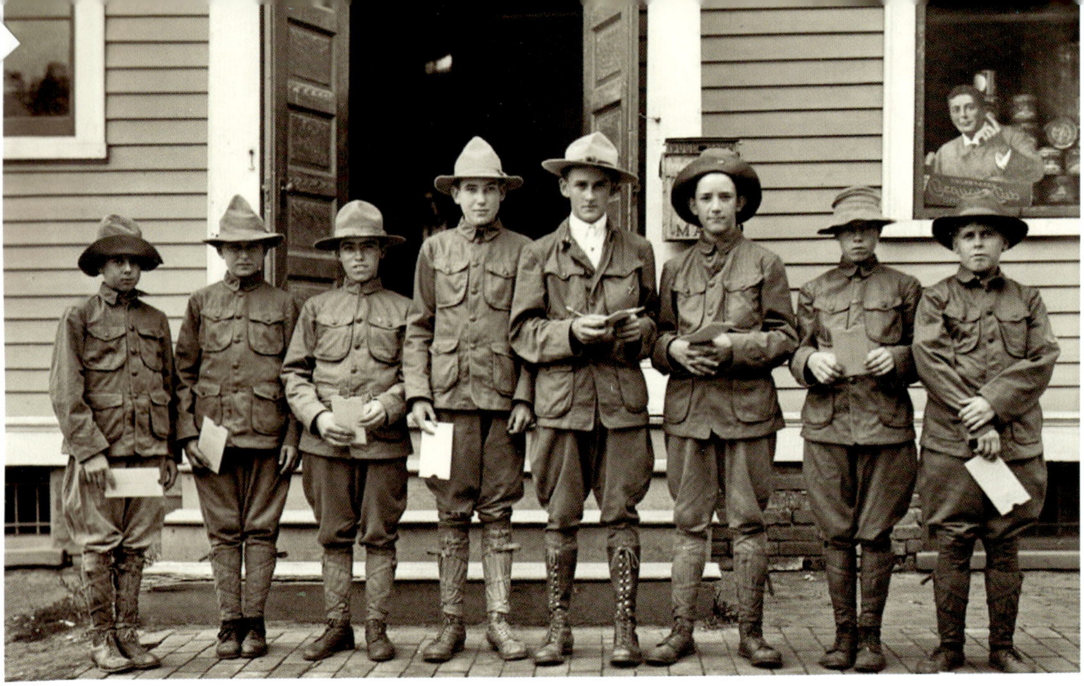

CONTINUED INNOVATION: In 1910 an innovative movement began that brought kids out of the city and into the woods. Boy Scouting's impact upon the character of generations cannot be overstated or overlooked. As the world changed, a solution to provide meaningful life-changing adventures became more complex. Remaining relevant requires continuous adaptation to the needs of young people. In recent years Scouting has become more inclusive and broader in its reach. New England Base Camp is the center of a new effort to adapt our camps in a way that meets the needs of young people and their families. It is a program development laboratory that seeks to become more effective. At its core its embraces social evolution and program innovation. Yet, its foundation is still directed towards creating the spirit of adventure that fills the hearts and imaginations of all who walk the trails.

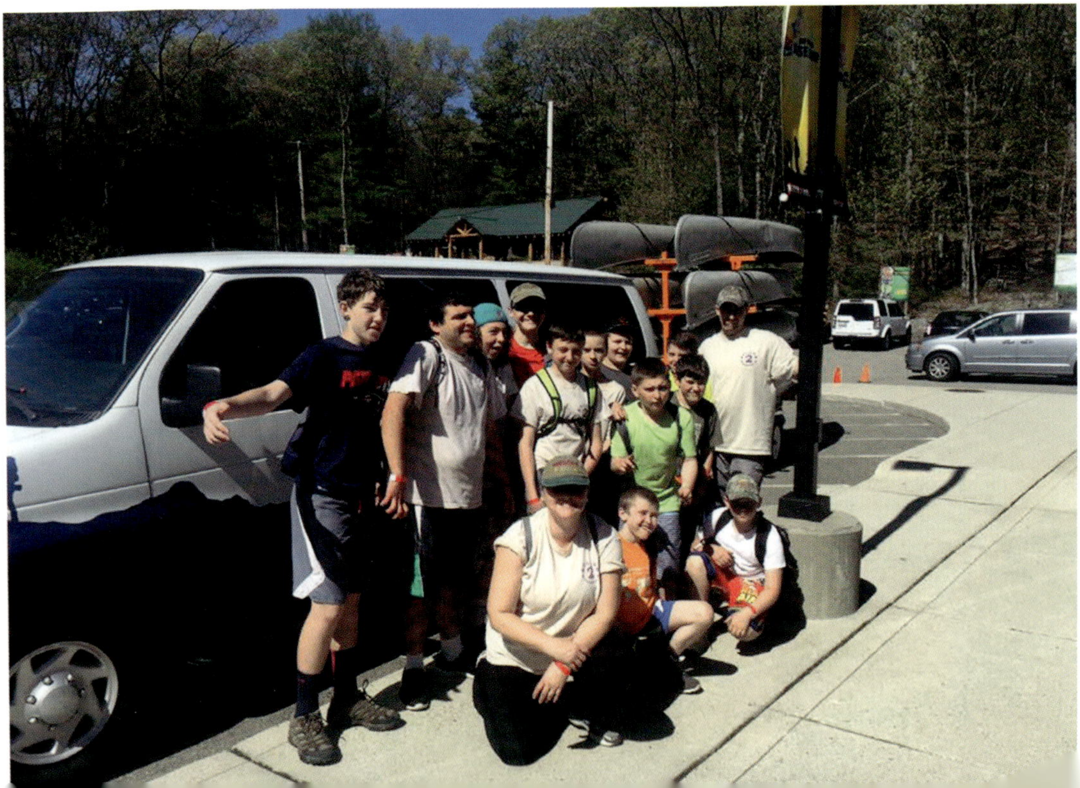